Revealing the
INVISIBLE

The *Teaching/Learning Social Justice* Series
Edited by Lee Anne Bell, Barnard College, Columbia University

Critical Race Counterstories along the Chilcana/Chicano Educational Pipeline
Tara J. Yosso

Understanding White Privilege: Creating Pathways to Authentic Relationships Across Race
Frances E. Kendall

Elusive Justice: Wrestling with Difference and Educational Equity in Everyday Practice
Thea Renda Abu El-Haj

Revealing the Invisible: Confronting Passive Racism in Teacher Education
Sherry Marx

Revealing the
INVISIBLE

Confronting Passive Racism in Teacher Education

Sherry Marx

Routledge
Taylor & Francis Group
New York   London

Routledge is an imprint of the
Taylor & Francis Group, an informa business

Routledge
Taylor & Francis Group
270 Madison Avenue
New York, NY 10016

Routledge
Taylor & Francis Group
2 Park Square
Milton Park, Abingdon
Oxon OX14 4RN

© 2006 by Taylor & Francis Group, LLC
Routledge is an imprint of Taylor & Francis Group, an Informa business

Printed in the United States of America on acid-free paper
10 9 8 7 6 5 4 3 2 1

International Standard Book Number-10: 0-415-95343-X (Softcover) 0-415-95342-1 (Hardcover)
International Standard Book Number-13: 978-0-415-95343-6 (Softcover) 978-0-415-95342-9 (Hardcover)

Library of Congress Cataloging-in-Publication Data

Marx, Sherry.
   Revealing the invisible : confronting passive racism in teacher education / Sherry Marx.
      p. cm. -- (The teaching/learning social justice series)
   Includes bibliographical references.
   ISBN 0-415-95342-1 (hardcover) -- ISBN 0-415-95343-X (pbk.)
   1. Teachers, White--United States--Attitudes. 2. Student teachers--United States--Attitudes. 3. Race awareness--United States. 4. Racism in education--United States. 5. Multicultural education--United States. 6. Teachers--Training of--United States. I. Title. II. Series: Teaching/learning social justice.

LB1775.2.M275 2006
370.71'1089--dc22   2006008023

Visit the Taylor & Francis Web site at
http://www.taylorandfrancis.com

and the Routledge Web site at
http://www.routledge-ny.com

Contents

Series Editor's Introduction

The Teaching/Learning Social Justice Series explores issues of social justice in classrooms and communities to show the essential connections between theory and practice. Central are the stories and lived experiences of people who strive both to critically analyze and challenge oppressive relationships and institutions, *and* to imagine and create more just and inclusive alternatives. My hope is that the series will balance critical analysis with images of possibility and be accessible and inspiring to a broad range of educators and activists. The series seeks to address those who believe in the potential for social change through education and who seek stories and examples of practice, as well as honest discussion of the ever-present obstacles to dismantling oppressive ideas and institutions.

In *Revealing the Invisible: Confronting Passive Racism in Teacher Education* Sherry Marx engages in a fascinating microanalysis of racism and white privilege through analyzing conversations with white preservice teachers as they tutor children of color in predominantly Latina/o schools in the Southwest. Through transcribed, in-depth dialogues with nine white, female tutors, Marx guides us through the process of their unfolding racial identity and emerging consciousness of their position as white teachers vis a vis the students of color they tutor.

Marx is concerned with understanding "the dominant face of teaching," one that is framed by color-blind discourse and unexamined negative assumptions about children of color and their communities. Noting the "inescapable influence of racism" she argues for teacher education to directly address racism and white privilege.

The author then outlines her approach to working with white students, emphasizing the importance of building sufficient safety and trust so that they are willing to open up and speak honestly about their racial assumptions. "Just like new speakers of English, new speakers of racial matters often feel quite stupid in a new language about race. They have fragile egos and worry about saying the wrong thing. Without support and patience, these factors can easily lead to silence – silence that reinforces reliance upon color-evasive and color-blind discourse in ways that maintain inequality." Having established a safe relationship, the dialogues she reports do indeed open up the tutors' assumptions about the invisibility and neutrality of whiteness, their association of color with deficits and fear, and the ways in which they see themselves as saviors and role models for the children of color with whom they work. However, they are not necessarily critical and indeed often "massaged each others' racist thoughts and comments in a safe and self-congratulatory way." Marx decides that she must take a more "gently confrontational" stance.

Asking the tutors to examine the transcripts of their own spoken words for racist content and pushing them to take responsibility for the words they have spoken proves to be a powerful intervention. The confrontations seem to create a breakthrough for several students as they recognize the low expectations they have for their tutees and the internalized racism that shapes these expectations. They begin to understand the effects their racism can have on the students they teach and realize that they are not automatically good teachers, let alone role models and saviors.

Marx convincingly argues that teacher education programs and field experiences that do not directly address student misperceptions about race and racism are likely to contribute to the construction of white self-images as role models and saviors to the detriment of their ability to teach all children well. She urges for direct teaching about racism and white privilege in ways that problematize both the beliefs teachers hold about racial others and the idealistic images they construct of themselves.

Several useful recommendations for structuring antiracist teacher education include: reflection and dialogue that encourage students to enter field experiences as learners rather than authorities, opportunities to learn valuable skills from members of the communities in which they tutor, assignments that require them to critique their own suppositions, and developing trusting relationships with supervisors who can directly confront racist ideas. She also argues for requiring courses in second language learning and the history of racism to counter the "pedagogy of amnesia" that supports color-blind ideology and to help students learn to notice the stereotypes and inequality in standard curricula. She also urges the necessity for creating measures for antiracist teaching developed in collaboration between white researchers and researchers of color to insure that teachers are truly prepared.

In this engaging book, Sherry Marx takes the reader on a journey through white consciousness, her own and that of her students, to show the damaging effects of unaddressed racism and white privilege on the capacity of white teachers to effectively teach students of color. Marx also models a process for inviting the kind of honest dialogue that can directly engage misperceptions and assumptions that usually remain unspoken, and shows how to confront students in ways that move them to take responsibility for their racism so as to be more present to the strengths, capacities and learning needs of students of color. From the evidence of several of the young women we get to know here, such approaches to anti-racist teacher education are quite promising.

Lee Anne Bell

Acknowledgments

I am grateful to the many individuals and organizations that have directly and indirectly influenced the work that has gone into this book. I would first like to thank the preservice teachers who participated in this project. I greatly appreciate their honesty, their kindness, and their willingness to share their thoughts and experiences with me. I remain impressed with their accomplishments.

The arguments I make throughout this book have a particular resonance when I relate them to the predominately Latina/o high school students, many of whom were non-native speakers of English, I taught in California after finishing this research project. As I revised this book, I thought of these students and the many ways they influenced my own understanding of the issues I present here. I am grateful for having been able to work with them as their teacher. I would also like to thank my former colleagues at this high school for helping me to become a better teacher.

The many university students I have taught over the years in Texas, California, and Utah have also influenced my teaching and my understanding of the issues presented here, although in a very different way. As I wrote each word, I thought about these students, most of whom are planning to become teachers, and hoped that they would find these words meaningful and relevant. In many ways, this book is written specifically for them. I would also like to thank my colleagues at Utah State University for their support.

In their readings of various early drafts of this book, my good friends Tracy Koncilja, Heather Whitaker-Shaddeau, Brent Shaddeau, and Julie

Pennington offered many insights that have made their way to this final version. I would also like to thank my editors at Routledge, especially Brook Cosby and Catherine Bernard, for much perceptive advice and Lee Bell, the editor of this series, for her insightful suggestions and much appreciated encouragement.

The influences of my wonderful family permeate my work and life. I want to thank Stacey and Greg Guilford and Steve and Felicia Marx for their continuous support and encouragement. I want to thank my parents, Charlie and Karen Marx, for shaping many of my views about the world and for continuing to inspire me as teachers and parents. I thank them too for carefully reading and rereading this work for me.

Especially, though, I would like to thank my wonderful husband, Zsolt Ugray, for making this book possible by being such a supportive partner in every sense of the word. We had two small children during the completion of this book—including one born between chapters 3 and 4—and I would not have been able to take a shower, let alone publish a book, without his help. Of course our children, Zsófi and Austin, make it all worthwhile.

I am very grateful to the University of Texas for supporting the data collection aspect of this project through the Gordon Whaley Fellowship. I also thank Peter Lang Publishing, Inc. for allowing me to use information previously published in Marx, S. (2004). Exploring and Challenging Whiteness and White Racism with White Pre-Service Teachers. In V. Lea & J. Helfand (Eds.), *Identifying Race and Transforming Whiteness in the Classroom* (pp. 132–152). Peter Lang. Long Island University Press also has allowed me to use information previously published in Marx, S. (2003). Entanglements of Altruism, Whiteness, and Deficit Thinking: White Preservice Teachers Working with Urban Latinos. *Educators for Urban Minorities*, 2(2), 41–56. Information from the following articles published by Taylor & Francis is likewise reprinted in this book: Marx, S., & Pennington, J. (2003). Pedagogies of Critical Race Theory: Experimentations with White Pre-Service Teachers. *Qualitative Studies in Education*, 16(1), 91–110 and Marx, S. (2004). Regarding Whiteness: Exploring and Intervening in the Effects of Racism in Teacher Education. *Equity & Excellence in Education*, 37(1), 1–13.

Introduction

When I was a student teacher, I taught under the supervision of a teacher who was renowned in her school district for being an outstanding professional. Mrs. D. was a twenty-year high school teaching veteran. She was also pursuing her master's degree in education and had set her sights on a Ph.D. in the near future. She was a leader in the local Writing Project and had just published an article in a highly esteemed professional journal. Moreover, several of her students had received major regional and national scholarships over the years. Indeed, every new school year, numerous parents clamored to get their children into her classes. These parents had educated themselves about good teachers and trusted that Mrs. D. was their child's best bet for a bright future. Considering her achievements and her reputation, this certainly seemed like a safe bet. And it was, for many.

For others, no amount of preliminary research, parent-teacher conference attendance, or homework supervision assured their children's success in Mrs. D.'s class. The children who sat in the back left corner of first period were all making Cs and Ds. Two of these high school freshmen, Tasha and Alisa, were failing. In third period, the "upper track," only Ophelia was failing, but Mrs. D. still advised that I "watch out" for her, as well as for Kwame, a straight-A student. She described both students as reckless and untrustworthy. When any of these children would forget their homework or misunderstand directions, she would bite her lip and harshly whisper, "No work ethic!" the moment they left the classroom.

The situation that disturbed me most, however, concerned Raquel, a freshman stuck in the lower track although she excelled in every assignment. A straight-A, thoughtful, quiet student, Raquel was clearly a mature young lady. Her parents were very supportive and concerned about her education. I know this because I met Raquel's mother, a beautiful woman with her daughter's same reserved demeanor, at a parent-teacher conference. In what I thought of as a trusting, thoughtful gesture, Raquel's mother had brought Raquel along with her so there would be no secrets about her progress in school. Mrs. D. seemed delighted to see both mother and daughter. She flattered Raquel and described her many successes to her mother. Raquel's mom listened carefully, also praised her daughter, and then finally asked the question, "So, do you think Raquel is where she needs to be?" I had often wondered this myself, as Raquel would obviously

1

do well in the upper track. The lower track did not challenge her nearly enough.

Mrs. D. attentively nodded her head while she listened to the expressed concerns. Raquel remained respectfully quiet. After a moment of thoughtful reflection, Mrs. D. turned her gaze to Raquel, smiled widely, and said, "I think Raquel is exactly where she needs to be." Raquel's mother, grateful for Mrs. D.'s honesty and care, smiled, thanked Mrs. D., and then ended the conference. She seemed satisfied with her daughter's situation, and appeared to trust that Mrs. D. knew best. The moment they left, I turned to Mrs. D. and asked her why she didn't want to move Raquel up to the higher level. Her smile disappeared as she harshly whispered, "She is not advanced material" and curtly slammed her gradebook shut. This statement clearly summed up Mrs. D.'s thoughts about Raquel, Ophelia, Kwame, and the other kids who were doing poorly in her classes. In a very real sense, she slammed her gradebook shut on all these kids, all these African American kids.

It is true that Mrs. D. was a successful teacher, but only to the White students in her classes. Given the facts that Whites account for 90 percent of American school teachers (National Education Association [NEA], 2003), that we live in a segregated society where Whites, Latinas/os, African Americans, and other ethnic populations tend to live with and go to school with others of their own ethnic or racial background (Donato, Menchaca, & Valencia, 1991; Trueba, 1998), and that nearly 70 percent of teachers live outside "the attendance areas of [their] school buildings," with almost half living outside the school districts where they teach (NEA, 2003, p. 97), it is no wonder that White teachers often have little understanding of their students of color. Because students of color now account for 42 percent of the U.S. student population (National Center for Education Statistics, 2005a), this is an issue no educator can ignore.

Given this information, some might argue that Mrs. D. simply needed some lessons in cross-cultural teaching in order to be successful with her students of color (e.g., Cazden & Leggett, 1981; Diller & Moule, 2005; Lynch & Hanson, 1998; Michaels, 1980; Philips, 1983). Others might argue that if she only became aware of her own culture, she would realize how she taught to that culture, unintentionally marginalizing the cultures of others (Spindler & Spindler, 1982, 1989, 1990, 1993, 1994; Spindler, 1997, 1999). Given her reputation for "professionalism," she may have even been willing to undertake these challenges. However, changing her teaching approach would certainly be easier than changing the racism that twisted her perceptions of her students of color. Although she would surely deny any accusation of racism, her actions clearly belied its influence on her beliefs. Lack of cultural awareness could not explain why Mrs. D. held such low expectations for her students of color or why she worked against them. However, the racism that is ingrained in U.S. culture explains her expectations very well. Just as we are all influenced by our culture, we are all influenced by the racism that is an inescapable part of it. Acknowledging this fact is an essential step in understanding the beliefs and practices of White teachers such as Mrs. D.

In all the time I spent with Mrs. D., I wished she could have *heard* the words and thoughts that came out of her mouth. I wished she could have somehow *seen* these words to understand how devastatingly full of doubt and disgust they were. Unfortunately, Mrs. D. is not alone in her beliefs. The racism that influences teacher perceptions of children of color is much more prevalent among educators than anyone is willing to admit. With that in mind, this book is an attempt to open up critical dialogue about race and racism in education practices in the U.S. today. It is my hope that initiating discussion of these issues will comprise a step towards changing them.

In this book, I present an in-depth qualitative exploration of the racist beliefs and actions of White female teacher education students. I also offer an intervention for challenging and, perhaps, changing these beliefs. With the educators presented in this book, I attempted to do just what I had not done with Mrs. D. That is, I listened to them talk about students of color and I observed their interactions with students of color. As I did so, I heard comments and witnessed actions that were infused with subtle and obvious racism. I then brought my observations to their attention. My intention was to help these educators gauge the weight of their own words and thoughts, critically reflect on the racism underlying them, and ponder how racism might affect their future work with schoolchildren. In doing so, I took the advice of Scheurich (1993) and made an effort to talk with other White educators "about our own racism" (p. 5).

Helpful Definitions

Working definitions of race, racism, Whiteness, and other racial terms are helpful at this point. In the section below, I explain the ways that I understand these terms and the ways that I use them in this book. The definitions I offer are not facts, nor are they undisputed. Many scholars, authors, and others define them differently, and use their definitions to make specific points. What I offer here are the definitions I find most useful and the ones that frame the analyses I present.

Race

Like Frankenberg (1993, p. 11), "I have found most useful those analyses of race as a socially constructed rather than an inherently meaningful category, one linked to relations of power and processes of struggle, and one whose meaning changes over time" (see also Chabram-Dernersesian, 1997; Lopéz, 1995; Nakayama & Krizek, 1999; Omi & Winant, 1986, 1994; Rodriguez, 1998; Scales-Trent, 1997; Twine, 1997; Wetherell & Potter, 1992). Believing in the socially constructed nature of race is believing that, "humans rather than abstract social forces produced races" (Lopéz, 1995, p. 196). That is, racial categories are products of time and space, not genetic categories with rigid definitions. That explains why the U.S. Census currently defines "White," "Black," "African American," "Negro," "American Indian," and "Alaska Natives" as racial groups but "Spanish, Hispanic, or Latino" as ethnic groups (U.S. Department of Commerce, 2001, p. 1–2). Many Latinas/os are unhappy with the racial categories used by the U.S. Census, feeling that their own racial backgrounds are omitted in the paperwork. As a result, nearly 50 percent of those who checked "Hispanic" as an ethnic group on the 2000 U.S. Census refused to "identify themselves by any of the five standard racial categories," writes Mireya Navarro in the *The New York Times* (Navarro, November 9, 2003). "As the Hispanic population booms," continues the author, "the fluid ways that . . . Latinos view their racial identities are drawing more attention and fueling the national debate over racial classifications — what they mean, what they should be and whether they are needed at all." This is an exceptional, contemporary example of the socially rather than biologically constructed nature of racial categories.

Offering another illuminating example, Banks (2003), writes,

> Two individuals with nearly identical physical characteristics, or phenotypes, can be classified as members of different races in two different societies (Nash, 1999). In the United States, where racial categories are well defined and highly inflexible, an individual with any acknowledged or publicly known African ancestry is considered Black (Davis, 1991). One who looks completely Caucasian but who acknowledges some African ancestry is classified as Black. Such an individual would be considered White in Puerto Rico. (p. 17)

The racial category of White is similarly a construction of history. Italian, Jewish, and Irish immigrants to the United States, for example, were not considered White 100 years ago. Articles on the debased nature of the "Irish race" frequented American media during the large wave of Irish immigration in the early 1900s (Ignatiev, 1995; Leonardo, 2002;

Takaki, 1990). Even today, while Jews are typically considered White in the United States, they often are considered to be people of color in other countries (Brodkin, 2000). Intermarriage over several generations gradually transformed European "races" into the general White American population that now makes up the dominant racial/ethnic group in the United States. This dominant group has a shared history in European immigration and assimilation into the British-inspired structures and morals of the American system (Alba, 1990; Takaki, 1990). To be White in the United States is, essentially, to be a person of some European descent who is thoroughly assimilated into the dominant culture and who receives the benefits of racial privilege, which will be discussed further below.

I capitalize the term White throughout this book, signifying its status as a proper noun used to name a particular ethnic/racial group, recognizing the socially constructed, dynamic nature of racial categories (see also American Psychological Association, 2001). By capitalizing this term, I purposely draw attention to the race, ethnicity, and power shared by Whites in this country. I also purposely do not distinguish between race and ethnicity as some other authors have done (see Kolchin, 2002) because both terms connote socially constructed categories that change over time and often overlap.

Racism

In this book, I use Wellman's (1977) definition of racism as "a system of advantage based on race" (Tatum, 1999, p. 7) that benefits Whites in the United States. This understanding of racism takes into account the United States's history of slavery and racial inequality that has always privileged Whites as it has denigrated people of color. It also sheds light on the institutionalized nature of racism. That is, rather than being defined just as an "irrational" feeling of hatred against individuals due to their skin color (for a critique of the "irrational" perspective, see Haberman & Post, 1992; and Sleeter, 1993), racism is described as a system that "clearly operates to the advantage of Whites and to the disadvantage of people of color" (Tatum, 1999, p. 7). As such, racism is understood to be widespread and ingrained in society, rather than manifested only in the actions of a few "irrational," hate-fueled individuals. Through this perspective, racism is perceived as an entity that affects everyone in society, benefiting some and victimizing others. Using this understanding of racism, there is no such thing as "reverse racism" (Tatum, 1999) because multicultural hiring practices and policies such as affirmative action do not systematically advantage people of color over Whites; rather, they seek to limit the pervasiveness of White privilege. Whites remain in the dominant social and power position. This understanding of racism is directly connected to critical race theory (CRT), which is a perspective that emphasizes the systemic—even normal—state of racism in the United States. Those who adopt CRT argue that this system is always in place, whether or not we admit to it or agree to it (e.g., Delgado, 1995a; Ladson-Billings, 1999; Ladson-Billings & Tate, 1995; Solórzano, 1997, 2001, 2002; Scheurich, 1993; Tatum, 1994, 1999).

Whiteness

Perhaps because Whiteness is often understood by what it is not rather than by what it is (Fanon, 1967), Whiteness is described more often than it is defined. Sometimes, it is described as separate from White people and White culture. For example, Leonardo (2002, p. 31) describes White people and White culture as neutral categories, but Whiteness as a negative "racial discourse" that serves to reproduce White privilege and racism. McIntyre (1997, p. 45) uses the term *White talk* to describe similar discourse, Bonilla-Silva (2003) prefers "color-blind racism." Others, such as Giroux (1997) describe Whiteness as racial performance, something that can be enacted to reproduce racial inequity (see also Chubbuck, 2004). In her synthesis of Whiteness literature, Chubbuck (2004, p. 302) suggests that Whiteness is "directly connected to institutionalized power and privileges that benefit White Americans." Through this perspective, Whiteness is something that antiracist Whites can and should reject (see also Ignatiev & Garvey, 1996).

In this book, I take the stance that Whiteness is much more than racial discourse. Rather, I understand it as an amalgamation of qualities including the cultures, histories, experiences, discourses, and privileges shared by Whites. Many of these qualities can be described similarly to the descriptions offered above. However, I suggest that because all Whites are necessarily influenced by the often-invisible racial privileges intertwined with White culture, even as they/we benefit from them, Whites cannot reject Whiteness. As Scheurich (1993) and Thompson (2003) point out, no one gets to be the "good White" who is no longer affected by racism just because he or she recognizes and rejects it. With this understanding of Whiteness, I suggest that racism and certain discourses, such as White talk and color-blindness, can be rejected by Whites, but the amalgamation of Whiteness cannot. That is, no White person can escape its influence, though they/we can learn to be critical of it and to work against the racism related to it.

White Privilege

The ways that Whites are advantaged in society because of their/our race is described as "White privilege." These advantages can be as obvious as being able to find bandages and pantyhose that match the "flesh" color of a White person's skin, or as subtle as not being pulled over by police for no apparent reason while driving—or even walking, as was the case for a Latino high school student of mine—and not routinely being followed by security in department stores (see McIntosh, 1988/1997 for more examples). Because most White people believe these privileges of being trusted rather than distrusted are experienced by everyone, they are often reluctant to believe in the notion of White privilege. The term "White racism" also is used by some scholars to highlight the racial privileges that Whites consciously and unconsciously benefit from and perpetuate in society. This term deliberately links White privilege to a system of racism.

Prejudice

In discussions of racism, the term prejudice inevitably comes up. Tatum (1999, p. 5) defines prejudice as "a preconceived judgment or opinion, usually based on limited information." She suggests that "we all have prejudices, not because we want them, but simply because we are so continually exposed to misinformation about others." Many—if not most—Americans tend to consider prejudices inconsequential, negative thoughts that are not nearly as dangerous as full-fledged racism. They reserve their examples of racism for unabashedly hate-filled individuals and groups such as the Ku Klux Klan. Many of the preservice teachers with whom I have worked offer similar examples. Consider the comments of Rachel,[1] for example:

> When I think of somebody who's racist, I think of the Ku Klux Klan, Nazis. . . . I think of, you know, a general hatred for all minorities. . . . Total hatred. Extinction of a people. You know, lynching, hate crimes. And, I think prejudice is making snide remarks, treating people maybe differently but not hating them necessarily. Treating them differently than you treat somebody of your own.

The young teacher education students presented in this book tended to think of prejudices as harmless thoughts just barely connected to racism. I find it important, however, to emphasize the connections between the two. Prejudiced thoughts are good indicators of the unacknowledged racism and privilege that shape the thoughts of White Americans. If there were no racism, racial prejudices would not exist.

Discrimination

A definition of racial discrimination is hard to pin down in the education and social sciences literature. Traditionally, discrimination has been perceived as a harmful act against a person committed solely and obviously because of race, such as the violent acts against African Americans by Whites that were tolerated and even condoned by much of the White public during the Jim Crow period, which lasted from about the 1890s until the U.S. civil rights movement of the 1960s (Klarman, 2004). This understanding of discrimination is clearly tied to the overt, hate-fueled form of racism that is not so common in U.S. society today. However, like that understanding of racism, the description of discrimination as overt and hate-fueled is not so useful in efforts to discuss the more passive, institutionalized nature of racism today. Feagin and Vera (1995) offer definitions of discrimination that emphasize "group power and institutionalized factors" (p. 11), such as Pettigrew's (1975) description of "an institutional process of exclusion against an out-group" (p. x) and J. R. Feagin and C. B. Feagin's (1978) description of "practices carried out by members of dominant groups which have differential and negative impact on members of subordinate groups" (pp. 20–21). In contemporary times, these practices are often conducted without the conscious intention of the perpetrators. Rather, they are interwoven with negative "racial myths," "fictions," and other "ideological constructions" (Feagin & Vera, 1995, p. 12), including White privilege, that shape one's understanding of reality. Because racism has such a negative connotation in the minds of most Americans, Feagin and Vera argue that "few Whites are willing to accept 'racist' as a personal trait" (p. 13). As a result, no matter what discriminatory acts, intentional or unintentional, Whites may commit against people of color, such as denying housing, jobs, or a chance to excel in an advanced academic course, they are likely to deny that racism has anything to do with it. As Bonilla-Silva (2003) suggests, there now seems to be "racism without racists." Thus, definitions of discrimination, such as those above, that highlight group power are much more useful in understanding contemporary racism in the United States.

The Role of Racial History and Language in the United States

Understanding present-day racial dynamics necessarily requires an understanding of America's racial history. The United States has a long history of racial inequality that is anything but a secret. Africans were brought to the United States as early as 1619 as slaves and remained in bondage until as late as 1865 (Kolchin, 2003; Takaki, 1990). All non-Europeans who entered the United States purposely for labor—Chinese, Mexicans, etc.—were meant to be temporary residents (Takaki, 1990). When the work was done, they were expected to leave. The Chinese Exclusion Act of 1882 and its 1904 extension, for example, kept Chinese immigrants out of the United States until the repeal of the act in 1943 (Enrolled Acts and Resolutions of Congress, 1789–1996; Gabaccia, 2002; Takaki, 1990). This is the most well known of many exclusionary acts throughout the history of the United States, beginning with the Naturalization Act of 1790 which limited U.S. citizenship to "free [W]hite person[s]" and ending with the Immigration Act of 1965, which eliminated "natural origins," i.e., race, from criteria by which citizenship is granted (Debates and Proceedings in the Congress of the United States, 1789–1791; Suárez-Orozco & Páez, 2002).

The future of people of African descent, if they were someday freed from slavery, was ambiguous in the first hundred years of U.S. nationhood (Takaki, 1990). Plans to send former slaves back to Africa, to a new nation-state, or to give them "40 acres and a mule" were never resolved. Jeffersonian-era policy towards Native Americans involved their removal to the Rocky Mountains and westward, "incorporation" into society, or extermination (Takaki, 1990, pp. 62–63). "Indians as Indians," writes Takaki, "could not be tolerated in the republican civilization the American Revolution had created" (p. 63). Using the words of Jefferson, he summarized that "[t]he new nation must have a 'homogenous' population—a people with the same language and laws, good cabins and enclosed fields, owners of private property" (p. 63). Being more specific, Benjamin Franklin described the ideal homogenous population as "the lovely White" (Takaki, 1990, p. 14).

After slavery and until the civil rights movement of the 1960s, African Americans and other people of color in many parts of the United States were legally prohibited from living near or going to school with Whites. Although these legal forms of separation have been abolished in the years since, the structures they created still remain. Most Americans still live in racially segregated communities. Most White children still go to predominantly White schools. Most African American and Latina/o children still go to predominantly African American or Latina/o schools, or a combination thereof (NEA, 2003; Trueba, 1998). This separation is the residual effect of the legal segregation of days gone by, and it seems to be getting worse rather than better (Trueba, 1998). Despite the historical significance of these school demographics, few Americans see the connections between the past and the present. Similarly, few Americans today give racism the weight it deserves in structuring much of our society. Rather, many of us—especially those of us who are White—believe racism is a thing of the past that does not have much of an influence on our present-day lives (Sleeter, 1992b). In fact, for those of us who are White, seeing the effects of racism on *our* lives requires a conscious effort.

Part of the obliviousness Whites have regarding their/our part in racism is linked to the language we use to talk about racism. The language of racism has been intricately tied to the ways different races have historically been characterized in the United States. At the moment, racism has exceedingly negative connotations. Without a doubt, Mrs. D., like the preservice teachers discussed later in this book, would consider the charge of racism the worst kind of insult and even disgrace. Tatum (1999, p. 11) notes, "For many White people, the image of a racist is a hood-wearing Klan member or a name-calling Archie Bunker figure," something that most Americans can point out but something most Americans, at this point in our history, are not. No professional in the United States, especially no teacher, could publicly identify with these racist archetypes and keep her or his job. Tatum explains that these types of images of a "racist" person

> represent what might be called *active racism*, blatant, intentional acts of racial bigotry and discrimination. *Passive racism* is more subtle and can be seen in the collusion of laughing when a racist joke is told, of letting exclusionary hiring practices go unchallenged, of accepting as appropriate the omissions of people of color from the curriculum, and of avoiding typical race-related issues. Because racism is so ingrained in the fabric of American institutions, it is easily self-perpetuating. All that is required to maintain it is business as usual. (p. 11)

Passive racism explains the racism of most White Americans today. They/we buy into it and reproduce it, even as they/we condemn active racism. Passive racism is so ingrained in American institutions, philosophies, and practices that it is often times completely invisible to the Whites who benefit from it. Frequently, it is invisible to the people of color who are victimized by it as well (Bonilla-Silva, 2003). They/we cannot see it because it is embedded in nearly every aspect of all of our daily lives. As Scheurich (2000) suggests, it is as invisible and prevalent as oxygen in the air. Tatum (1999) prefers the term smog. We all breathe it in and it becomes a part of who we are. No one is immune to its grasp.

Three Racial Discourses and Paradigms in the United States

Because passive racism is the most common form of racism in the United States today, it is the focus of this book. While active racism is certainly harmful and hateful, at the present time, it is generally considered unacceptable. Passive racism, in contrast, is widely accepted and unchallenged. Indeed, it was the accepted norm of my own student teaching experience. This passive acceptance of racial inequality is a relatively new kind of acceptable racial discourse in the United States. According to Frankenberg (1993), it has only been prevalent since the late 1960s. Omi and Winant (1994) suggest that American racial thought can be divided into three chronological paradigms. Frankenberg (1993) adds that each of these racial paradigms is accompanied by a particular "racial discourse" that articulates, and thus perpetuates, each paradigm. As I outline the three racial paradigms below, I will also discuss the racial discourse that Frankenberg (1993) attaches to each.

Biologically Different Paradigm

The first U.S. racial paradigm presented by Omi and Winant (1994) begins with the earliest European American settlers and lasts well into the 1920s. In this first paradigm, people of color were constructed as biologically inferior to Whites. Frankenberg (1993) writes that slavery was rationalized through the discourse of the first racial paradigm, as was the statement that enslaved persons would be considered three-fifths human in article 1, section 2, clause 3 of the U.S. Constitution (Bell, 1995). Because biological inferiority discourse was the accepted racial discourse at this time, White people did not question their superiority to people of color. It was simply the standard, dominant paradigm/discourse. Frankenberg terms this dominant acceptance of racial inequality "essentialist racism." This means simply that White people and people of color were thought to be biologically—or genetically—different, with Whites the acknowledged superior group.

Foley (1997) writes that this philosophy eventually fell out of favor due to five main factors. First, the Great Depression threw members of the White middle class into poverty, something that biological superiority arguments could not explain. Second, Hitler's "racial purification program" (p. 114) was based, in part, on the work of U.S. eugenicists. Many American scholars, quick to distance themselves from Hitler's ideologies, distanced themselves from the study of eugenics as well. Third, many anthropologists, in particular Franz Boas, were critical of the White racial superiority model and philosophically against it. Many dedicated their work to discrediting it. Fourth, Foley notes (p. 114), citing Valencia and Guadarrama (1985), "There was a sharp decline in research activity dealing with intelligence testing during the 1940s" because many intelligence researchers left their work to take part in World War II. The final factor that Foley discusses is the contribution of noted child psychologist Jean Piaget who "incorporated both genetic and environmental influences in his theorizing as to how children cognitively develop" (p. 114). In any case, Blum (1978, p. 65) notes, "By 1945, racial theories were no longer considered scientifically respectable. Most psychologists decided that the hypothesis of [B]lack genetic inferiority should be abandoned" (as cited by Foley, 1997, p. 114). Despite these recommendations, however, the racial inferiority paradigm was so pervasive and so entrenched in the American psyche that in 1915, 50 years after slavery was abolished, 408 African American children in Missouri public schools were assessed as possessing two-thirds the intellectual ability of White school children (Pyle, 1915, as cited by Pearl, 1997). These arguments linger today as the popularity of Herrnstein and Murray's (1994) *The Bell Curve* shows. This book, which seeks to "prove" the genetic intellectual inferiority of people of color, became a national bestseller in 1994. Though widely condemned by anthropologists, educational researchers, and geneticists, the notion of the biological inferiority of people of color remains an undercurrent in U.S. thought today.

Ethnically Different Paradigm

The second racial paradigm delineated by Omi and Winant (1994) is that of "ethnicity" rather than "race" as the foremost marker of difference among people. Beginning in the 1920s, this view placed emphasis on cultural rather than biological differences between Whites and people of color. Frankenberg (1993) explains that "Within this new paradigm, belonging to an ethnic group came to be understood more behaviorally than biologically..." (p. 13). That is, ethnic backgrounds and cultures, more than genetics, were thought to influence a group's economic achievement, the most common marker of "success" agreed upon by the larger society. However, as Frankenberg notes, "Since a cultural group continued to be understood in terms of descent rather than practice, one could add that biology continued to underwrite conceptions of identity" (p. 13). This is the case because the first racial paradigm was never completely wiped out in American thought.

The belief in the power of an individual to transcend her or his culture in order to assimilate and then succeed in the United States arose during this second paradigm of dominant racial understanding. The notion of meritocracy is central to this culture-centered paradigm. Within this framework, the best and brightest are expected to "rise to the top" of society based on their intellectual strength and ability to work hard. Race, per se, is not considered an inhibiting factor. Moreover, society, in this view, is considered neutral; that is, it is thought to have no effect on an individual's attempts to succeed. Along with this acceptance of fundamental equality among all races came the view that "we are all the same under the skin" (Frankenberg, 1993, p. 14). This ideology is frequently termed "color-blindness" based on the reasoning that individual characteristics eclipse any influence race might have on a person's life (see also L. Bell, 2002; Bonilla-Silva, 2003; Leonardo, 2002). Displeased with the term "color-blindness," Frankenberg suggests that the same ideology can be better characterized as "color-evasiveness" and "power-evasiveness"; that is, the dominant discourse purposely moves away from open discussion of color/race and power inequality. Naturally enough, cultural deficit models were soon generated to explain why some groups had a harder time succeeding than others.

The culture of poverty theory, proposed by Lewis in 1965, proves to be a particularly devastating cultural deficit theory. Foley (1997) summarizes this theory by explaining that

> [Lewis] emphasized that people living in poverty tend to create a unique, self-devastating lifestyle or way of life marked by a host of negative values, norms and social practices. The culture of poverty that is allegedly passed on to successive generations consisted of 70 traits which can be compressed into four clusters: 1) basic attitudes, values and character structure of poor people; 2) the nature of the poor's family system; 3) the nature of the slum community; and 4) the poor's social and civic relationship with the larger society. (p. 115)

Mexican Americans, African Americans, and Native Americans were considered, by subscribers to this theory, to live in cultures of poverty that prevented them from assimilating into "mainstream" American society and succeeding educationally and economically. Moreover, as Foley notes, this cycle is understood to be self-perpetuating; thus, from the perspective of this theory, it is nearly impossible for anyone in a culture of poverty ever to become economically successful.

Another cultural deficit model associated most closely with John Ogbu classifies American minority groups into three categories: "autonomous," "immigrant," and "castelike" (Ogbu, 1992, p. 8). According to this model, autonomous groups are "people who are minorities primarily in a numerical sense," such as "Jews, Mormons, and the Amish" (p. 8). Ogbu writes that no "non-White" (p. 8) groups in the United States are considered autonomous. "Immigrant or voluntary minorities," he continues, "are people who have moved more or less voluntarily to the United States – or any other society – because they desire more economic wellbeing, better overall opportunities, and/or greater political freedom" (p. 8). While these people have initial difficulties in adjusting to their new home, their problems with educational success are not "lingering and disproportionate" (p. 8). Involuntary or castelike groups, in contrast, "are people who were originally brought into the United States or any other society against their will," such as through "slavery, conquest, colonization, or forced labor" (p. 8). Their troubles with education are "greater and more persistent" (p. 8) than those experienced by the other two groups. While this is a complex theory, Ogbu gives much attention to the ways that castelike group members keep themselves from experiencing educational success. He suggests they do this when they, "interpret school learning as a displacement process detrimental to their social identity, sense of security, and self-worth" (p. 10) and, consequently, reject much of schooling. He writes that "involuntary minorities do not seem to be able or willing to separate attitudes and behaviors that result in academic success from those that may result in linear acculturation or replacement of their cultural identity with White American cultural identity" (p. 10). Thus, rather than "acting White" (p. 10) members of involuntary, castelike groups prefer to fail. Group members contribute to this mindset by undervaluing education, accepting failure, and not taking responsibility for being in control of their own success. Ogbu suggests that involuntary immigrants emulate voluntary immigrants to resolve these issues.

While the theory of voluntary and involuntary immigrants is often taught in the social sciences, it does not make for common discourse in popular American culture. The theory of the "at-risk" child does. The "at-risk-of-failure" construct is perhaps the most embraced form of cultural deficit thinking in American education today. It seeks to pinpoint children who are "predisposed to dropping out" of school for reasons such as language background, family income, family structure, age as compared to peers, and other "person centered explanation[s] of school failure" (Valencia & Solórzano, 1997, pp. 195–196). A child who grows up in a household where the dominant language is not English is automatically labeled "at risk," as are students who receive free or reduced-price lunch. Therefore, in some schools, nearly all children are considered "at risk." An excellent example of the harm this label can do is the blunder the Austin, Texas, Independent School District (AISD) committed in 1994. In the early part of this year, AISD labeled all its English-language learners and low-income children "at risk" and sent letters stating this home with more than 33,000 children (Valencia & Solórzano, 1997). Indeed, letters went home to "46 percent of the total 72,000 AISD student enrollment" (p. 197), regardless of the grade point average of the child—something that many would argue is a better indicator of school success. Straight-A students and their families were particularly hurt and offended.

The culture of poverty, the voluntary/involuntary, and the "at risk" theories of cultural difference all "blame the victims" for their own hardships in the United States. They also consistently blame the *same groups* of people for their economic disadvantages. Each of these theories perpetuates the notion that low-income children of color, especially those who speak a nonstandard variety of English, such as Black English Vernacular or Tex-Mex, or a native language that is not English, are destined to fail in education. Despite their different appellations, these theories are remarkably similar to one another. All three are cultural deficit models. While each one has been lambasted by anthropologists and some education researchers (e.g., Valencia, 1997; Trueba, 1988), cultural deficit thinking remains firmly entrenched in the American mindset. I know this because several of my own students, young women and men born long after the culture of poverty theory was discredited, have remarked upon the challenges children from the "culture of poverty" present. They have also discussed the need for special programs for "risky" children. Moreover, each time principals come to my teacher preparation classes to recruit volunteer tutors, the first issues they discuss are the percentages of their students who are low income, African American, Latina/o, English language learners, or otherwise "at risk." Thus, cultural deficit models are certainly "alive and well in the contemporary period" (Valencia & Solórzano, 1997, p. 198), no matter how thoroughly they have supposedly been discredited.

Economically and Nationally Different Paradigm

While the biologically different and culturally different paradigms remain an undercurrent in American thought even now, by the mid-1960s, "*class*-and *nation*-based paradigms of race began to take form" (Omi & Winant, 1994, p. 12). Omi and Winant (1994) explain that

> These theoretical challenges originated within the [B]lack and other racial minority movements which rejected two central aspects of the ethnicity approach: the European immigrant analogy which suggested that racial minorities could be incorporated into American life in the same way that White ethnic groups had been, and the assumption of the fundamental, underlying American commitment to equality and social justice for racial minorities. (p. 12)

Frankenberg (1993) suggests that with this third paradigm, racial discourse had come full circle, from a discourse of difference, to a discourse of similarity, back to a discourse of difference. This time, however, the differences were asserted by people of color rather than by the dominant, White group. Frankenberg explains that "Where difference within the terms of essentialist racism alleges the inferiority of people of color, in the third [paradigm] difference signals autonomy of culture, values, and aesthetic standards, and so on" (p. 14). Far from being a panacea for race relations in the United States, however, this third paradigm has spawned a kind of backlash of "furor over 'multiculturalism' and 'political correctness'" that has left many White Americans resentful of what they see to be a "new form of racial hegemony" that "disproportionately benefit[s] those concentrated at the bottom of the socioeconomic ladder, where racial discrimination has its most damaging effects" (Omi & Winant, 1994, p. 148; see also Kincheloe, Steinberg, Rodriguez, & Chennault, 1998; Leonardo, 2002). Omi and Winant (1994, p. 12) add that this backlash has "marked the resurgence of ethnicity theory," which, in their words, "once again reigns supreme. . . ." An indication of this backlash is that, while many White Americans are now willing to admit that there is structural racism in our society, many of them/us see only the structures that benefit people of color. This has certainly been true for many of the preservice teachers with whom I have worked.

The Significant Role of Color-blindness

Linked to this backlash and the resentfulness many White Americans feel toward people of color is the exacerbating contribution of color-blind or color-evasive language, what Frankenberg (1993, p. 145) describes as the "dominant language of race in the United States" today. Color-blind language prevents Americans from openly discussing race without having their/our words infused with politics, judgment, and emotion. Indeed, this racial avoidance discourse is so common among Whites and so effective in derailing efforts to address racism, that Leonardo (2002) considers it the essence of Whiteness. After all, a White person can rarely mention racism without encountering defensiveness and anger from other Whites (Helms, 1990). I have experienced this reaction myself countless times by just mentioning that I study the racism of White teachers. One friend responded by giving a 15-minute, red-faced, monologue that started with affirmative action and ended with the comment, "I guess I'm just a bad person." No one has heard the topic and responded with the neutral statement, "That's nice." This topic is not neutral because race in the United States is the antithesis of neutral.

Accordingly, a White person talking about her or his concerns with White racism risks losing in-group membership with other Whites. Helms

(1990, p. 54) explains that, "Significant White persons in one's environment may use the socialization pressures available to them to ensure that the White person learns the rules of being a socially accepted White person." One of these rules is knowing not to talk about race. Citing Boyle (1962) and L. Smith (1961), Helms (1990, p. 57) suggests that if a White person in an early stage of racial identity consciousness interacts with people of color continuously, "sooner or later significant others in the person's environment will make it known that such behavior is unacceptable if one wishes to remain a member in good standing of the White group." This shunning of antiracist discourse by the dominant culture enables the everyday, passive, "business as usual" form of racism to continue generation after generation (Bonilla-Silva, 2003; Helms, 1990; Leonardo, 2002; Tatum, 1999).

At the same time antiracist discourse is considered divisive and controversial, color-blind language is considered neutral, and even politically correct, by much of the dominant culture. Frankenberg (1993, p. 142) explains that, "'color-blindness'—a mode of thinking about race organized around an effort not to 'see,' or at any rate not to acknowledge, race differences—continues to be the 'polite' language of race." However, in a country as racially stratified as the United States, it is impossible not to "see" race. Rather, as Frankenberg explains, "This discursive repertoire is organized around evading difference or acknowledging it selectively, rather than literally not 'seeing' differences of race, culture, and color" (p. 76). Color-blind language superficially accepts diversity with the provision that it not be significantly different from the White norm and, most importantly, that it not *challenge* the White norm. The trouble lurking behind this philosophy is succinctly expressed by Sleeter (1993, p. 167), who suggests, "People do not deny seeing what they actually do not see. Rather, they profess to be color-blind when trying to suppress negative images they attach to people of color. . . ." Indeed, school policies that delineate White, Western-centered curricula and White, middle class values work to suppress anything other than mainstream White culture (Alba, 1990; Banks & Banks, 2003; Calabrese, 1989; Takaki, 1990). Moreover, statements such as "all children are the same," and "all children should be taught the same," comments I hear among preservice and practicing teachers all the time, are misnomers. A more accurate description of this kind of teaching philosophy is believing that "all children are White under the skin."

This philosophy was certainly embraced by the school where I did my student teaching. At Midwest High School, an African American student was suspended for wearing dreadlocks. Although his hair was short enough to expose his ears, a mandate of the school's official dress code, his hairstyle was deemed too "ethnic" for the school. After three days of suspension, the young man returned with a military-type buzz. After this incident, dreadlocks were banned in the school's newly revised official handbook. Thus, Midwest High revealed its color-blind/color-evasive philosophy that diversity should not be too diverse, and that any style other than mainstream White style is, in reality, unacceptable. In a nutshell, this inequity is what lies in the heart of color-blindness, the most common racial philosophy embraced by the dominant American culture today.

In analyzing the history and complexities of American racial thought, it has been helpful for me to think of each paradigm as a house that has slowly deteriorated and then been partially rebuilt. Frameworks of each structure remain; thus each newer paradigm is built on the rotting foundations of those previous. None has ever been totally removed, and the decay of the first paradigm eventually seeps in and spoils the cosmetic improvements of the more recent construction. In order to draw attention to the foundation of our racial paradigm and discourse so it can be excavated, examined, and thoughtfully rebuilt, rather than covered over yet again, we must talk about it. At the same time, the color-evasive, color-blind nature of race and racism today make that a difficult endeavor. Because color-blind is the more well-known term, I use it in this book more often than color-evasive.

Implications for Education

Once we begin to "name" (Freire, 1970/2000) race, racism, and Whiteness in the US, and once we take a closer look at their influences on American society, the fact that 90 percent of American schoolteachers are White and 42 percent of American schoolchildren are people of color becomes an alarming issue (NEA, 2003; NCES, 2003a). Included in the growing number of children of color is the growing population of people age five to 24 who speak a language besides English in their home, estimated to be 17 percent in 1999 (NCES, 2003b). During the same year, at least 8 percent of American school children received English language services in school (NCES 2003a). In contrast, 97 percent of teachers are estimated to be monolingual in English (Darling-Hammond & Sclan, 1996). This discrepancy between teachers and their students is also clearly reflected in traditional teacher preparation programs, where Whites make up the majority of teacher education students and the vast majority of teacher educators (NEA, 2003). White women remain the majority of teachers and future teachers alike (NEA, 2003). Indeed, like most teacher educators, I have found myself working almost exclusively with idealistic young White women throughout my career. As Ladson-Billings (1999, p. 226) asks, given this population, "Where are the voices to challenge the dysconscious racism[2] (King, 1991) so prevalent among prospective teachers?" With so many White teachers, teacher educators, and teacher education students, there are very few voices, indeed, to challenge these often subtle, yet pervasive forms of racism.

Confronting Whiteness and Passive Racism

The purpose of this book is twofold. Its first objective is to better understand how Whiteness and passive racism influence the ways that White educators make sense of children of color, particularly children who are learning English as a second language. The second objective is to challenge these negative influences by confronting the beliefs of educators with the intention of changing them. This second objective is perhaps the more important of the two as much attention has been given to Whiteness and the passive racism entangled within it in recent years, but little has been done to actually intervene in these entities. The intervention offered in this book is, consequently, a jump into unchartered waters.

Chapter 1 discusses the groundwork necessary to set up critical discussions of race and racism with Whites, as they/we are much more used to avoiding these topics than addressing them. I then introduce the nine White women, all students in a class I was teaching, who spent a semester talking with me about the English-language learning schoolchildren of Mexican origin they tutored as a requirement for my class.

Chapter 2 explores the ways that Whites make sense of Whiteness, weaving together the literature on the topic with the stories of the nine tutors I got to know. I then contrast that with the ways Whites make sense of color, highlighting the positive associations made with Whiteness and the negative associations made with color. I also examine the role model and savior constructs tutors used to describe their own roles in working with English-language learning children of color.

Chapter 3 focuses on the ways that the tutors defined racism and the stories they told to illustrate their definitions. Their stories show that racism is a label they were willing to give to others, but never themselves. This chapter explores the arm's length at which Whites tend to keep the construct of racism.

Chapter 4 discusses the dilemma I faced as a teacher educator learning about the racism of my own students and the impact this racism was having on the children tutored. In this chapter, I introduce the intervention method I used to draw the racism of the young women to their attention, and I present the stories of each woman as she experienced the intervention.

Chapter 5 presents an analysis of the steps tutors seemed to pass through as they experienced the intervention, including the forward and backward dance of admissions and denials. I then discuss themes that arose in the intervention, all of which point to the benefits of confronting racism.

Chapter 6 discusses the sense of empowerment tutors gained through the experience of being confronted with their own passive racism and concludes with recommendations for improving teacher education by addressing issues of Whiteness and racism in university curricula and field experiences.

I hope the information shared in this book will be helpful to educators seeking to better understand the influences of Whiteness and racism on the education of American schoolchildren of color, particularly English-language learners. I also hope the stories shared in this book can offer guidance to those hoping to disrupt and change these negative influences.

CHAPTER 1

Talking about Race

Because contemporary White Americans have been conditioned not to think about race and, especially, not to talk about it, facing the topic can be a challenging, frustrating, and even frightening experience for many. Preservice teachers in the multicultural issues in education classes that I teach often feel defensive when the word *race* is introduced in class. The topic makes them uncertain and sometimes angry. In the beginning of each semester, White students spend a lot of time arguing that race should not be the primary marker of diversity. Also, many argue that race is overemphasized in the field of education and that, in reality, we are all individuals with much in common and little that separates us. On some points, I agree with them. For example, I agree that race is neither the only marker of difference nor the only kind of diversity. In these classes, we talk about numerous aspects of diversity including socioeconomic class, gender, sexual identity, and more (see Adams, Bell & Griffin, 1997; Banks & Banks, 2003). However, I recognize the color-blindness that influences students' discomfort with the topic of race and, in a continual effort to dismantle color-blindness, I persistently call race to the students' attention and weave it into most every topic we discuss in class. Because the majority of my students and teacher education students around the country are White, I give a lot of attention to Whiteness. This makes students uncomfortable. But, as time goes by, most of them begin to develop language with which to talk about race, and many open their eyes to the influences of race on everyone's life.

A color-conscious repertoire of language and tools would be in contrast to the color-blindness embraced by most members of U.S. society, including most practicing teachers. The "color-blind" teachers with whom I have worked readily dismiss the notion that race has any influence on their students or themselves. At the same time they reject the influences of race, they often point to the underachievers in their classes, the "problem students," and the students who "don't fit in," many of whom are children of color. Sometimes *all* of these students are children of color. In these cases, race is definitely having an influence in the classroom. Across the United States, there is an achievement gap between White children and children of color. As recently as 1999, just over 7 percent of White students age 16 through 24 were considered to have dropped out of high school, while this was the case for nearly 13 percent of African American students and nearly 27 percent of Latinas/os (NCES, 2001). At the same time, Whites continue to outperform African Americans and Latinas/os in reading and math at every grade level measured (NCES, 2003b) and to attend college at higher rates (U.S. Census, 2003). Given the number of children of color who receive most, if not all, of their education from White teachers, race is an incredibly important topic that teachers must be able to think about and discuss.

Expectations and Race

The beliefs teachers and preservice teachers have about students make their way into the classroom even when the teachers themselves are unconscious or "dysconscious" (King, 1991) of their thoughts. Unacknowledged, passive racism certainly had an effect on Mrs. D's teaching. It is also evident in many of the schools that I visit today and in the tutoring experiences of my teacher education students. Not long ago, I taught a teacher education class that focused on issues related to English-language learning school children (ELLs) in the United States, including second language acquisition and teaching strategies for ELLs. This class was required for all elementary education and bilingual education majors. For the sake of simplicity, I call this course "Second Language Acquisition," or SLA. As a requirement for the course, all students tutored an ELL in a local public school or library for 10 hours during the semester. Because of the southwestern location of our university and the segregated nature of our town, nearly all of the children were of Mexican descent and from low socioeconomic backgrounds. This was usually the first experience the teacher education students had working with children whose linguistic, cultural, ethnic, and economic backgrounds were quite different than their own. Like most teachers, my students tended to be White, middle class women who spoke only English and who grew up in what Fuller (1994) terms *monocultural* environments; they had very little experience with racial or ethnic diversity.

While teaching this course, I discovered that many of the White students in the class had exceedingly low expectations for the ELLs they tutored. To learn more about their beliefs, I interviewed fourteen students in the class—nine Whites and five Latinas/os—about their tutoring experiences (Marx, 2000). While the White students professed to care deeply about the children they tutored and described the kids as "bright," all nine nonetheless predicted that the kids they tutored would drop out of school before graduating. Saliently, all of these kids were in elementary school. In contrast, all five Latina/o students I interviewed predicted that the children they tutored would be able to succeed in college at least to the extent that they, themselves, had. Some even predicted that the children would go further than they had educationally and economically. Although the White and Latina/o teacher education students shared many similarities in the ways they talked about the children they tutored, the differences in expectations between them were stark. After these interviews, I made substantial changes in the course syllabus and the way I taught the class. As the semesters went by, the low expectations and misunderstandings of ELLs became much more subtle, but they continued to surface semester after semester.

Believing that simple lack of information about ELLs and second language acquisition could not explain the low expectations White students consistently held regarding the children of color they tutored, I decided to probe deeper into the beliefs of the White students in the class to learn more about the factors contributing to these low expectations for ELLs. Because so many of my students had pointedly addressed the racial, ethnic, and cultural backgrounds of the children they tutored when sharing their beliefs about them, I knew I had to specifically focus on race and racism. As a result, one fall semester I explained to the students in the SLA class that I wanted to learn more about the beliefs of White, female, preservice teachers who spoke only English regarding race, racism, Whiteness, and the children they tutored, and I appealed to the class for volunteers. I chose students with these characteristics because they represent the dominant face of teaching, and their beliefs about children of color and English-language learners need to be better understood.

Creating a Trusting Discussion Environment

When I decided to talk with SLA students about race, racism, and their own White identities, I took into consideration the politically charged nature of any discussion of race in the United States and the pervasiveness of color-blindness and color-evasive language. To enable the young women to talk *about* race rather than just talk around it, I knew that I would have to create a trusting environment where they would feel safe sharing their honest thoughts. In addition, because most White Americans are so inexperienced talking about race, I knew that I would have to explicitly focus our conversations on race and continuously pull us back to the topic if necessary.

As I gave attention to the construction of a trusting environment, I realized that any White person invited to talk about race, ethnicity, and racism, in many ways, would be asked to speak a new language. Our society has become that adverse to talking about these issues. My background as an English as a second language (ESL) teacher reminded me of some foundational advice given to new teachers in my subject area:

> Overtly display a supportive attitude to your students. While some learners may feel quite stupid in this new language, remember that they are capable adults struggling with the acquisition of the most complex set of skills that any classroom has ever attempted to teach. (Brown, 1994b, p. 23)

Just like new speakers of English, new speakers of racial matters often "feel quite stupid in this new language." They have fragile egos and often are worried about saying the wrong thing. Without support and patience from others, these factors can easily lead to silence. Silence reinforces reliance upon color-evasiveness and color-blindness, entities that maintain racial inequity and should be deconstructed and discontinued (L. Bell, 2002; Bonilla-Silva, 2003; Frankenberg, 1993; Leonardo, 2002; Omi & Winant, 1994). In order to facilitate language that is race conscious, rather than race blind, patience and empathy are critical.

Although I respect and value the work of those antiracist educators who take a more confrontational approach to issues of race—such as McIntyre (1997), O'Brien (2004), Berlak and Moyenda (2001), and others—my approach is to develop mutual trust and respect with those willing to talk to me about such sensitive issues as race and racism before engaging in confrontation. While I believe that confrontation has an important place in intervention, the confrontation style that I share in this book is firm but gentle and respectful, something I will discuss at length in chapter 4. However, when first getting to know someone and in first broaching the topics of race, racism, and Whiteness, I take a congenial, information-gathering approach that is devoid of confrontation. This approach enables me to establish qualities that are critical to successful qualitative inquiry, such as mutual trust (Coenen, 1987; Boog, Coenen, Keune, & Lammerts, 1996; Gonzalez et al., 1995), dignity and respect (Lincoln & Guba, 1989), and optimal rapport (Brooks, 1989; Glesne & Peshkin, 1992; Jorgensen, 1989; Miller, 1952; Spradley, 1979).

In addition, my own background as an ESL teacher strongly influences my beliefs in the importance of trust. In ESL pedagogy, a safe, risk-embracing environment is the fundamental setting for successful language learning. The notion of an "affective filter," first proposed by Dulay and Burt in 1977 and adopted by ESL researchers and practitioners, uses the metaphor of a filter or wall that "goes up" and blocks out the learning at hand when affective factors such as anxiety, self-confidence, and attitude are activated. High anxiety creates a high filter. Conversely, when the affective filter is "low" or "down," the learner is open to receiving new information. As a teacher of ESL students, English-speaking high school students, and teacher-preparation university students, I have seen the value of a trusting learning environment for all kinds of subject matters, not just language.

Without a trusting, mutually respectful relationship between investigator and participant, participants cannot be expected to share their honest feelings about controversial topics. Confrontation at the early stages of discussion would likely lead to defensiveness and an even firmer embrace of color-evasive language for most Whites. At the same time, it could easily inspire those not yet committed to taking a deep, difficult look at race and racism to adopt the racial backlash about which Omi and Winant (1994), Helms (1990), and Kincheloe and Steinberg (1998), among others, have written. Racial backlash is characterized by a defensive attachment to White privilege and a renewed rationalization for racism. For example, rather than continuing to examine their own contributions to racial inequity, Whites experiencing racial backlash might suggest that African Americans or Latinas/os deserve the inequities they experience due to their own anger, untrustworthiness, ignorance, laziness, ineptitude, etc. Once a White person adopts racial backlash, it is very difficult for her or him to critique this stance, shake it off, and move forward in examinations of Whiteness, including White privilege and racism (Helms, 1990). In my own experience, I have witnessed confrontations that resulted in a renewed attachment to racism. Thus, it was very important for me in this project not to contribute to racial backlash.

The trusting, safe, discourse environment that I sought to create with my students was the first step that I took in avoiding backlash and creating a mutually respectful environment. I did this by getting to know the women for several weeks through the SLA class before asking them to talk with me. In this class, I modeled patience and guidance when politically charged topics such as bilingual education, English-language education, and school equity came up. By the time I met with the individual women, they had gotten to know me as an instructor fairly well. Also, in our first conversations, I asked them about their own racial and ethnic backgrounds, their own experiences with diversity, and their own expectations about tutoring children of color who were learning English. These were nonthreatening, reciprocal, conversations that enabled us to get to know one another.

Storytelling

As a means of building trust and sharing our realities with one another, the women I interviewed and I shared the stories of our beliefs, our plans, and our lives. This storytelling served as a powerful means of conveying information rich in context and feeling. The value of storytelling as a way to better understand the human condition has been described by several qualitative researchers, including Connelly and Clandinin (1994), Foley (1997), and Parker, Deyhle, and Villenas (1999). Many more qualitative researchers choose to use the term *life history* to describe the historical accounts of individuals that situate the stories they tell in time and place (see Ball & Goodson, 1985; Behar, 1993, 1996; Frankenberg, 1993; Goodson, 1981, 1983; Henry, 1998; Schultz, 1997; and Valdés, 1997). Connelly and Clandinin (1994, p. 8) suggest that life stories "function as arguments in which we learn something essentially human by understanding an actual life or community as lived." Ball and Goodson (1985, p. 24) add that through life histories, a teacher's career can "be studied in the context of the whole life." Because teachers' careers with children are intimate, holistic, and laden with values and beliefs, studying their perspectives through the highly contextualized method of storytelling seemed the most appropriate means to learn more about the future teachers who agreed to speak with me.

The stories the women and I shared also marked our own places in time and space. That is, they situated us as humans socialized by our lifetimes in the late twentieth and early twenty-first centuries, the places we grew up, the families and friends who nurtured us, and, necessarily, the Whiteness and racism that characterize our privileged status in the United States. As we talked, our stories constructed and then conveyed our realities. As Richard Delgado (1995b, p. 65) writes, for any event or situation, "there is no single true, or all-encompassing, description." Rather, all events are interpreted differently by different people; moreover, as we tell the story of what we have seen, "we participate in creating [it] (p. 65)." Although we have constructed this reality, we do not necessarily see our own handiwork. Very often, we consider our own interpretations to be the "truth." Delgado writes that membership in a particular group, where stories are shared and passed down to future generations, adds to the validity of these stories and serves to reify them. These stories often become a great source of pride because they "create their own bonds, representation, shared understandings, and meanings" (p. 64). They also, in the case of the dominant group, "remind it of its identity in relationship to out groups, and provide it with a form of shared reality in which its own superior position is seen as natural" (p. 64). Delgado labels the stories we tell and retell to maintain our superior position in society "stock" stories (p. 66). López (2001, p. 31) explains that, "These stock stories are so customary, so ingrained in our collective psyche, that they assume a normality that is often taken for granted." Indeed, these stories become our "truths."

Storytelling is used in this book in many ways. First, every time students and I met, we shared the stories of our lives, our tutoring experiences, and our beliefs about different things. Second, students shared the stories of their tutoring experiences and the connections they made with their own lives in the journals I collected three times over the semester. Third, in this book, I present the stories students told as well as the stories of our conversations as I try to construct complex, rich portraits of the women who graciously agreed to share aspects of their lives with me. Finally, the whole book is a story unto itself, unfolding as this investigation did. I cannot emphasize enough that trust was a fundamental element of our storytelling. Moreover, the more we shared ourselves through our stories, the more trusting we became of one another (Freire, 1970/2000). In Freire's words, we created a "dialogue," where I was something of a "teacher-student" and students became "students-teachers"; that is, we learned from and taught one another many things.

As I taught the SLA class and the semester progressed, I met with the nine women who volunteered to talk with me individually for interviews, at least three times and up to ten times, for an hour or two hours each time. In an effort to emphasize that these conversations were not related to their grade and to also facilitate a trusting environment, we met in coffee shops around campus or in my home.[1] One young woman actually stated that she felt "safer" meeting in my house where no one could overhear her talk about race. In the first few conversations, as discussed above, the young women talked about their own racial and ethnic backgrounds and their experiences with diversity. I introduced the notion of Whiteness to them and asked them to talk about their White identities. As their tutoring experiences got underway, we talked specifically about the schools and the children with whom they worked. In addition to our conversations, I observed the tutoring sessions of all 9 women once and collected their tutoring journals, as well as those of all 76 of their classmates, several times over the course of the semester. I also tutored a child in one of the local public schools where I saw many of my own students tutoring. All these ways of collecting information about the tutoring experience helped me to gain a strong understanding of the ways that race, racism, and Whiteness were influencing the ways that White education students were making sense of the children they tutored.

Instructor and Student Relationship

Although I built positive rapport with SLA student volunteers and I tried in many ways to circumvent the power I held as their instructor, by meeting in coffee shops and my home, by speaking casually, and by being consistently receptive to student thoughts and ideas during interviews and in class, in the end I was still the instructor and they were still the students. There was no getting around it. Thus, in getting to know the students who volunteered to talk with me, I reflected on my positioning constantly so as not to abuse my authority or fool myself into believing I had neutralized it. In light of this positioning, I sought to learn more about my own students with an ethic of responsibility akin to Noddings's (1984, 1994, 1999a, 1999b) ethic of caring. The caring relationship described by Noddings (1999a, p. 207) occurs when A, the "carer," "is nonselectively attentive, receptive to B [the cared-for]" and "experiences and exhibits motivational displacement," while B, the cared-for, "acknowledges that A cares." She also cites Mayeroff (1971, p. 1) in adding: "To care for another person, in the most significant sense, is to help him grow and actualize himself." For teacher-researchers investigating their own students, the responsibilities they have to respect their students, to be absolutely trustworthy, and to constantly work in their students' best interests are essential aspects of research. These responsibilities are also essential aspects of good teaching. Teacher-researchers have the double responsibility of being ethical teachers and ethical researchers simultaneously. The notion of an ethic of responsibility, I think, articulates this positioning well.

White Teacher Education Students

The nine White women who agreed to talk with me about race were representative, and not so representative, of "mainstream" future teachers. In reality, there is no such thing as a wholly "mainstream" person, as each of us has our uniqueness as well as our multiple positionalities and identities (Banks & Banks, 2003; Frankenberg, 1993; Kincheloe, et al., 1998). The simple fact that these women were interested enough in issues of race to talk with me sets them apart from the "mainstream" in some ways. Moreover, they spoke at length about how their gender, their religion, and their upbringing influenced their beliefs and their expectations in unique ways. When we talked about being members of the dominant White group, we also talked about being marginalized as women. Three women discussed being marginalized as Jews. Two also talked about being marginalized due to their low economic status. Conversely, two talked about their privileges growing up in wealthy families. Some were excellent students who aced all papers and tests; others had attendance problems, and one even apologized for occasionally sleeping in class. Concerning grades, they were A, B, and C students. The best way, I think, to convey the uniqueness of these nine women is to give a brief description of each that reveals something of each woman's background and character. Each of these short portraits, inspired by the descriptive narratives Valdés (1997) shares in her study of Mexican immigrant families, is meant to give readers a glimpse of the humanity and uniqueness of each young woman. They are introduced below in alphabetical order by the pseudonym each chose for herself.

Amy

Like several of her classmates, Amy turned 21 during the semester we got to know each other. She was about five feet five inches tall with dark, thick, wavy hair highlighted with copper streaks. Her skin was dark enough that, in the Southwest, she was sometimes mistaken for a Latina or someone from the Middle East. Most often when we met, she was dressed in jeans and a sorority sweatshirt. Amy gave me the impression of being an introspective, somewhat shy, young woman. She explained that,

> I am shy when I am around people that I don't know, but once I get to know them, I come out of my shell. . . . I am always the person that my close friends go to if they are having a problem and they need to talk about it. I am like "the good listener" when it comes to things like that.

Indeed, Amy did seem to be a very sensitive listener. She listened very carefully to my side of our conversations, and she often thought long and hard before she articulated her thoughts.

Amy grew up in San Antonio, Texas, in an environment she described as suburban and middle class. Although San Antonio is a predominantly Latina/o city, Amy always lived in predominantly White areas and attended public schools that were racially and economically mixed. While her neighborhood was predominantly White, it was also largely Jewish. Amy was Jewish and had attended Hebrew school since she was a little girl. While her Jewish identity was important to her, she still considered herself White. Although she grew up in San Antonio, she never had any close friends who spoke Spanish as a first language or learned English as a second language. When reaching, she could think of a girl of Puerto Rican descent with whom she carpooled sometimes when she was a child, but this was her only meaningful experience with a person of a different racial or ethnic background. Moreover, while Amy had traveled to Israel and Poland, she always traveled with groups of Jewish Americans. Because she always traveled with people who were, in her words, "just like me," she did not consider her travels to be challenging experiences with different cultures.

Amy's mother was a teacher and her father was a lawyer who worked in real estate. Amy had wanted to be a teacher her whole life. She planned to get a master's degree in religious education and eventually teach at a public suburban elementary school. She explained that "My dream job would be a kindergarten teacher in an elementary school like the one that I went to." The desire to teach in schools similar to the ones they attended was a common theme among these preservice teachers. For her field placement during the SLA class, Amy tutored at Mayan Elementary.

Ashley

Ashley also turned 21 during our semester together. She was confident, articulate, and over six feet tall. Her blonde hair, blue eyes, and very fair, rosy skin revealed her German heritage. Ashley grew up in a small town on the Texas-Mexico border. Her native language was Tex-Mex, the mix of English and Spanish that is the predominant language of the Rio Grande Valley. Her family was one of just a few White families in the area. Although her father was a firefighter and her mother worked as a church secretary, Ashley described her family's economic situation as "upper class" compared to her classmates and neighbors.

Ashley grew up as something of a "minority" in her small town; thus, when she came to our university as a freshman, she felt completely out of sorts with, and overwhelmed by, suddenly being a part of the White majority. As she explained,

> When I got here, I was staying in the dorms and everybody around me was White. Everybody. And I'm not used to that. I'd never seen so many White people, because in high school you just don't

see that. I mean I had maybe—oh, there were maybe 20 of us out of 400 kids. It was nothing compared to this. And *here they're all White!*[2] It made me feel *really* uncomfortable. For instance—it made me feel insecure that I was —that I was different from them, I guess. I don't know why it made me feel like that. And I came up here with several Hispanic friends who I'm not even really friends with any more because . . . I don't know, I guess my friends are just—all changed White.

As Ashley explained, around so many White people, she had at first felt out of place. Because her native language was Tex-Mex, she did not know the English words for common items such as sandals and gum, and she considered this an embarrassing deficiency. In our university town, she broke up with her Latino boyfriend of four years and slowly lost touch with her Latina/o friends as she began to embrace a new White identity. The semester we got to know each other, all of her friends were White, and she hated going back home to the Valley.

Although she had initially struggled with it, Ashley now loved being a part of the dominant White culture. When we met, she planned to teach second grade in a middle- or upper-class area far from the Rio Grande Valley, preferably in a White, suburban area, though she changed her mind several times as the semester unfolded. Through jobs, internships, and school programs, Ashley had worked with children nearly as long as she could remember. During this semester, she was a live-in nanny, a volunteer tutor, and a day-care teacher. At times, she stated that she needed a break from children. Because she felt pressured by her education program and her family to use her Spanish skills to work with impoverished Latina/o children, she felt that she particularly needed a break from Latina/o children. When we met, she absolutely refused to speak Spanish. As a devout Christian, she thought she would try something new and work as a missionary in Australia the next summer. She was very excited about this because it would be her first trip outside the American South. For her field placement during the SLA class, Ashley tutored at a public library tutoring program.

Becky

At 28, Becky had several years of work and military experience behind her. She was a confident, take-control kind of person. Her years managing Old Navy and Gap stores had outfitted her very well; she was always impeccably dressed, and her short, dark hair was always stylishly coiffed. Her dark hair and eyes made a striking contrast with her very fair skin. Becky grew up in an all-White community in Connecticut and attended public schools until sixth grade. At that point, since she was facing a teacher she did not like and a "rough" group of students, her parents transferred her to a private Christian school where she "blossomed." Becky loved her new school, explaining that,

> Kids in public school—they don't all come from the same, the same values as others. You know there's a lot of peer pressure and aggression, and in the *private school* I felt *safer* because they all came—pretty much came from the same background as I did.

Throughout our interviews, Becky expressed her beliefs in the importance of Christian values, a strong work ethic, and integrity. The "way you are raised," she often said, has the most significant effect on a person's life.

Although her initial plan had been to become a child psychologist, over the years, Becky changed her major to education because she remembered that her high school English teacher had told her that she would make a wonderful English teacher. I wondered if Becky had had some kind of epiphany that brought her back to school at an older age, and I asked her about it. Shaking her head, she firmly corrected me, clarifying that she had been pursuing her undergraduate degree every year but one since she graduated high school ten years ago. When her parents refused to help her pay for college, she immediately went to work, drawing her undergraduate experience out to 10 years.

When I asked her where she would like to teach when she finished college, she explained that she was looking for a school that was

> probably something that I'm used to, what I was brought up with. You know, probably like the schools I went to growing up . . . mostly White children, but that's because that's what I'm familiar with. I haven't experienced it. Of course being in [the Southwest], you're going to have a variety—I'm not opposed to that because I grew up having friends that were mixed races, so. . . . My first year, though, I probably want to be with something I'm more comfortable with.

Due to her age, her military and management experience, and her desire to teach high school, Becky was atypical of many of her classmates. However, her plan to teach White children from middle-class homes mirrored the intentions of most of the women presented here. For her field placement, Becky tutored at Benitez Elementary.

Claire

Claire was 22 when we met and wanted to be a teacher "since forever." She told me that she "loved kids" and had always enjoyed working with them as a tutor, babysitter, and lifeguard. After a family tragedy the year before our semester together, Claire had failed school. She was slowly building back up to a full-time course schedule and thought that talking with me outside of class about racial issues would motivate her to succeed in our class.

Claire grew up in a middle-class White neighborhood in a central part of our university town. From first through third grades she attended an elite private school that is well known for its wealthy clientele. For reasons she does not know, her parents transferred her to public school in fourth grade. In junior high school, she was bussed to the east side of town, which is predominantly Latina/o and African American. As she explained, in junior high, "Whites were definitely a minority. So it was very, very different." As an English-speaking, blue-eyed blonde, she did not easily fit in at first. After a period of adjustment, however, Claire became good friends with many of the Latinas in school

In high school, Claire once again met many of her friends from elementary school. Several of these friends had a hard time adjusting to the diversity of the public high school, where 60 percent of the student body was White. Although Claire had many close relationships with people of color in junior high school, in high school, most of her friends were White. Once at our university, she realized that she no longer had any close friends of color. She was, however, a strong believer in diversity. As she explained,

> I think you have to be. I do have some friends that are very, very close-minded. But anywhere you work, there is going to be diversity. Look at this [university].[3] You just get used to it. I don't really have an opinion either way.

Claire explained to me several times that she considered diversity to be "the norm" of things today. In describing the racism of her grandparents and even her parents, Claire made it clear that "I have definitely become more adapted."

Attending diverse schools had made a strong impact on Claire. She was very aware of her Whiteness, as her friends in junior high school and the children she tutored on the east side of town frequently remarked upon it. In thinking about schools where she would like to work, Claire was open-minded about teaching in both private and public schools, and White schools and diverse schools. She was interested in teaching in any of the several kinds of schools she had attended. For her field placement, Claire tutored at Benitez Elementary.

Elizabeth

Elizabeth also turned 21 during our semester together. She was extremely interested in the topics of White identity and racism. During that semester, she was also taking classes in cultural anthropology and sociocultural influences on learning. These classes, along with the class she was taking from me, were making a strong impression on her. Several times, Elizabeth stated that these classes and this opportunity to talk about race were together some kind of a "sign" that she needed to reevaluate her thoughts about Whiteness, culture, and "normalcy." She was blue-eyed and blonde, with long, thick hair that would tumble down to her waist if she didn't tie it up in a complicated fashion each day. She dressed consistently in light-colored Oxford shirts and jeans, and described her look by saying, "I dress like a White girl. Basically. I mean . . . I don't look diverse." She was so quiet in class that, if she had not volunteered to talk with me, I never would have guessed she was so interested in the topics we discussed.

Elizabeth grew up in the wealthy Dallas suburb of Plano, an area she called "a White suburban Beverly Hills." When she was little, her parents owned a successful business and were quite wealthy. In sixth grade, however, the business failed and her parents went bankrupt. They lost their house and cars, and Elizabeth's mother returned to work as a teacher. Despite the bankruptcy, Elizabeth continued to go to school in the same wealthy neighborhood. The experience changed her, though. She began to feel like something of an outsider. In the end, she believed that this experience brought her "down to earth," although it was a difficult struggle at the time.

Elizabeth talked at length about how much she valued the diversity she encountered at our university. Before coming to school and taking so many sociocultural and multicultural classes, she had never wanted to travel abroad. Now, however, she was very excited about possibly going to Spain and thought that a new cultural environment would be good for her. She was very critical of the wealthy, "sheltered," "normal" people she had grown up with in Plano, so she surprised me when she said that she planned to teach elementary school there. She realized her inconsistencies and laughingly explained that "Even though I like the diversity, I still want to go back to Plano." In trying to pin down what was drawing her back to the White suburban Beverly Hills, Elizabeth suggested that

Maybe it's because—when I was little, everything was *so great*. . . . It's just that I have *really good memories of childhood*. . . . I want to teach in either the school that I went to or at a school . . . which is a lot like it. Which, they are all basically the same. . . . I'm sure they were good—they were good schools because they were in Plano.

As her words convey, Elizabeth was a complicated young woman who was struggling with many different perspectives at the same time. She was ready to do some serious reflecting on the topics covered in her classes and in our conversations. For her field experience, Elizabeth tutored at Willow Elementary.

Gen

Although she looked about 25, Gen was 35 years old when we met. She had long, wavy brown hair, dark skin, and dark eyes. Although the color of her skin revealed her mixed Mexican, Native American, Norwegian, and Irish heritage, Gen considered herself White. She did not like to "classify" people according to their racial or ethnic heritage and explained that "I don't really consider myself anything. If I have to, I am White." She stressed several times that race was never really an issue in her school or home experiences. Indeed, throughout our time together, it was hard for Gen to "see" race or racism. During our first interview, when I asked her if she had any close relationships with people of color, she answered that race was "really not an issue" in her relationships because she was mostly a loner growing up. However, as we got to know each other, she shared that her boyfriend of eight years was Japanese American and that her step-mother was African American. Also, one of her closest and oldest friends was an African American man. Gen had always attended diverse schools, had always lived in multicultural neighborhoods, and had always had very close relationships with many people of color. However, she did not seem to realize this until we talked about her background at length.

In addition to her unusual White positioning, Gen had an unusual educational background for a teacher. As an army brat, she went to five elementary schools in three states from first through sixth grades. After her parents divorced, she moved with her mother to Corpus Christi, Texas, where she stayed, but lived in three different low-income to middle-class neighborhoods. Although she liked schoolwork itself, she had a very difficult time with many of her teachers. Her struggles culminated in high school when she quit tenth grade three times and then dropped out of school altogether. She did earn a GED, but life after high school was a mixture of bartending, drugs, and lots of wild times. As she said,

> That is the irony of it. And I get made fun of by my family: "You want to be a teacher? You? The dropout?" I was a party animal. I was bad. I was a teenager that did all the bad drugs and alcohol. . . .

A daughter, a stable relationship, and maturity eventually settled her down.

Gen's inspiration to become a teacher did not come from childhood dreams or a favorite teacher of her own. Rather, she was inspired by her daughter's third and fourth grade teacher. As she explained,

> I was really impressed with the way she handled her classroom. And she was very nice and the kids just. . . . I would watch the kids and how they would respond to their teachers, and it was like, I could do this. And it also comes down to a personal feeling that I want. . . . I need to do something that is fulfilling.

Gen's desire to become a good teacher clearly transferred to her tutoring experience where she put in more than double the time required for the class that I taught. She also tutored at another school for another teacher education class at the same time. The teachers she worked with at both schools raved about her devotion to the children and her help in the classroom. Gen was very open-minded about where she wanted to teach. She enjoyed her tutoring experiences so much she was thinking about applying to work in the schools where she volunteered. These mixed race, low-income schools were very much like the schools she had attended as a child. For the SLA class, Gen tutored at Johnson Elementary.

Megan

Megan was just 20 during our semester together, and her most marked characteristic when we first met was that she was very shy. Blue-eyed and blonde, she grew up in a middle-class, mostly White, suburban area of Dallas that bordered a wealthy community. According to her memory, the public schools she attended had an equal mix of White, Black, and Latina/o students, mostly from the upper-middle class. Although she considered her own family middle class—her father worked in insurance and her mother worked in retail—she shared that, in school, "most of my best friends were upper-middle class." While her high school had a mix of races, Megan had little close contact with people of color other than basketball teammates and student council members. She remembered that her school was tracked, with children of color filling up the lower levels.

It was surprisingly easy to talk to Megan about Whiteness and race. She was very interested in these topics and told me that an African American culture class she had taken the previous summer prompted her to think about the White role in racism for the very first time. She was already aware of Wellman's (1977) definition of racism as a system advantaging Whites, and she thought it made a lot of sense. Because she was very interested in different racial and cultural groups, towards the beginning of the semester she was planning to apply to a teaching program that recruited volunteers to teach in low-income urban or rural areas. She was very excited about this plan and explained,

> I really want to do that for two, I think two years—it's a two-year program. I really want to go somewhere far off, that's just different from anything I've ever known, maybe New York or California, New Mexico, just somewhere, work with those kids. I think that, I don't know, that that's just something that would give me a real [takes a deep breath], I don't know, sense of . . . just something different than what I've known.

More than anything else, a sense of adventure was pulling Megan to this exciting teaching experience.

In the very next breath, however, she clarified that her long-term plan involved teaching in an area much like the one where she grew up:

> And then, I'm sure, eventually, later on [starts laughing] when I get married, I want to settle in a smaller town. I've always wanted to live—my parents grew up in a small town. And, so, I know where I'll want to end up. Teaching or, you know, married, or whatever. But, I want to do that first.

So, like nearly all the women with whom I talked, Megan was planning to eventually return to a school much like the one she attended as a child. The adventure she sought for herself would be a temporary situation focused on giving to those less fortunate than herself. After that, she would go back to her roots. For her field service, Megan tutored at Willow Elementary.

Michelle

With fair skin, long dark hair, dark eyes, and the confident, purposeful air of a much older school administrator, something she planned to become, I was surprised to learn that Michelle turned just 21 during our semester together. She had a very strong personality and commandeered our relationship right away. She called when she needed to talk; she arranged meetings when she needed advice; and she stopped me after class when she thought I needed advice.

Michelle came from an upper-middle class Jewish family and grew up in a wealthy, predominantly White, Jewish neighborhood. The diamond earrings, faux tortoise-shell sunglasses, and expensive clothes she wore each time we met belied her wealthy background. From first to sixth grade, she attended an elite Jewish day school; after sixth grade, she attended well-respected public schools in upper-middle class areas while she continued "religious school on Tuesday nights and Sunday mornings." Although she remembered her schools as being "99 percent White," Michelle did have experiences with English-language learners because she was very close to wealthy, "high-class" relatives from Mexico. Michelle had many fond memories of "helping" these relatives. In her words,

> I always tutored them growing up. . . . And we are like their tutors; my family is like their tutors. . . . So I try to help them as much as possible, just be their older friend, they call me "Cousin Michelle." Really, if I told you how we are related, it is just so far back; but we are very close. . . . We are so close and its kind of like we always rely on each other and I would always have the boys in the summer. I used to have summer camps for them, and we used to have lots of activities, go swimming, and . . . we always helped them and I tutored them a lot.

In addition to these relatives, Michelle and her family also sponsored an immigrant Russian family and helped them acclimate to American life. She explained that

> My family did adopt a Russian family, we had a Russian Jewish family when I was much younger . . . and when they came to America, we were their first friends and we basically took care of them; I mean they were very nice. . . . We had them over all the time for dinner and my dad would help the father do his résumé. . . . So that was a great experience for me, because everyone in my school was well-to-do. Not *well-to-do*, but had everything. And, I met these people at such a young age that didn't have anything. So, I think it made me appreciate, honestly, what I had so much more. . . .

This same helping philosophy transferred to Michelle's past and present tutoring situations in her desires to be a strong, positive influence on the lives of children.

Michelle planned to teach for a few years and then become an administrator for a Jewish day school, much like the one she attended in elementary school. She had very fond memories of that school and stated that "I would definitely send my kids there. Like, there is no doubt in my mind." A very proactive person, Michelle was well on her way towards making her dreams a reality. For her field experience, she tutored at Mayan Elementary.

Rachel

Rachel was another student with a strong personality. She was 22 when we met and had thick, wavy, dark hair that fell just past her ears, fair skin, freckles, and hazel eyes. In addition to diamond earrings, she wore a little silver stud in her nose and a bejeweled *chai* pendant attached to a gold chain that signified her Jewish faith. She would reach into her neckline and pull out this pendant each time we met. She told me that she did this because she did not always feel "safe" publicizing her Jewish identity. As she explained, "I identify myself as Jewish as much as I can without doing it to the wrong people." Rachel felt that she had a strong dual identity, a cultural Jewish identity, and an ethnic White identity. Specifically, she said,

> I mean somebody wouldn't necessarily look at me and say, "Oh she's Jewish." I know that I am and that's how I identify myself, I guess. I mean, not as far as ethnicity goes. I fill out a survey, I say "White."

Rachel also described herself as "a liberal" who was "into helping." In fact, she said that she volunteered to talk with me because she thought the topic was interesting and because she wanted to "help" me.

Rachel grew up in Houston and spent the early part of her childhood in a predominantly White area. Over the years, the neighborhood started "getting run down," so her parents decided to move, and Rachel transferred to a wealthy White public school. However, she hated this school and explained, "I couldn't compete with those people. . . . And I hated it. I hated the people. I hated the way I felt—it was very *White*." According to her memory, her parents moved back to the original neighborhood after just one year partly because Rachel hated her new school so much. This time, though, Rachel found herself attending a much different school. Whites were the minority and, although she felt more comfortable with the diversity, she believed the education was deficient. She talked a lot about how her high school education did not prepare her for university work. In fact, she failed out of our university during her sophomore year, in part, she believed, because she was not well prepared academically. After returning to school, Rachel changed her major from social work to education and maintained high grades and high interest in the field.

In looking back at her school career, Rachel felt as though she received the best education from the Jewish elementary school she attended as a child. At the beginning of the semester, she was very devoted to private education. Her initial plan was to teach at a private school where she felt that the "parents would care" and the children would be well behaved and have values similar to her own. Later in the semester, however, Rachel changed her mind and became more interested in teaching at a diverse public school because, in her words, "I would have more to offer a school like that." When I asked her to explain, she said, "I want to feel, you know, like I'm helping, and I feel like I would feel that way more at a school like [the public school where she was tutoring] than at a private school." However, she felt that it was very important that she send her own future children to a private school, preferably Jewish, where the atmosphere would be "safe" and "calm." She wanted her own children to develop "a strong Jewish identity" through Jewish day school or supplementary Hebrew school. Rachel tacked back and forth between the merits of public and private education for herself and her own future children throughout our semester together. For her field experience, she tutored at Smith Elementary.

The Tutors in Sum

Overall, the young women had many similarities. Amy, Michelle, and Rachel, especially, had a lot in common because they were good friends who together had decided to talk with me about race, racism, and the issues of identity that were part of the interviews. The most striking similarity of all these tutors, except for Ashley, was that they planned to eventually teach or work as an administrator in schools similar to those they had attended as children. Ashley's desire to teach in an upper-class, predominantly White school was strongly influenced by her own school experience in a low-income, predominantly Latina/o region. Like all the other women discussed, Ashley hoped to eventually work in a school where the children would be racially, culturally, and economically similar to herself. In addition to this similarity, most women expressed a strong desire to "help" children who were less fortunate than themselves. Consequently, they found tutoring in schools with large populations of English-language learners and children of color from low socioeconomic backgrounds to be very rewarding. Several of them also mentioned how important it was for them to be good "role models" for the children with whom they worked.

Because the SLA class was required for most students in the class, SLA students were not necessarily interested in diversity issues. Those volunteering to talk with me about their tutoring experience likely had more interest in diversity than most; however, the stories they shared above reveal that they were not strongly dedicated to the topic. While they were excited to work with children who were different from themselves and to talk with me about the experience, most planned to work with White, middle-class children in White, middle-class areas in the future.

As I got to know these women, I found that I had something in common with each of them. At 20 years old, Elizabeth and Ashley were making plans to travel abroad for the very first time, something I had done at 20 as well. Ashley was considering teaching abroad, a move that had started my own teaching career. Becky, Gen, and I agreed that getting our teaching credentials a little bit later than average was a benefit to us and the children we taught. Claire and I discovered that we were members of the same college sorority. I could relate to Amy's sensitive nature, as well as to Michelle's, Rachel's, and Ashley's assertiveness. All women were excited about becoming teachers and truly valued their tutoring experience. Because we shared these many interests, our conversations were typically warm, engaging, and filled with laughter. In addition to being able to relate to these women, I also grew to like each of them a great deal. I looked forward to meeting them in and outside of class, as their vibrant personalities and their desires to become better teachers were always evident.

My Own Story

Because I am a White, female educator from a middle-class background who is fluent only in English, I understand many of the life experiences and feelings about race and racism the women above and other students have expressed over the years. I have much in common with most of my teacher education students. These commonalities allow me to be something of a "cultural insider" (Foley, 1998, p. 116) in any discussion of Whiteness. I definitely know what it is like to live the White experience. Like the White student teachers with whom McIntyre (1997) worked, I was taught directly and indirectly that I could be something of a "White knight" (p. 121) all my life. Like them, while growing up I thought of myself as "having good parents, good values, a good education . . . In contrast, [I] saw students of color as not having—as somehow deficient" (p. 121). This was due in part to the lingering effects of the United States's historical association of goodness with Whiteness (Franklin, 1751; Omi & Winant, 1994; Takaki, 1990). It was also due to the distance that characterized my relationships with people of color, something very similar to the distance described by most of the young women above (see also Hartigan, 1999; Frankenberg, 1993).

I grew up in a rural region of Kentucky populated mostly by low-income White farming families. African American families lived primarily in the small town that served as our county seat. While I was growing up, the only English-language learners in our county school system were occasional European exchange students, though, since that time, increasing numbers of Mexican nationals have migrated in and out of the region. My middle school had a large African American population, but I never became close friends with any of the African American students. Also, although about 15 percent or so of my high school was African American, only three African Americans were in any of my "honors" classes. The private liberal arts college that I later attended enrolled only four students of color during my time there. When I pursued my teaching certification through a masters of arts in teaching program at an urban-centered public university several years later, there was only one African American student and no other people of color in my cohort of 54. The lack of diversity I experienced throughout my educational experience is fairly common for Whites, due to the segregated society in which we live (Donato, Menchaca & Valencia, 1991; Trueba, 1998). It was easy to think of my Whiteness and the Whiteness of these institutions as normal or, rather, not to think of it at all.

The neutrality of my race was disrupted for the first time when I moved to Japan to teach English. I realized that I was White when my Whiteness suddenly became a marked characteristic. It seemed that wherever I went in Japan, strangers would call "Hello!" to me; they would sit down, uninvited, next to me at the beach to practice English; and they would often tap on my car window at red lights to ask about English lessons. Though these strangers likely equated Whiteness with "Americanness," this new attention to my Whiteness truly unsettled me. My Whiteness was so arresting that I startled myself sometimes when I unexpectedly glimpsed my own reflection in shop windows. On occasion, I gasped with great surprise when I saw another White person. It was not possible to deny my Whiteness when I lived in Japan, although I certainly tried to do so. Many times I emphasized that I was "just normal" and not necessarily a product of my Whiteness or my home culture. This may sound unbelievable to people of color who frequently realize the parameters of their racial in-group very early in their lives (Scheurich, 1993). However, it is true that undisrupted Whiteness causes "we Whites [to] operate as if we are oblivious to our racial positionality and its effects in terms of the inequitable distribution of resources and power within our society" (Scheurich, 1993, p. 8). In fact, obliviousness characterizes much of Whiteness. Like the teacher education students with whom I work, I did not grow up "in a structural position [that allowed me] to either see the effects of racism on [my life] or the significance of race in the shaping of U.S. society" (Frankenberg,

1993, p. 9). I was oblivious. In Japan, however, my Whiteness attracted a bright spotlight that illuminated my presence every day, everywhere I went. It was impossible to deny.

Since my time in Japan, I have given considerable effort to examining my own White identity and to Whiteness as a concept. It is a never-ending study. In this sense, I am quite different from my students. Very few White college students (or White people for that matter) have critically examined Whiteness. Teacher educators interested in examining this issue with pre-service teachers must realize that they begin this exploration from a very different perspective than their students.

Conclusion

In endeavoring to open up conversations about race, racism, White tutors, and the children of color they tutored, I kept all of the above information in mind. I knew I would be entering into unchartered waters and that the women I spoke with would likely feel uncomfortable talking about issues related to race in a direct manner. I realized that I would have to build trusting relationships with them in order to open up these dialogues. I also realized that each tutor was an individual who was influenced by her own unique background, just as I am an individual influenced by mine. Taking all this information into consideration, I began this project with excitement and not a small amount of trepidation, curious about what I was getting myself into.

CHAPTER 2

Illuminating the Invisible

Describing Whiteness has sometimes been expressed as "illuminating the invisible" because it envelops so much of what White people and many people of color consider normal rather than a marker of White culture, interests, language, etc., as my own story in the previous chapter illustrates. Because Whiteness is perceived by Whites as the status quo and the "normal" experience, it manifests itself as "raceless" (Chennault, 1998, p. 314). Ethnic restaurants, hair salons, neighborhoods, and even identities, for example, are typically considered entities possessed by people of color, rather than Whites. In addition, though "ethnic groups," i.e., racial/ethnic groups that are not White, are often understood as having shared histories and cultures that have been influenced by time, political movements, geographic change, and more, Whites and Whiteness are considered to be somehow impervious to these same influences (Rodriguez, 1998; Frankenberg, 1993).

Frankenberg (1993), Kincheloe and Steinberg (1998), and Shome (1999), among others, note that the phenomenon of racelessness and imperviousness are linked to colonialism. Western expansion into "the heart of darkness" (Conrad, 1902) and lands populated by mysterious and frightening "vile race[s]" (Shakespeare, 1611), such as "Blacks and Tawneys" (Franklin, 1751), and other "savages" (Conrad, 1902), has influenced Western literature and thought from (at least) the time of the British empire to the present. The success of Western imperialism has encouraged the dominant group, Franklin's "lovely White" (Franklin, 1751), to continually envision itself as civilized, good, moral, and upstanding, most especially in contrast to what it is not: the person of color, the Other (Kincheloe & Steinberg, 1998; Leonardo, 2002; McIntyre, 1997; Said, 1987; Takaki, 1990). Succinctly summarizing these points, Leonardo (2002) writes that, "The Orient is written into history by the Occident. Simultaneously, the Occident invents itself by inventing its Other" (p. 45, citing Said, 1979).

In Franklin's day, the purity of the White race was synonymous with the purity of virtue (Takaki, 1990). White Americans are still influenced by these ideologies, despite their/our protestations to the contrary. The legacies of colonialism, racial domination, and hegemony lend to the construction of White Americans and White American society today. To put it concisely, "The development of White identity in the United States is closely intertwined with the development and progress of racism in this country" (Helms, 1990, p. 49). This is a point on which Whiteness scholars agree. Although a White person making this connection for the first time would likely be shocked, when Whiteness is deconstructed, it clearly can be discerned that racism lies at its heart.

The Invisibility and Neutrality of Whiteness

In meeting with the young women from the SLA class who agreed to talk with me about race, racism, and Whiteness, I took the opportunity to explicitly ask them what Whiteness meant to them. In deconstructing their understandings of the subject—something most of them had never before done—the women shared thoughts that represent two aspects of Whiteness found in the literature on the topic: invisibility and neutrality. These two different ways of understanding Whiteness will be discussed below, followed by a discussion of how the young women understood the contrasting construct of color.

Amy and Gen, more than any other tutors with whom I talked, were confounded by the notion of Whiteness. This perspective on Whiteness is most common among Whites who have never thought about their own racial positionality. For Whites like Amy and Gen, Whiteness is entirely "invisible," so it is nearly impossible to describe (Chennault, 1998; Hartigan, 1999; McIntosh, 1988/1997; Rodriguez, 1998; Giroux, 1998; Proweller, 1998; Wildman & Davis, 1997). Amy's reaction to the invitation to, "Tell me about your White identity," illustrates her bewilderment. She stared at me, opened her mouth, lifted her hands in the air, and tried to call forth words that just would not come. She finally gave up and admitted that, "I've never been asked questions like this before! I don't know how to answer that one." Amy could not think of a single way to describe Whiteness, except to finally point out the color of her skin.

This means of identifying with Whiteness, however, was problematic because Amy's skin color was dark enough that, in the Southwest, she was often mistaken for a Latina. While she felt that her Whiteness was indisputable, she could not articulate any of its parameters. Likewise, Gen could not identify a single characteristic of White culture. In fact, she asked, "Do we have a culture? I mean, because we are all so different. We all come from so many different places. I really don't know how to answer that." Neither Gen nor Amy had ever thought about being White; consequently, White culture and White identity were completely invisible to them.

No other woman with whom I talked was rendered speechless by the invitation to discuss White identity and culture. Rather, everyone else was able to illustrate Whiteness by subtly or obviously contrasting it to color. Whiteness, for these women, was described as neutral and normal. Elizabeth's thoughts about White culture offer a good example of this perspective. She was able to define the borders of Whiteness by describing all things that were normal to her growing up. As she explained,

> We had White friends, we went to a White country club, and we did normal, American activities. We went to swim team. We were in Girl Scouts and Boy Scouts and dance and gymnastics and we were just—we had three kids and a dog. We had a swimming pool. Maybe that's how I see White people at least.

Although our southwestern town is not extremely racially diverse, to Elizabeth, it was much more diverse than the "White Beverly Hills" of her hometown. She went on to explain that her childhood community was so White that, now

> Even if I see someone whose skin is White, I still might not even think of them as White because I come from *such* a suburbia. You know? It's just like the All-American place [claps hands with each word in 'All-American place']. So, that's what I think of as White, I guess.

Elizabeth assessed Whiteness as the normal, "All-American" suburban experience. Before she moved away from White suburbia, and spent some time thinking about it, Whiteness had been completely invisible to her. Now that she lived in a more diverse area, however, she recognized her home culture as the more "normal" White experience.

Claire, Megan, and Michelle likewise began to see the borders of their Whiteness by spending time with people of color. All three professed to feel somewhat out of place in schools where Whites made up the minority of students and teachers. Claire's comments illustrate this feeling most clearly. In a predominantly African American school where she used to tutor, an African American girl named Rolanda had called her "White girl," much to Claire's mortification. When this happened, Claire immediately said, "Rolanda, I do have a name. I am Claire." I asked Claire how she felt about the appellation "White girl"; she confessed, "I was kind of *stunned*." Being marked as White upset Claire's sense of racial neutrality and made her feel uncomfortable. She did not want to be White; she just wanted to be normal. As she explained, "I guess I just don't really think I am that different from anyone else just because of skin color at all." Becky expressed similar sentiments when she said that, regarding children of color, "They are people. I'm a person. And . . . I just like kids. So, I just talked to them. You know, I don't really think about [racial and cultural differences]." This desire to shrug off the marker of race is a very common feeling among Whites.

Rachel's ability to articulate her Whiteness came not from comparing her identity to people of color but by contrasting her White identity with her Jewish identity. She explained that her Whiteness allowed her to "blend in" with the norm, while her Jewish identity marked her as different from the norm. In her words, this dual identity allowed her to consciously "play both sides of the fence." With this understanding, Rachel seemed to consider the obliviousness of Whiteness as a kind of racial safety net that was available to her when she needed it.

Ashley took a similar kind of refuge in White identity. Unlike the other women with whom I talked, she remembered thinking that the predominantly Latina/o border community where she grew up was the normal experience. When she first moved to our predominantly White university town, Whiteness was marked for her and her own background was neutral. However, over time, she embraced White culture and the advantages it gave her. This led her to begin assessing the negative aspects of the culture she left behind as characteristics, or markers, of color. When I asked her to describe White culture, for example, she paused for several moments and then answered, "higher class." She went on to explain that

> In the [Rio Grande] Valley, you have White, kind of working class, but you really don't have White poverty because you have a lot of Hispanics having babies, and they usually end up at the poverty level, and they're all on welfare down there—everybody. The White class hung out together . . . there was like, you know,

10 to 20 people. And, they all hung out, and then you have the Hispanics who just *associated* themselves with the White people and kind of hung out with us too.

Ashley readily contrasted the negative aspects of her home culture with the positive aspects of her newly adopted White culture. She rejected the race, culture, economic status, and language of her home culture, as she rejected her old Mexican American friends. Ashley recognized the higher social status of Whiteness and gladly embraced it. In fact, she felt that Whiteness represented not just "the norm," but also a superior "class." The more time she spent in our university town, the more normal Whiteness felt to her, and the more negatively marked her home culture became.

The Contrasting Markedness of Color

In addition to being invisible or neutral, the White racial group is also commonly perceived by Whites as being extremely complex and ambiguous (Katz & Ivey, 1977; Nakayama & Krizek, 1999; Tatum, 1999). This perception is tied to the belief that White culture is not a cohesive entity but rather, an amalgamation of very different individuals with little else in common but skin color (McIntyre, 1997; Rains, 1998; Scheurich, 1993; Tatum, 1999). In contrast to their own complexity, Whites often perceive cultures of color to be homogenous, tight-knit entities with clear parameters (Feagin & Vera 1995; Frankenberg, 1993, 1997). Frankenberg (1993, 1994) explains that the very ambiguity of White culture is evidence of its colonial past. Groups that are named, bound, and encouraged by the dominant culture to remain "pure" and "preserved" (1993, p. 193) like Native Americans, Inuit, and other native groups, are most likely to be groups that have been marginalized by colonialism. In its dominance, White culture remains unmarked. Indeed, many Whites profess to feel resentment and even envy regarding the imagined cohesiveness of these "other" cultures. Many of the women with whom I talked, as well as many other students I've taught over the years, expressed such thoughts. Omi and Winant (1994), Apple (1998), Kincheloe and Steinberg (1998), Leonardo (2002), and others describe these feelings as evidence of a backlash against the progress of racial minority groups. The more I talked to the young women about race and Whiteness, the more evidence I found for the existence of racial backlash.

Elizabeth's words most vividly illustrate this negative perspective. Although she had a relatively easy time talking about White culture in our first interview, by our second interview her understanding of Whiteness had grown much hazier. The more she thought about it, the more ambiguous it became. After several quiet moments, she passionately exclaimed, "*I don't really know what American culture is!* That's my whole deal." In a frustrated manner, she tried to describe her thoughts:

> I have started to think about this all the time, how it's such a *big deal.* Everything is, you know, being politically correct and not insulting someone else's culture. Helping them preserve it or incorporating their culture. But . . . I just think that for White people . . . it's just hard. It's such a big emphasis on fitting into your group and to your culture and to your ethnicity. But for White people, we are just clumped in one. So, I think White people are just lost. And they don't know where, you know, they don't know where they fit in. . . . It just makes me wonder where I fit in. You know? Or where—where—because White people—their groups are religious or . . . subgroups, like, deaf people have a set culture, gay people have a set culture—or whatever—but, I'm not deaf. I'm not gay. I'm not blind.

As her words indicate, Elizabeth felt she had no culture in contrast to people of color and White subgroups. This lack of culture was something that troubled her deeply. She admitted that she was envious of the strong cultures other groups seemed to share. She wanted to be part of a cultural group, but explained that she didn't know where she fit in since she had no ties with her Welsh and Scottish heritage, nor any subgroup qualities. The pervasiveness of the dominant White culture, a culture of which she was very much a part, completely eluded her, as did the historical oppression experienced by the groups she perceived as having strong cultures. In fact, her interchangeable use of the terms "American culture" and "White culture" gives even more evidence for the dominance of White culture in the United States and her membership in that racial category. By using these terms interchangeably, she was equating them. The participants in Frankenberg's (1993) study on White women describing Whiteness spoke in the same manner.

In contrast to the complex, dynamic understanding of culture adopted by critical scholars and many multicultural educators, Elizabeth had a superficial understanding of culture. Whereas Erickson's (2003, p. 32) description of culture includes everyday habits, norms, expectations, and the "sedimentation of the historical experience of persons and of social groupings of various kinds," upon which these everyday experiences are built, Elizabeth thought of culture as voluntary remembrance of shared history, traditions, and cooking, something Alba (1990) found to be the typical ways that Whites define ethnic identity. Perhaps because she did not recognize the oppression of the traditionally marginalized groups she described as cultural, Elizabeth did not see her own role in the larger, White, oppressing culture.

Amy expressed similar sentiments after unsuccessfully trying to put White culture into words. Finally, she explained that

> I think that if somebody was Hispanic or African American and they were asked the question, "Do you consider yourself this race or ethnicity?" they'd [say], "Oh, you know, there's this *history* and everything." And . . . I just . . . I just don't feel like I can say anything. I don't know. It's hard thinking of anything.

Like Elizabeth, Amy did not know much about African American or Latina/o history, but she did consider it something that tied these people of color together. As a White person, she could not relate to this kind of cohesion.

Becky also shared this same perspective on the cultures of others and admitted that "I almost envy that, you know, all that support [people of color seem to give one another]." Laughing, she went on to say,

> Growing up I wished my mother was more *ethnic*. You know, like Polish. My friend's mother was Polish and she was an awesome cook, and I thought, gee, if my mom was Polish or my mom was, you know, if she was Mexican, we'd have all this wonderful food . . . .

This desire for a more "ethnic" mother shows Becky's superficial understanding of culture, as well as her belief that people who did not consider themselves White shared a more defined, cohesive culture.

Ashley's similar understanding of culture led to feelings of both respect for and frustration with the Latina/o culture with which she grew up in the Rio Grande Valley. She explained that "I just don't like being down there. People are really culture-[centered]. They are really big in their culture. They are very proud, very, very, very much so." Although she claimed to admire the pride of her home community, she could not relate to it and felt out of place in the midst of it.

These contradicting feelings of respect, envy, and resentment were common among most of the women with whom I talked and many White SLA students. In fact, the day I introduced the notion of White culture in class, using Peggy McIntosh's (1988/1997) article on White privilege as a starting point, a White student, Johanna, immediately expressed her thoughts that Whites had no culture. She voiced her feelings that while Latinas/os shared religious and familial bonds, and African Americans shared a strong community, Whites were so diverse that they did not share any of those markers of culture. To help Johanna better understand White culture, a Latina student voluntarily pointed out aspects of Latina/o culture and then invited Johanna to point out similar aspects of her own culture. This invitation just made Johanna more confused. Next, an African American male student volunteered that all the elements of diversity Johanna had just talked about in White culture were elements he could see in African American culture. He then criticized the term "African American community" as labeling something that did not exist. As this class wrapped up, I felt very proud of the SLA students for intelligently negotiating such complex ideas. I thought the class had gone amazingly well. However, later, when I talked about this class session with the women I interviewed, several of them only remembered what Johanna had said about a diverse, indefinable White culture. None of them remembered any comments made by the students of color. It was as if those students had not spoken at all. The White women's beliefs in a dynamic, indefinable White culture that contrasted sharply with the static cultures of people of color remained unshaken. Discussing the tenaciousness of preconceptions, Pajares (1992) writes that "There is substantial evidence to suggest that beliefs persist even when they are no longer accurate representations of reality" (p. 317, citing Nisbett & Ross, 1980). He goes on to add that Nisbett and Ross "could find no literature showing that individuals pursue, even in minor ways, strategies that aid in the alteration or rejection of unreasonable or inaccurate beliefs." The words of these young women certainly give evidence for this disappointing assessment.

The Entwined Nature of Whiteness and Racism

Although Whiteness has ties with skin color, discourse, economic class, ethnic heritage, geographic location, and membership in the most dominant social group, these ties are inconsistent and debatable (see Bell, 1995a; Frankenberg, 1993; Hartigan, 1999; Leonardo, 2002; Lopéz, 1995; Twine, 1997). What does remain consistent and fundamental is the solid connection between Whiteness and racism (Helms, 1990; Frankenberg, 1993; Leonardo, 2002). Some argue that the United States officially established White racial superiority as an American ideal when enslaved people were counted as three-fifths human and all other people of color were omitted in the U.S. Constitution of 1787 in regards to how the population would be counted for purposes of taxation and representation (Bell, 1995a; Chennault, 1998; Goldwin & Kaufman, 1988). The privileges attached to Whiteness have been, and continue to be, perpetuated in subtle ways through American institutions and popular culture, as the earlier discussions of essentialist racism, cultural deficit thinking, and the "at-risk" child have illustrated. McIntosh (1988/1997, p. 291) likens the privileges of White Americans to "special provisions, assurances, tools, maps, guides, code-books, passports, visas, clothes, compass, emergency gear, and blank checks," that are unearned benefits of being born White. The color-evasive era we live in today exacerbates the invisibility of these privileges and dis-suades efforts to discuss them as particularly linked to race.

However, because Whiteness and racism are so thickly woven together, just talking about Whiteness and race with Whites can readily illuminate beliefs in the inferiority of people of color and the superiority of Whites. In fact, showing our racism is a lot like showing our accent. It is some-thing that is neutral to our own ears, yet marked to those from a different place. Because I am further along in my understanding of race, racism, and Whiteness than the women with whom I talked, in our conversations, I was something of an "out-of-towner" who could hear the racism that accented their words. At the same time, I recognize that racism accents my own words and perspective as well, in ways I do not even realize (Scheurich, 1993). Recognizing this difference in sensitivity to racism, throughout our discussions I emphasized to the women I interviewed that I wanted to gather a better understanding of their deep-seated beliefs, and, in order for this to happen, I needed for them to speak honestly. Such talk requires a conscious effort to avoid color-blind language. I also suggested that the women avoid the constraints of "politically correct" language if they found it cumbersome. I assured them that no fail-safe language existed that would make our conversations easy. But I promised that I would not use their own words to "malign" them and I emphasized that pseudonyms, rather than real names, would be used in any portrayal of them. It is likely because of this purposely constructed, trusting environment that the comments of the young women who spoke with me were less assuaged by color-evasive language than is typical. Their honest words, harsh at times, give some insight into the beliefs they likely would not have voiced other-wise. The ways in which racism was entangled in their words as they dis-cussed people of color and English-language learners are discussed below.

Associating Color with Deficits

Thinking of children of color and English-language learners in terms of what they do not have—that is, in terms of their deficits—is extremely common among White Americans, perhaps especially among educators (see Valencia, 1997). Deficit thinking is very often perpetuated in colleges of education where preservice teachers learn that children of color and English-language learners are hard to teach and overrepresented in special education and remedial classes (Artiles, Harry, Reschly, & Chinn, 2002; Banks & Banks, 2003; Cummins, 1986, 1994; Delpit, 1995; Wink, 2000). Even though classes in multicultural education and diversity are meant to improve the education of the teachers who will work with all kinds of children, they oftentimes reinforce prejudices and stereotypes, rather than disrupt them (Sleeter, 1992b). Because deficit thinking is so pervasive, it would be the exception, rather than the rule, to think outside of it. One might even consider it a characteristic of White culture. Not surprisingly then, all the women I talked with showed some signs of deficit thinking concerning people of color. The ways in which they did so are outlined below.

Deficits in Culture   The deficit thoughts of most young women concerning the cultures of people of color were illuminated when they contrasted these "other" cultures with their own. Rachel, for example, described the students who dropped out of the urban, racially diverse high school she attended as "*demographically,* I guess, [different from] me and my friends." Michelle was more explicit when she described the predominantly African American school where she tutored the semester before we met, and its students, as "trashy." She was dismayed that the kids looked like "they just rolled out of bed" each time she saw them. Michelle then contrasted this school with the predominantly Latina/o school where she tutored during our semester together. She described the Latina/o kids as "cleaner," better dressed, and more appropriately concerned with their appearance than the African American children. When I asked her how these schools compared to those she attended, she took a deep breath and exclaimed, "Gosh, I went to a private Jewish day school!" And left it at that. Although Michelle did not specifically state the superiority of her own upper-middle-class White background, these feelings certainly came through in our discussions about children of color.

Ashley clearly stated her thoughts about the Latina/o border culture where she grew up by saying, "I feel like I'm settling for less when I go home." Just talking about her hometown brought a frown to her face. Expressing similar thoughts about the cultural deficits of Latinas/os, Claire suggested that her Latina/o friends made it to college despite "their backgrounds, their environment." All the women who talked about the deficits of other cultures did so with ease. They seemed to assume that I would naturally agree with the characterizations they offered.

Deficits in Language   In addition to deficiencies in culture, nearly all women, at some point or another, commented on the deficient nature of the home language of the child they tutored. This was of particular interest to me because language, of course, was the focus of the SLA class in which we all participated. Michelle, for example, termed the language used by the two kids she tutored "slang," "street language," and "poor English." She also denigrated the support she felt their parents' gave this language. Her deficit thoughts were vividly demonstrated when I observed her tutoring Valerie. Trying not to distract them too much, I sat a little ways away from Michelle and Valerie as I observed and listened to their interactions. Michelle was tutoring Valerie in reading and they were taking turns reading the pages of a popular children's book. Michelle hugged Valerie many times and showered her with praise so frequently that she often disrupted Valerie's reading. I listened to Valerie carefully and made mental notes of her English skill. She seemed to be doing a very good job with the book she was reading. After she finished the whole book, Michelle encouraged her to show the tutoring director her accomplishment. Valerie excitedly ran over to him with her book, and he responded by giving her a big hug. I was pleased to be observing such a supportive learning environment. However, as I watched this interaction, Michelle turned around and tried to catch my gaze. She leaned in to make sure she had my full attention, scrunched up her face and said, "See? This is what I mean." Absolutely mystified, I waited for her to explain. She took a deep breath and exclaimed, "Her English is so poor!" She then mimicked Valerie's accent several times to illustrate her point, adding that Valerie's accent was "just kind of street—I think of it as just kinda more of a street talk. Sometimes," she added, "her grammar is real bad. She has the Mexican talk." Her assessment of the second child she tutored, Cristobal, was even more unfavorable. As she said, "Oh, Cristobal is worse. He's like a street . . . urchin." By this, she meant that Cristobal, a fourth grader, talked in a "slangy" way and dressed "like a gangster."

Ashley's feelings about Tex-Mex were similar to Michelle's feelings about "street Mexican talk." In talking about her own native language, she said, "I don't like Tex-Mex, Sherry!" When I asked her to articulate the feelings behind this statement, she took a deep breath and passionately cried, "Augh!! Tex-Mex is *low*." She then explained,

> It's like if you take a genuine Hispanic and a White person and you mix them together and you have an offspring kid. The kid's both, you know. The kid's kind of a mix. So Tex-Mex is just kind of a, you know, it's a *mix*! It's not really a genuine thing! Either speak English or speak Spanish! Just don't speak both.

Ashley's feelings about the Tex-Mex language mirrored her feelings about the border area—and the border people—where she grew up. She could not imagine anything worse than speaking a mixed language or being a "mixed" person. Although her passionate abhorrence of Tex-Mex is striking, Ashley is not alone in these feelings. English speakers north of the U.S.-Mexico border and Spanish speakers south of the border often disparage this mixed language and the border people who speak it. These social stigmas are a part of her culture, and they have influenced Ashley's perception of language, land, and people.

One theme we revisited many times in the SLA class was the importance of encouraging maintenance of the home language in order to both scaffold the second language with the first and support strong family units. The literature in second language acquisition strongly supports this "additive" perspective (e.g., Collier, 1995; Lambert, 1974; Trueba, 1988, 1998). Over the years, however, I have found that many students resist this particular bit of information because it contradicts their own opinions and previous beliefs (Marx, 2000; Nespor, 1987; Pajares, 1992). Thus, despite our continued attention to this topic in class, SLA students often associated home language use—even the existence of a non-English home language—with deficiency, as the women described in this section illustrate.

For example, during one of our meetings, Rachel shared that, "In all the articles we've read, [I've learned that] it's important that the home have an open mind about these kids learning English." While I did not disagree that language teaching is benefited when families support their children's English learning effort, I did disagree that our course articles focused on that topic. In contrast, I told Rachel that our class had consistently advanced the perspective that the teacher should encourage home language use and then add in English. None of the articles we read in class advanced the perspective Rachel stated. As I clarified this for her, Rachel listened to me but then tried to better explain her point by saying that, "I don't want the kids to—just because their parents don't care, [to learn a] 'they don't care' kind of attitude." This clarification revealed Rachel's embrace of deficit thinking regarding the home language and families of the children she tutored even more clearly. After all, she had no evidence that the parents did not care about English, education, or the successes of their children. She just assumed that this was the way things were for ELLs.

Sentiments such as those shared by Michelle, Ashley, and Rachel regarding the families and home languages of ESL students are very common among preservice and practicing teachers. Whenever I discuss language acquisition and ELLs with other Whites in class or in social gatherings, I am met with the response that the parents of ELLs are "against" their children learning English and so sabotage the education of their children. This reaction always stuns me as I have never found this to be the case in my own experience, nor have I read any evidence of this in the literature on second-language acquisition and ELLs (e.g., Trueba, 1988, 1998). I suggest that this perception among teachers, preservice teachers, and the American public is more evidence of the pervasiveness of deficit thinking in the United States, as well as a characteristic of White culture and Whiteness.

In addition to misunderstanding the value of the native language and the ways in which it affects the acquisition of a second language, many educators working with ELLs make another critical mistake: they forget English-language learners are wholly functioning beings in their native language. Thus, they associate lack of English skill with lack of intelligence and sophistication (Cummins, 1986, 1994; Marx, 2000). Moreover, they assume learners of English are "empty slates" with no prior world knowledge at all (Cummins, 1994). This misunderstanding certainly contributes to the tragic overrepresentation of English-language learners in special education classes (Anstrom, 1996; Artiles, Harry, Reschly, & Chinn, 2002; Cummins, 1986, 1994).

When I first talked to White and Latina/o students in the SLA class, a few years before the students I am discussing here, one young White woman stated that a child's father could not "teach you about the world" if he was Mexican (Marx, 2000, p. 216). She suggested that a mentor like herself, middle class, White, and English-speaking, would be best suited for that kind of undertaking. Moreover, a few of my students over the years have admitted that they thought ESL was some kind of acronym for "slow." They did not realize this acronym represents a language program or class(es) rather than a person. The young women I am discussing in this book did recognize that the children they tutored were proficient and functioning in their native languages, but they thought of these native languages as less sophisticated, less valuable, and even less real than English. Just as Delpit (1995) suggests, the tutors who thought of the children's native languages as deficient also consciously and unconsciously expressed their disdain for other speakers of the child's language, particularly her or his family and friends.

Deficits in Families   Unfortunately, deficit thinking regarding the families of children of color and ELLs is as pervasive as it is heartbreaking (Rogoff, 2003; Trueba, 1988; Valencia, 1997). So many Americans associate success with seamless assimilation into the American way that families who choose to retain aspects of their home culture, such as language and values, are often misunderstood and, thus, disparaged by those in the dominant culture, including teachers (Frankenberg, 1994; Marx, 2000; Sleeter, 1992a; Trueba, 1988). The women I interviewed were no different. Megan, for example, explained that she was drawn to a particular teaching program because the kids served by the program, in her mind, came from families that did not support them. She described these families as, "mostly Black families—or Hispanic—a lot of kids, single parents, [who] live in bad, bad neighborhoods." As a teaching volunteer, Megan felt that she would be able to fill the void left by uncaring, unsupportive parents. This dual role of teacher and parent was a particularly attractive aspect of the position for her.

Michelle shared similar opinions about the shortcomings of the parents of an African American child she had tutored the semester before we met. Like Megan, she relished stepping into the role of parent. As she said,

> I just think Christina had no one to talk to; I think that was the big problem. . . . I felt so bad for her, but I loved her because she never really gave me any discipline problems; I think that's why I liked her so much. . . . It was amazing . . . she kind of became a part of me; she was like my little sister.

When I asked her how this child responded to all her attention, Michelle gushed,

> Oh I think she—I think it made her so much better. I think it finally gave her something to hold on to, someone that she liked that was in her life. . . . So I think it really helped her a lot with her home life too.

Michelle was clearly elated at being liked by her tutee. As she said, Christina was very generous with her attention, affection, and appreciation. However, Michelle interpreted Christina's attention and appreciation as evidence that the child appreciated her *more* than she did her own parents. Michelle seemed to feel a kind of competition with Christina's parents, hoping that Christina would love her more, and need her more, than she did them. I wonder what Christina's mother, a teacher in the school where Michelle tutored, would make of this assessment. Rather than filling a hole in Christina's life, it seemed that, by showering affection on Michelle, Christina was likely filling a need of Michelle's to feel generous and important.

Becky likewise felt that she was stepping into the role of parent when she worked with her tutee. After just a couple of meetings with Paulo, she was convinced that, "He speaks English fluently," although she was not qualified to make that assessment. She also went on to say that his mother did not speak very much English at all, so when she tried to help Paulo with his homework, she only confused him. Becky concluded, then, that, "The parental, you know, aspect of it, is missing." She emphasized that, "He really tries hard," and that she "felt bad" for him because of all his struggles. While Becky was critical of Paulo's parents, she made no comment about his school situation. Paulo's teacher had been on leave for several months and her position was filled by a series of substitute teachers who were never able to gain control of the classroom. The teacher who recommended Paulo for tutoring was a friend of mine who commented on the "chaotic" nature of the classroom; she thought that private tutoring would give him some much-needed academic guidance. Although I shared this story with Becky before she became Paulo's tutor, she nevertheless placed all blame for his struggles squarely on the shoulders of his parents.

Claire assessed the parents of a former tutee in similar ways. In particular, she was dismayed that they seemed to care so little for education. As she explained,

> One thing I noticed was that his parents did not read to him. They basically hired me, and I told them I would do it for free—they paid me a little bit—but they basically wanted somebody else to do it.

As our discussion about Juan continued, she mentioned that his parents did not speak English. She did not make a connection between their lack of proficiency in English and their inability to read with Juan in English. Nor did she consider how much they must have cared about their child's education to hire a tutor for him.

Similarly, Rachel suggested that the parents of the children she tutored did not care enough about education to help their children succeed. She based this assessment on the fact that she assigned homework once and the children never returned it to her. This judgment was extreme given the fact that Rachel had only been in the classroom a few times, just once a week and not on a regular schedule. Her authority for assigning homework was dubious at best. Rather than critique her own role in this situation, however, she leaped immediately to the parents.

Like her classmates, Elizabeth also spent a lot of time thinking about the deficits in the home life of the child she tutored, although she acted out her thoughts in a quite different manner. Rather than adopt a substitute parent role, she decided not to ask her tutee, Martin, any personal questions, in order to avoid opening up a discussion about his "hard family life." She explained that she did not want to "embarrass" him. Because she and Martin never "broke the ice," their relationship was awkward for much of the semester. Elizabeth was not alone in these thoughts; a few SLA students also raised this issue in class. They wanted to know how to talk about a child's life without embarrassing him or her. This belief that a child of color who was learning English would necessarily have a "hard," unhappy home life that she or he would be "embarrassed" to talk about is ample evidence of the pervasiveness of deficit thinking in the dominant U.S. culture and a problematic characteristic of Whiteness. So are the demeaning observations that "It's not them. It's not their fault," comments spoken by Elizabeth, Ashley, Rachel, Becky, and several SLA students.

I am disheartened whenever I hear comments such as these. In addition to illuminating deficit thinking, they highlight a great deal of ignorance on the part of the tutors that was largely impervious to the articles we examined and the discussions we had in class. I can use Martin as an example to illustrate this. By coincidence, Martin was the child that I tutored weekly. Believing in the importance of getting to know students in order to assess their skills, their needs, and their funds of knowledge—that is, the wealth of family and cultural knowledge they bring with them into the classroom (Gonzalez et al. 1995)—I asked him all kinds of questions about himself, and we developed a warm relationship. By getting to know Martin, I found out that his brother was a straight-A student at the school and that the two boys had a loving, competitive relationship; that his mother cried with pride whenever he made good grades; and that he was so close to and respectful of his father that he chose his name, Martin, as his pseudonym for this book. I found no evidence at all that Martin had a "hard" family life, nor anything shameful about his home life. Indeed, Martin had a warm, loving relationship with his family about which he was proud to talk.

Deficits in Esteem and Intelligence   Based on their judgments of the children they tutored, it is not surprising that several tutors also commented on the perceived "low self-esteem" of their tutees. Elizabeth, for example, thought that Martin might be "insecure" because he read too quickly; she felt that he was trying to "prove that he knew everything" rather than just accepting his low level. She was more pleased with the reading style of another child whom she described as much more "modest" than Martin. This little girl, she felt, "doesn't make herself out to be something she—you know, [is not]." What Elizabeth did not know was that Martin was a fourth grader who could read at the fourth-grade level. However, he was reading second-grade level books in the reading tutoring lab. The director of the lab did not monitor his work enough to know that he was reading far below his ability. Martin was indeed trying to "prove" that his skill surpassed his assigned level by two grades. Rather than being insecure, he was very self-confident and wanted to show off his ability to his tutors. I know this because I got to know Martin. Because he sailed through the second- and third-grade books,

I finally talked with the tutoring director, who agreed to move him up to the fourth-grade level—where he still read strongly. By not carefully monitoring his skill level, Martin's tutoring program was doing him a serious disservice. In that particular government-funded tutoring program, children were encouraged to read at very low levels and admonished when they wanted to read more challenging materials. In these ways, this tutoring program worked against the success of the children it was meant to serve. Because nearly all tutors were volunteers with little or no teaching experience, the failures of this tutoring program were difficult for them to assess. Martin took advantage of this lack of expertise to read the "easy" books that did not challenge him. Ironically, he thought his quick, fluent reading made him look smart, while his tutor thought this made him look foolish and insecure.

Rachel made similar mis-assessments of a little girl she tutored just one time. She told me that she felt the lesson had been completely unsuccessful because she could not get the child to read anything in English. In her words, the child repeatedly said, "I could read this if it were in Spanish," which additionally frustrated Rachel. Clearly, the little girl knew her intelligence was being judged by her English skill, rather than her intellectual ability. Rachel did not realize this until we talked about it several days after the lesson. Like Elizabeth, she thought the child was trying to "fool" her, and wished she had just gone along with the lesson.

Elizabeth and Rachel were not the only ones to negatively assess the esteem of the children they tutored. In her final assessment of Paulo, Becky wrote:

> I wanted him to have a positive self-concept. There were many instances where I could tell that he had a poor self-concept. He'd put his hands over his eyes and slouch in his chair when he pronounced a wrong word. Paulo would complain that his handwriting was messy even though I could read it clearly. Paulo needs positive reinforcement and encouragement.

Here, Becky associated Paulo's language skill with his general self-concept. While it was likely his English proficiency that frustrated him, she assumed he was a generally insecure person.

In addition to esteem deficits, Claire, Becky, and Gen indirectly suggested that people of color might not be as intelligent, or work as hard, as White people. Gen suggested that our university had a low enrollment of African American students (3.9 percent in 1999) because they had unsupportive families; they were insecure; they did not like to work; and they did not "want to be there." Becky suggested that there were few people of color in her military squadron because, in her words, "If you had a higher intellect, you'd be put into fields like administration, medical—I was put in medical." Because of these deficit-laden assessments of people of color, it is no wonder that they believed that the children they tutored had low self-esteem. Anyone would have low self-esteem if their/our lives were as miserable and deficient as these tutors imagined them to be.

Associating Color with Fear   Because the women I spoke with associated people of color with deficits in culture, language, families, intelligence, and character, it is not surprising that many of them also talked about people of color with statements characterized by fear. Though they worked with Latina/o children, the fearful stories they told resemble the same old fictions about people of color originally spread across the United States to rationalize and maintain slavery (Davis, 1995). These fictions about the simpleminded, lustful, debased, lazy, and untrustworthy nature of those of African descent were extremely effective and became solidly entrenched in the American psyche (Davis, 1995). Although slavery has been abolished for nearly 150 years, because the United States was meant to be an all-White country (Debates and Proceedings in the Congress of the United States, 1834; Franklin, 1751; Takaki, 1990), all people of color in the United States shoulder the weight of this stigma to varying degrees. Whites still often view African Americans and other people of color as inferior people who are unable to take care of themselves or others (Berlak & Moyenda, 2001). Sadly, some people of color believe these fictions as well and internalize racism (Berlak & Moyenda, 2001; Tatum, 1999). Although the specifics of these retold stories change with each new generation, the message that people of color have deficiencies that cause them to be dangerous remains an undercurrent in U.S. society. The following comments of the young women with whom I spoke illustrate the resiliency of these fictions and the fear they generate.

Becky expressed fear the most frequently. In the first few weeks of class, she told me that she wanted to teach secondary school, so I suggested she tutor at a high school where I had contacts. When I mentioned the school, Becky gasped and said she would never tutor there because it was too "scary." Later, I suggested she try another school that was just up the road from my house. Becky recognized this school as being at an intersection where "there are always big accidents," and then said that her boyfriend, a police officer, cautioned her against volunteering there because

> They find the stolen cars there. So he thinks that there are hoodlums and criminals going to the school, and there may be. And he said something like that too, "You're not experienced. You could be putting yourself in a dangerous situation."

Her boyfriend was not the only source of Becky's fears. During our first interview, she described the private school that made her feel "safer" as a child. I asked her why she used the term "safer," and she explained that, "Because in public school . . . I saw catfights between girls in the hallway, and boys would always try and touch you and kiss you . . . ." Because she had described her school as economically elite, I asked her, "Even in a middle-class or upper-middle-class school?" She answered,

> Well, they bussed people in. . . . I did have one—one little Black girl that was in my class when I was little and we used to play. She would come to my house and play with me. I think that scared the neighbors. I don't know. But . . . these Puerto Rican girls would go at [it] in the hallway, and there was a Black boy that liked me, and he would try and touch me and kiss me.

In the stories she told, people of color were always constructed as "scary." Even the "little Black girl," who did not frighten her, frightened others. When I asked her about this association of fear with color, she thought for a moment and then clarified her point by saying, "The Puerto Rican girls—I think I was a little scared because they were kind of aggressive. But, I didn't think I equated it to their race. I just was scared of them." She then explained that an African American boy she dated also frightened her with his aggressiveness. In her words,

> When I was in seventh grade I had a *Black* boyfriend. And [sigh] it was okay except, kind of, I guess it was a little scary because he did try to go, you know, little kids, they are experiencing things and he was trying to . . . push himself on me. I was like, "Uuaa!"

Nationwide, it is estimated that 80–90 percent of secondary school girls experience sexual harassment in school (Stein, 1999), so it is not surprising that Becky had negative stories to tell about fighting off unwanted romantic advances. In fact, sexual harassment was the second most common act of violence committed in U.S. schools during the 1999–2000 school year, with 127,568 cases reported (NCES, 2005b). Only vandalism was more common. Interestingly, schools with the smallest percent of "minority enrollment" (p. 67) reported the greatest number of incidents. No research has shown that males of color sexually harass females more often than White males (Stein, 1999). It may be that Becky's passive racism caused her to remember her experiences with this Black boy more vividly than any experiences of sexual harassment she may have endured that were committed by Whites. Throughout our conversations, Becky continuously claimed that she was not intimidated by the race of the people she discussed. However, she also consistently associated color with danger and even disgust. Her refusal to "name" the racism associated with these judgments was a clear sign of color-evasiveness.

Because of her feelings about people of color, it was not surprising that Becky felt uncomfortable spending ten hours on the east side of town. She explained that she felt relatively safe as long as she remained in her car; however, the very thought of her car breaking down on the east side of the highway made her shiver. Although she was afraid of the area, Becky did claim to feel "safe" at the elementary school where she tutored because, in her words, "I'm bigger than them." As an afterthought, she added that, "They patrol it a lot too." Further signifying her fears, Becky referred to the schools in the east part of town with high populations of people of color as "high-risk schools" where the lives of teachers were often in peril. This interpretation seemed to be something of a connection to—or a misunderstanding of—the "at risk" construct. Because of her embrace of these beliefs, it is no wonder she was afraid to be on the east side of town.

Amy and Michelle also professed to feel afraid in the neighborhood where they tutored; their school was just one block north of Becky's. Amy described these fears by recounting how she felt driving through downtown, across the interstate, into the east side of town and to the school:

> Driving . . . this probably sounds so bad . . . but driving up to the school, the area made me a little nervous; but then it was ten o'clock in the morning. I know—me, personally, I wouldn't want to be in that area at nighttime.

Michelle likewise described how vulnerable the neighborhood made her feel and laughed as she shared that she and Amy made sure their car doors were locked when they drove to Mayan Elementary each week.

Ashley and Rachel also talked about the fear they felt in neighborhoods of color, particularly African American neighborhoods. When we were talking about a city Ashley had visited with an African American part of town, she found it important to state that, "We [White people] weren't *welcome* there," although how she knew this when she was too afraid to go to the African American neighborhood remained unclear. In contrast, Rachel wore the "dangerous" neighborhood where she lived like a badge of honor, laughing at her friends who were afraid to visit her on the east side of the highway. She talked about the crime, the police sirens, and the people of color who hung out at the local gas station in the late hours. Several times she used the terms "afraid" and "scared" to describe her feelings about the area. Rachel's neighborhood did sound dangerous to me until she mentioned the corner where she caught the bus to school each morning. That was the same corner where I caught my bus. It turned out that Rachel and I lived across the street from each another. Had she left out the bus stop, I never would have recognized the neighborhood by her description.

Several women rationalized their fears of people of color by explaining that as single females, they were particularly susceptible to danger; thus, they had to be careful in dubious areas. They described their avoidance of people of color, particularly men of color, as a safety measure. Becky said she was most frequently propositioned by African American men. Ashley had the worst experiences with Latinos. These fears led them to further distance themselves from people of color and to associate people of color with aggressive, uncivilized behaviors, which, in turn, intensified their fears.

In their book about the costs of racism, Feagin and Vera (1995) suggest that the fear caused by racism drains the U.S. economy financially and emotionally. Financial drains are caused by the high costs of increased security measures and the numerous lawsuits that result from racial discrimination. Emotional drains are paid by all people who feel they must live in fear of color, such as the young women described here. The pervasive crime of sexual harassment against women also leaves an indelible mark on women of all races and, naturally enough, often causes women to be fearful of men. However, no evidence exists that males of color sexually harass more often than White males. The influences of racism in our society may leave the U.S. public to believe this is the case, however. Although all people are affected by racism, there is no doubt that people of color pay the largest price, as they are continuously dehumanized by racist fictions and they often live in fear of Whites and the existing power structure (Berlak & Moyenda, 2001; Feagin & Vera, 1995; Obidah & Teel, 2001).

Maintaining Distance In addition to feeling a great distance between themselves and people of color, the tutors discussed how they planned to maintain this distance throughout their lives by "sticking with" their own race. Although this desire seems reasonable and benign, its link to racism must be acknowledged. The United States has a long history of racial separation that is firmly connected to the notion of keeping the White race pure. Miscegenation laws (i.e., laws that prohibit marriage between Whites and people of other races) were introduced in Virginia as early as 1662, sanctioned by the U.S. Supreme Court in 1883, and not wholly overturned until 1967 (Ross, 1997; Scales-Trent, 1997). Just 1.5 percent of married couples responding to the 2000 Census checked that they married outside their race (U.S. Census, 2000a). Scales-Trent (1997) suggests that, if the southern United States had not legally codified "the 'one drop' rule" that labeled every person with any amount of African heritage, no matter how remote, "Black," and if intermarriage between Blacks and Whites had not been outlawed, "the concept of race" could have been "eliminated altogether" (p. 476). Instead, now, almost 350 years after the first miscegenation law was enacted, 97 percent of Whites still prefer to marry within their own racial group (U.S. Census, 2000a).

The young women I talked with shared their embrace of racial separation in many ways. Ashley frankly stated that she wanted "to marry somebody White . . . to have White kids. And I want to have a White family." After spending four years with a Latino boyfriend, she realized that,

> I don't want my kids to have the—or look different from me, I guess. I want them to have the blonde hair, blue eyes, and *look* like me. And I want them to just not have interracial parents. I want them to have, you know, be completely from a White background and . . . I guess, follow along in it.

Although her mother wanted her to keep speaking Spanish, to teach Latina/o children, and to spend more time at home in the Rio Grande Valley, Ashley preferred to live and work with Whites in a White majority area. She was relieved that she and her Latino boyfriend had broken up.

Becky also admitted that when "I look for somebody to date, I look for a White man. . . . I'm attracted to the same thing that I am, you know? Plus, I want to please my family, so that's kind of a trickle-down from them." She emphasized that she had "never had a problem being friends with somebody of a different race," but marriage was different. Both Ashley and Becky had dated people of color, but both planned to have White families in the future.

Claire did not share this strong desire to keep her own race line pure; however, she did realize that her life was becoming very White-centered. She kept in touch with her White friends from elementary school, but lost track of her friends of color from middle school and high school. During the semester we got to know each other, her closest friendships were with sorority sisters and fraternity friends, nearly all of whom were White. Megan's comments were very similar; although she said that she was "open-minded" about such things as "marrying a Black man," she also honestly admitted that she "wouldn't seek it out" because of the difficulties such a relationship might entail. She added that meeting a partner of color would be difficult because her social, academic, and religious circles were almost exclusively White.

In addition to not wanting to marry outside their race, nearly all the women discussed the importance of living in communities like those where they grew up, and sending their own future children to White majority schools. Racial diversity was a very low priority for nearly every one of them, something they could easily imagine living without. Because separation is the norm in our society (Scales-Trent, 1997), the desire to lead racially segregated lives is anything but controversial. However, its relationships to racism and Whiteness should not be denied.

Associating Whiteness with Superiority

As the young women articulated the deficits in the cultures, families, characteristics, and languages of the children they tutored, as well as the other people of color and learners of English they described, they silently praised their own White culture, families, characteristics, and English fluency. As they did this, it became clear that the perceived deficiency of color went hand-in-hand with the perceived superiority of Whiteness. Just as Fanon (1967) contrasts "blackness, darkness, shadow, shades, night, and the labyrinth of earth" with "the bright look of innocence, the White Dove of peace, [and] magical, heavenly light" (pp. 188–89, as cited by Jones, 1997, p. 255), the women with whom I talked contrasted the deficiencies of color with the inherent goodness of Whiteness. Like the participants in McIntyre's study on White identity, "for these young White females, being White is normal, typical, and functions as a standard for what is right, what is good, and what is true" (McIntyre, 1997, p. 135). Believing their own backgrounds to be right, good, and true, SLA students also believed themselves to be "White knights" (p. 123) who could greatly benefit the deficient lives of people of color through their own upstanding qualities as role models and saviors.

Role Models and Saviors   Teachers, perhaps more than any other professionals, are socially constructed to be role models for children. This construction is so fundamental to education that it nearly goes without saying, although it has been spelled out now and again. The Ontario, Canada, Education Act, for example, explicitly requires Ontario teachers to be civil, moral, character, and spiritual role models for the children they teach. Clause 264 (1) (c) of the act delineates the following:

> It is the duty of the teacher and a temporary teacher . . . to incul-
> cate by precept and example respect for religion and the principles
> of Judaeo-Christian morality and the highest regard for truth,
> justice, loyalty, love of country, humanity, benevolence, sobri-
> ety, industry, frugality, purity, temperance and all other virtues.
> (Berryman, 1998, p. 1)

The United States leaves the specifics of teacher conduct up to individual school boards, which set the parameters of appropriate role models as minutely or as vaguely as they wish. Indeed, what constitutes a good teacher role model in this country depends on who is doing the constituting. In the education literature, teachers have been advised to act as "exemplary" role models of proper attitude (Carter & Rice, 1997; Onyekwuluge, 2000), proper character (Field, 1996; Foshay, 1996; Gibbs & Earley, 1996; Krajewski, 1999), proper professionalism (Moorehead, 1998), and even proper dress (Simmons, 1996). Moreover, much prescriptive attention has been given to the need for teachers to be especially good role models for those who have traditionally lagged behind White males in school, specifically girls (Edelman, 2000; Kimmel & Rudolph, 1998; McWhirter, Hackett, & Bandalos, 1998; Schwiebert, Deck, & Bradshaw, 1999) and children of color (Flagg & Flagg, 1988; Hale, 1996; Martinez, 1991; Shreffler, 1998; Stewart, Meier, & England, 1989). Teachers have even been pressed to share their role model skills with parents of color who, according to some, might not know how to be role models for their children otherwise (Lara-Alecio, Irby & Ebener, 1997).

As the abundance of this literature illustrates, people from every walk of life have different, and oftentimes passionate, ideas about what it takes to be a proper role model for children. Because teachers spend so much time with children each day, often more time than parents, the inevitability of them being constructed as role models, regardless of their own thoughts about the matter, may be inarguable. However, I find it surprising that many young people seem to want to become teachers specifically because they consider themselves to be good role models, regardless of their lack of experience with leadership, teaching, and/or children. Several of the women I talked with certainly shared this thought. Because they believed that the children of color they tutored were particularly disadvantaged and deficient, these women often expressed the extra importance of being role models when working with them. As they did this, they subtly elevated their own social status as they lowered those of the children they tutored.

Rachel, for example, stated that "I want to really make a difference in children's lives. I would like for kids to be able to see me as a role model, especially in an environment where they may not have anyone to look up to." Similar thoughts about her own exemplary qualities were reflected in her journal, where she wrote, "I really think we developed a good relationship, and that these kids look up to me." She also believed that, "[the kids] like it when I come to help them, and I know it is something they really look forward to all week." All these good feelings made her believe that she would "have more to offer a school like" the school where she tutored, where the children were mostly of color. Rachel never explicitly outlined her role model qualities; it was just understood that she had what the kids needed.

Michelle also felt strongly about being a role model for the kids she tutored. In her journal, she excitedly wrote that, "I felt as if I were doing a real 'MITZVAH' (the Hebrew word for good deed), I was really helping the world!" Michelle was thrilled the first time she worked alone with Valerie, and convinced that "Her English seemed to be improving, as well as her self-esteem." Michelle's ability to improve Valerie's reading and self-esteem in one 30-minute lesson would be phenomenal indeed. Rachel and Michelle were not the only SLA students to consider themselves miracle workers, able to move a child through several different reading levels in just a few days. Several SLA students talked in class about how quickly their tutees were advancing; many also wrote in their journals about how their role model qualities enabled this achievement. While the amazing academic results some SLA students professed to have with the children they tutored initially sounded wonderful, they were, in fact, suspect. After all, while SLA students had very large hearts, they had very little teaching experience. Few had any previous experience with English language learners or people of color. It takes a very good teacher, an excellent learning environment, and tremendous patience, commitment, and perseverance from children and teachers to truly reap such spectacular results. As I read journals, listened to class discussions, and observed tutoring sessions, I surmised that students were, in fact, reveling in the affection they received from very loving children and the satisfaction they gained from their volunteer experiences with these children. The affection and rewarding feelings flattered them and made them feel very successful.

In addition to viewing themselves as role models, many of the women I talked with and many SLA students thought of themselves as saviors for the children they tutored and construed the tutoring experience as a charitable endeavor. That is, they felt they were capable of, and responsible for, "saving" the children from the difficult lives they imagined through the self-sacrifice of volunteering to work with them. They demonstrated this mind-set when they described themselves as parental figures for the children, when they criticized the imagined families and home lives of the children, when they showered the children with small gifts and affection, and when they shared their motivations for wanting to help others, particularly English-language learners and people of color.

Rachel, for example, explained that her stepfather was her role model for wanting to work with "underprivileged" people of color. Mr. Merwin was a shop owner in a low-income, African American neighborhood in

Houston. When times were tough and business was bad, he retained all his African American employees, despite the profits it cost him. Emphasizing the self-sacrifice involved in this action, Rachel said that her stepfather was so appreciated and loved by his employees that they would say "God bless you Mr. Merwin" whenever they met him. She imagined herself being similarly self-sacrificing and benevolent in her work with children of color and ELLs. She also imagined similar grateful feedback from those she helped.

Michelle was also proud of her family's tradition of helping others. She shared that her family found it important to give "up our time and our money to help out other people, which I [think is] a great, charitable thing to do." She could easily list numerous friends, family members, and acquaintances she had tutored and otherwise helped over the years. For example, her family had "adopted" a Russian family when they first immigrated to the United States. When she was growing up, her father helped Mr. Revnik with his résumé, and her mother helped Mrs. Revnik put her household together and pursue her American professional credentials. However, once Mrs. Revnik earned her American credentials as a dermatologist, the family established a high socioeconomic position. This change of social position unsettled Michelle. She explained, "They are high rollers. [The daughter] drives a BMW. They have a Corvette. I mean *we* helped *them* when they came here. Now *look at them!* My mom was like, 'Oh my gosh.'" In a low, scornful voice, she added, "We don't have a BMW," and explained that

> [My mother] said it made her feel good . . . and inferior at the same time because—it made her feel good because we *helped* them out when they got here. *We* did something that ended up as a success. My family helped them. And she said it also made her feel inferior because these people came with nothing. They are already steps ahead. Not *steps* ahead, I mean, they are such high rollers. They live in this gorgeous, exotic house. . . . I mean it's *unbelievable* to her.

Michelle and her family's contradictory feelings of support and scorn for the people they helped offer an excellent example of the problems that come with the savior mentality. Michelle and her family expected the Revniks to maintain their low socioeconomic position and their dependency on Michelle's family indefinitely. They also expected an extreme amount of gratitude for the unquestionably helpful assistance they had given. Once the Revniks no longer needed help, Michelle considered them traitors of sorts, "high rollers" who overstepped their boundaries.

Claire's discussion of her tutoring experience similarly revealed her embrace of the White teacher-as-savior mind-set. As she talked about the importance of "helping" children in need, she pointed out that she rarely saw people of color tutoring. More often, she found them to be the tutored. As she said, "That's one thing that I noticed that I just thought was kind of interesting. I'm kind of curious as to why there aren't more . . . other races helping. I don't know. I just took note of that." Claire seemed to associate "helping" with the altruistic, charitable endeavors of good citizens. Because she rarely saw people of color giving of themselves in this way, she wondered if perhaps they were not as kindhearted as Whites.

Charity Work   Ashley, who grew up surrounded by low-income Latinas/os, clearly felt that tutoring English-language learners was charity work conducted by those interested in selflessly "saving" others; however, she felt completely drained by it and no longer wanted to sacrifice her own interests. She specifically did not pursue bilingual certification because, in her words,

> I don't want to get stuck teaching Hispanics all my life. Because, when people find out you have a bilingual degree, they're going to [say], "Oh, great!" And stick you with all the Spanish-speaking kids. I don't want to do that. That's not why I'm in teaching. I don't want to sit and teach people how to speak English all year long. I want to teach them to read stories and . . . creativity. I don't want to teach them how to speak English. There are people out there who want to do that. I don't.

Ashley believed that teaching Latina/o children required a teacher to sacrifice her own interests and professional goals for the sake of the children. Clearly, she considered work with English-language learners basic, uninteresting, charity work, in contrast to her perceptions of the more professional, challenging work that could be undertaken with White, native English-speaking children. The progeny of a border culture, she was also cognizant that teachers of White children had a higher status. Every time she worked with Latinas/os, warm feelings were meant to be the only reward. Ashley, for one, was "sick of" giving so much of herself for nothing.

Although the stories above illustrate the unique experiences and perspectives of different tutors, when analyzed together they paint a portrait that characterizes their belief that work with people of color and English-language learners was a charitable act that required self-sacrifice on their part. In sharing her story, each woman revealed her desire to help someone less fortunate than herself. However, this desire to help was entangled with the need for extreme amounts of gratitude and the acknowledgment of racial, cultural, linguistic, and social superiority. That is, those being helped were not expected to achieve the same social status as the helpers—ever. While the stories shared by Rachel, Claire, and Ashley highlight economic, racial, and cultural differences in status between themselves and the people they or their families helped, Michelle's story illustrates the stigma attached to English-language learners of any educational and economic background. Mrs. Revnik had been a dermatologist in Russia and her family was well educated. After moving to the United States, it took time for Mrs. Revnik to get her U.S. credentials and for the family to acquire English proficiency. When they did, however, Michelle and her mother were shocked at the family's economic and social success. Rather than being happy for this immigrant family who seemed to be attaining the American Dream, Michelle described this success as a kind of betrayal to her own family's efforts.

Instead of focusing on improving the skills and opportunities of the people they helped, tutors who embraced the role model and savior perspectives focused on themselves and their own feelings of self-worth, to the detriment of those with whom they worked. While volunteer experiences are certainly meant to be rewarding to the volunteer, tutors described in this section placed too much emphasis on their own good intentions and benevolence. In doing so, they constructed highly idealistic visions of themselves as role models, teachers, helpers, and even saviors. Simultaneously, they constructed highly deficient visions of the people they sought to help.

Self-aggrandizing "helper" images like those the tutors constructed of themselves are complex, as they are created by deficit, racist, misinformed constructs of the "other"—people of color and ELLs—as well as altruistic desires to help and save. Semali (1998) suggests that the desire to "save" is revealed as a characteristic of Whiteness when the disadvantages of color are contrasted with the advantages of Whiteness. Whites working with people of color for the first time may catch a glimpse of their own White privilege for the first time as well. Feeling highly uncomfortable in this privileged position, Whites often develop a strong desire to help and even save the folks with whom they are working. Feeling this unfair advantage, many SLA tutors showered the children with small gifts, brought them fast-food lunches, and thought of themselves as adoptive parents.

While those acting as benevolent role models and saviors are often lauded as self-sacrificing, well intentioned, and in possession of hearts of gold, this construct of the helper necessitates that the person helped is constructed as needy, dependent, and incapable of achieving on her or his own. When White teachers work with people who are commonly characterized as difficult, needy, and even expected to fail, they are often lauded for their intentions and their hearts of gold, no matter how unsuccessful their teaching efforts might be. As Jennifer Obidah (Obidah & Teel, 2001, p. 46) explains,

> It becomes easy for White teachers to eventually give up and say that the students are incapable of being managed or taught. And partly because of prevalent views of the students as failures, the White teacher is not reprimanded for giving up, but rewarded for even attempting to try in the first-place.

As a White teacher of students of color and ELLs, I have received praise from other Whites for "just trying with those kids" more often than I care to remember. Several of the women I talked with similarly illustrate the point Obidah makes.

Rachel, for example, experienced an unsuccessful lesson when working with a child for the first time. After the failed lesson, she wrote in her journal,

> I felt really bad for this kid, like, he was one of the children that might easily fall through the cracks. When I left, I was thinking a lot about him, and all I could think of was, "Where will the child be in 10 years?" In 10 years, I don't see him in a much different situation than today, unless he learns how to read and does not have such an apathetic attitude. . . . I saw a child who was not proficient in even his native language, let alone in English. . . . This child was not even able to follow along with what the other children were doing. He seemed to have another problem, which was his attitude, related to the sociolinguistic influences he must be receiving from somewhere. When I asked him about his background, he hesitated a lot, and it gave me the impression that he is not being encouraged to learn English from anyone, except maybe at school. . . . I think he would just as soon not learn English at all. Even when he seemed to be trying, I could tell he would get frustrated and give up. He did not want my help.

Rather than critique her own role in the lesson, Rachel pointed out that the child, whom she had never before met, was so far behind in fourth grade that he would be behind for the next 10 years. Through indirect, color-evasive language, she blamed his family for not encouraging him to learn English. She also negatively assessed the "sociolinguistic influences" in his life that might contribute to his struggles learning English without assessing her own contributions to these struggles. Her poor opinion of Miguel's lack of skills in his first language, something she was not capable of judging, as well as her thoughts about his "apathetic attitude," something that was surely a misunderstanding of his lack of English proficiency, were almost certainly felt by the child she was dismissing as an almost certain failure. Finally, she judged Miguel as difficult and not appreciative of her help. Rachel's inability to have a successful lesson seemed to be the true problem here, not Miguel's deficiencies.

Buying into the teacher-as-savior mentality, Michelle faced a different challenge in her tutoring situation. When she discovered that her tutees had tutors every day of the week, she was extremely disappointed. In her journal, she wrote,

> The only problem I faced with both Valerie and Cristobal is that I did not realize that they go to the [tutoring] program every day, and I was not their only mentor. It made me feel a little odd because they had been reading and making cards with different people all week. I kind of felt less important than I thought I was, but I will try to do the best that I can every time I am there with both of these students, and that is all that counts.

By sharing that she was disappointed that other tutors worked with the children she tutored and emphasizing that trying her best is "all that counts," Michelle revealed her embrace of the teacher-as-savior mind-set. Like the other women presented in this section, she was primarily concerned with the good feelings she gained from the lesson, not the children she tutored. Her negative comments about the children further illustrate this point.

While many preservice teachers bring these ideas about teaching with them into teacher preparation programs, schools of education that regularly stroke preservice teacher egos as they outline the needs of poor, "at-risk" students exacerbate this notion of "teacher as savior." As do schools and tutoring programs that entice volunteers to join their programs by showering them with thanks, praise, presents, and even cash incentives. One national, government-funded tutoring program SLA tutors worked with, for example, offered a several-thousand-dollar fellowship to *either* children or tutors each year. The most recent fellowship recipient was a volunteer. This same tutoring program had children decorate cards for their tutors with the message "You are a lifesaver" and an attached *Lifesavers* candy. Tutors breathed in this flattering, excessive praise and, naturally, became intoxicated by it. Assessing who was being helped most in this program, the tutors or the children, becomes a difficult task indeed.

Ramifications In the small study I conducted the year before getting to know the women portrayed here, the same themes of White tutors as role models and saviors and the tutoring of ELLs as charity work emerged (Marx, 2000). Several preservice teachers talked about the need for people such as themselves, all White women, to intervene in the lives of ELLs of color so the children could participate in the American Dream. One young woman suggested the need to "take [the child she tutored] out and show him places and explain why things are—and figure why this is this and that is that" (p. 216). Another suggested the need to "have someone English-speaking in [the child's] family," such as "a Big Sister" from the Big Brother, Big Sister mentoring association (p. 216). In contrast, Latina and Latino preservice teachers stressed the importance of families, teachers, and communities in helping children succeed. They were greatly offended by the suggestions of the White tutors to go in and take the children out. Elsa, for example, angrily responded to this suggestion, as retold by me, with the shouted statement, "No! *You* take *your* child and show *your* child the things he needs to know!" (p. 217). Nodding her head in understanding, Carola responded by first saying, "No." She then shared a story about the White nurses who visited her at home after the birth of her first child, some thirty years ago. All Latina mothers giving birth at that particular hospital were visited by nurses after they returned home. For this visit, Carola meticulously cleaned her home, baked special desserts, and made coffee. She kindly entertained her visitors when they arrived. After an hour or so, the nurses departed with the assessment that Carola was a good mother and that all was well. They did not even look at the baby. They did not know that Carola had locked the baby girl in her bedroom and purposely kept the nurses away to prevent them from taking her. Carola, in her mid fifties, and Elsa, in her early twenties, had heard and felt the desires of Whites to "help" them by intervening in their lives on many occasions. Such comments inspired fear in these two women, both mothers. They were fearful that their children would be taken away by Whites. These chilling effects are some of the negative consequences of the White teacher as role model and savior for children of color constructs.

CHAPTER 3

The Eye of the Beholder: Tutors Define Racism

In addition to asking tutors to describe Whiteness, as described in the previous chapter, I asked them what the word "racism" meant to them. Although I use an academic understanding of racism as a "system of advantage based on race" throughout this book (Tatum, 1999, p. 7; Wellman, 1977), I recognize that most Americans are not aware of that definition. Most Americans think of racism as irrational acts of hatred committed by obvious bigots (Tatum, 1999). Given this understanding of racism, few Americans would consider themselves racist. In fact, the term *racist* represents such a negative manifestation that it is often compared to the word *evil*. Thus, it is not surprising that Whites accused of racism commonly react with shock and hurt. Tatum (1999) writes that a White teacher compared an accusation of racism to being "punched in the stomach or called a 'low-life scum'" (p. 10). Indeed, several of my own teacher education students over the years have suggested that we use words other than "racist" and "racism" to talk about racial inequality. Those words, they emphasize, are just too loaded and insulting for any kind of rational discussion. No matter how academically we define these words in class, they tend to think of them as synonyms for evil: something they could never apply to themselves.

In order to better understand how the tutors I got to know understood racism, I explicitly asked them what racism meant to them. While the questions about Whiteness had seemed very strange, the questions I asked about racism seemed positively loaded. The first time I asked a tutor how she defined racism, she gasped and nearly choked out the words, "Oh, God." Clearly, she was apprehensive about stepping into such treacherous waters. Because of the politically charged, color-evasive nature of racial issues, this young woman and the other SLA students knew that anything they said might be used against them. Our dialogues began only after I assured them that I was aware of this dilemma, and I emphasized that my goal was to understand rather than judge them or use their words against them.

Racism

Megan, the shy young woman who planned to teach in a volunteer program in the future, actually had an easy time talking about racism. She was the only one who defined racism as a system of advantage that benefits Whites. Thus, she told me, people of color could not be "racist" because they did not benefit from the system. Tatum (1999) compares this understanding of racism to the notion of sexism. Because women do not systematically benefit from sexism, they cannot be termed *sexist*. These are academic understandings of racism and sexism that emphasize their systematic nature. To soften this language for my students, I often emphasize that we are all *influenced* by racism and sexism, with Whites and men being advantaged by these systematic inequities (respectively) and people of color and women being disadvantaged by them. Megan had learned about this perspective on racism in an African American culture class she had taken the semester before we met and thought it made good sense. In discussing racism, Megan was very much ahead of the other tutors. She had an easy time talking about racism both in the abstract and in her own beliefs and actions.

In contrast to Megan, all other women defined racism just as Tatum (1999) suggests most Americans do, as the beliefs espoused by Ku Klux Klan members, Nazis, and other groups that base their ideologies on hate. Claire, Elizabeth, Gen, and Amy also suggested that racism could be defined by feelings of superiority; that is, "looking at someone and automatically judging them" and "[thinking that] you're better than somebody for no good, solid reason." Becky, the young woman who had been active in the military before seeking her teaching credential, added,

> Racism is when you are so conscious of your own race, and the way you are brought up in that race, that you can't see another person's race.... Also, because you are so self-absorbed with

who *you* are. You can't be open-minded enough to see who other people are. [And,] obviously, ignorance. Ignorance springs about anger and fear and distrust and all that. . . . That's the way I think of it. Stupidity. When I think back to the Civil War and slavery and all that, people thinking that they are better than other races. It's just . . . uck! Makes me mad.

Becky's understanding of racism was actually very close to Tatum's (1999). However, she removed herself from it and judged it to be a problem that was pervasive primarily in the past. Like the other tutors, Becky agreed that racist groups and racist actions were deplorable. Indeed, she became visibly angry just thinking about the people who would advocate such hatred.

Prejudice

While all the tutors were angered by the notion of racism, several of them thought it was important to distinguish racism from prejudice. While they connected racism to repugnant, hate-filled acts and judgments, they thought of prejudices as much more benign and forgivable. Rachel, the Jewish woman with the "chai" pendant, for example, thought of racism as synonymous with "hatred," but defined prejudices as "treating people differently, but not hating them." Ashley, the tutor from the Rio Grande Valley, added that she saw a difference between "big prejudices" and "little prejudices," with little prejudices more forgivable than the big ones. Like Rachel, she emphasized that the little prejudices indicated dislike rather than hate. Amy, the sensitive young woman from San Antonio, emphasized the differences between the evil of racism and the relative innocence of prejudice by stating that "I don't think that just because somebody, every once in a while, has those [prejudiced] thoughts . . . that they should be considered a racist person." Like Tatum (1999, p. 5), these women generally described prejudice as, "a preconceived judgment or opinion, usually based on limited information."

With this rationale in mind, many women were quite tolerant of prejudices and, somewhat guiltily, even admitted to having them themselves. Claire spoke for many when she confessed that "I think I have a little bit of [prejudice] from the way I was raised. I mean, I'm not proud of that and I try to catch myself." Because the women seemed to believe that, in Tatum's (1999) words, "prejudice is like smog in the air . . . [and] . . . we are breathing it in" (p. 6), they were not terribly ashamed to admit small prejudices. Rather, many of them agreed with Amy's words that anyone who claimed to be 100 percent without prejudices "is lying."

The Clarity of the Racism of Others

Friends and Family

As they talked about racism, all the women told stories about people they considered racist to help illustrate their understanding of the concept. As they did this, they separated their own "open-minded," "more tolerant" ideologies from these other people and became more confident using the word "racist." For example, many women easily contrasted the overt racism of their grandparents with the subtle racism of their parents. As they did this, they characterized the views of their forebears as "understandable" because they were shaped by earlier, more overtly racist times. Omi and Winant (1986, 1994) and Frankenberg (1993) would likely agree with these assessments, pointing out the essentialist racism of the grandparents' generation and the "ethnicity" racism of the parents' generation. These scholars would also likely describe the beliefs of tutors that they, themselves, were not racist—as further evidence of the color-evasiveness that characterizes the present generation.

In addition to family members, the tutors could easily point out the racism they saw among their friends and acquaintances. For example, during our semester together, Rachel, Elizabeth, and Becky all claimed to be dating men they considered racist; Claire had just broken up with a man she characterized the same way. These four women admitted that the racism of these men sometimes embarrassed and angered them. Rachel and Becky both shared that they had occasionally confronted these men about their views. For example, Rachel described the man she was dating as "this guy I'm seeing, who *is* racist. He *is* racist . . . Sometimes I just can't stand the things that come out of his mouth." In trying to help him feel the weight of his words, she asked him, "How would you like it if somebody made derogatory Jewish comments to you? You wouldn't like it." However, while she found it easy to share her reprimands with me, she had a hard time relaying her boyfriend's reactions to them. That ambiguity made me wonder how stern her admonitions had been, and whether she had told me what she wished she had said rather than what she actually said.

The man Becky was dating, a police officer, made racist statements so frequently that she worried he would someday say the wrong thing to the wrong person and get himself in trouble. When I asked her if she thought of this man as racist, she skirted the question as she laughed and said, "He doesn't say as many derogatory things as my previous boyfriend." Returning to the question, she clarified that "I have called him racist. I have said, 'You are acting in such a racist way.'" Becky went on to explain that her boyfriend used various racial epithets whenever he referred to people of color. However, she emphasized that, "He doesn't really mean it to be mean. He just says that because everyone—that's what his family has always said." In fact, Becky was so determined to understand where his thoughts about people of color were coming from that she accompanied him on a police cruise through the east side of town one Saturday night. Although she disagreed with his racist words and beliefs, she was generally tolerant of her boyfriend and forgave this part of his personality. As her admonitions and comments indicate, she sought to separate his racist comments from her perception of the good-hearted man underneath them. That may have been her strongest rationale for continuing to date him when she disagreed with so many of his views. While countering racism was important to Becky and Rachel, it took a backseat to many other issues.

Unlike the tutors discussed above, Elizabeth, the young woman from the "White suburban Beverly Hills," seemed truly to struggle with the racism of her boyfriend. The seriousness of their relationship likely aggravated her concerns; they were planning to get married and she was worried that he would be a bad role model for their future children. She explained that

> I talk to my boyfriend like that a lot. [I tell him], "You are not even talking like that when we have kids. . . ." My parents didn't push [racist views] on me, so I don't want him to push it on them. Because if he is—he is racist around them, then they are going to grow up racist.

The idea of her children growing up racist horrified Elizabeth. The tension in their relationship due to his racism intensified during the semester. Elizabeth eventually decided to put off their marriage plans until they could better traverse their differing beliefs about people of color. She emphasized that his racism was the main reason for this decision.

Claire and Rachel also found it easy to discuss the racism of their friends. In talking about sorority and fraternity life, Claire said, "Yeah, there is so much racism"; she then explained that the "fraternity boys that I know . . . are rude to different races. [But,] there are a lot that aren't. There's a lot that aren't, or just don't show it." Claire did emphasize that her sorority sisters were much more "open-minded" about race; however, she also clarified that there were very few people of color in her sorority or in the university Greek system.

The racist person that Rachel talked about the most in our interviews and in class was a childhood friend of hers who was pursuing an alternative teaching certificate. Rachel often told stories about how this young woman dismissed the needs of her students of color and emphasized her desire to teach in an all-White school. Rachel said that she actively tried to change Alicia's beliefs by talking with her about the importance of helping all her students succeed. Rachel shared that in her last conversation with Alicia, "[I told her], 'Alicia, *I don't think that's right*,' and she said 'Your beliefs are obviously different than mine.'" Rachel was very upset with her friend and even thought about calling the principal of the school where Alicia taught to voice her concerns, although she never did.

Because Rachel talked about Alicia so often in class, Alicia was the example Gen gave when she talked about racism. Gen was the young woman who considered herself White although she was racially mixed and had a Mexican grandmother. She was positively amazed at the stories about Alicia. She explained,

> I didn't know that there were so many White teachers that had this kind of attitude. I never . . . it never dawned on me that that would be a situation. Because I know how I am, and I know how I want to teach and how I want to be, and, I guess, you would hope that everybody would be like that.

Gen's comments expressed the thoughts of many SLA tutors who were shocked and dismayed to hear about Alicia and the other educators who came up during our class discussions, such as Mrs. D., the teacher who had supervised my own student teaching experience. Like Gen, they assumed that most future teachers were as "open-minded" as themselves.

While Gen was concerned about the damage these actively racist teachers did to children, Amy was concerned and angry that people like these, in her words, gave "a bad name to White people who aren't like that at all, who could care less where you're from and what color you are." She was also worried that people of color who were discriminated against by overtly racist Whites "might put up generalizations over the whole White race when it only applies to such a small group of people that are really like that." Clearly, Amy felt that this kind judgment by people of color was very unfair.

People of Color

In addition to seeing the racism of family, friends, and acquaintances, several women pointed out what they perceived to be the racism of people of color. Due to her academic understanding of racism as a "system of advantage" Megan reserved the term "racist" for Whites. No other tutor did so. Ashley, for example, eagerly talked about the "racism" her family had experienced as one of just a few White families in her area of the Rio Grande Valley. She talked about the "discrimination" her father experienced as a White man working in a fire station that was otherwise entirely Latino. Specifically, she said that "He gets a lot of crap because he's White and everybody down there is Hispanic." In addition to feeling like a "minority," this experience made her feel like she "got treated like I was . . . underclass because I wasn't like all of them." Ashley still resented this feeling of being treated like a second-class citizen. It was part of the reason she did not like to go back down to the Valley. It also likely contributed to her understanding of Whites as "higher class" than Latinas/os.

No other tutor I spoke with had the experience of living as a White minority, so their views on "reverse racism" (i.e., the "racism" of people of color regarding Whites) were a little different. Gen, for example, had trouble defining racism so I asked her to think of some examples that would enable us to negotiate a way to characterize it. The only examples she could conjure included the story of a White friend of a friend who felt discriminated against by people of color at a local historically Black college and the story of White University of Texas law student applicant Cheryl Hopwood who, in 1996, won a lawsuit against the university on the grounds that affirmative action policies unfairly advantaged people of color over herself (Hopwood v. State of Texas, 1996). The resulting legal decision forced the University of Texas (UT) to end its affirmative action policy concerning student admission and resulted in a marked decline in "minority" applications and enrollment throughout the Texas higher education system and, especially, the UT School of Law (Texas House of Representatives, 1997; U.S. Commission on Civil Rights, 2003). Although Gen tried very hard to think of some examples where people of color were discriminated against by Whites, she could think of none, except for Alicia, the friend Rachel had described many times in class.

Rachel also found it easy to talk about what she felt was the racism of people of color. She shared a story about an African-American child, Shelly, who was her friend in elementary school. Emphasizing that she and her friends liked this girl very much, and welcomed her into their social group, she explained that the girl's parents eventually pulled her out of the group. She said, "Her parents kind of felt weird that she was friends with all the White Jewish kids." Remembering, she explained that

> My parents liked her *a lot*, they accepted her and wanted me [to be her friend]; they encouraged it, I think. At the same time they wanted me to have Jewish friends and White friends, they wanted me to get an idea of what is really out there.

In this story, Rachel emphasized the good-heartedness of her family in contrast to the senseless, racist actions of Shelly's parents who pulled her away from this nice group of people. The tokenism involved in her relationship with Shelly, highlighted by her characterization of people of color as "what's really out there," escaped Rachel when she told this story.

Becky, Claire, and Elizabeth also shared stories of the racism of people of color, emphasizing that they were "at least as racist" as Whites. Becky, for example, stated that, "Everybody has their biases and stereotypes about different cultures. Black people do too. In fact, I think they are almost equal [in racism], as far as Black against White and White against Black." Claire, the tutor who had had many Latina friends in junior high school, added that

> In my opinion, White people are more identified as being racist as compared to African Americans or Hispanics. I don't know if it's just the history or the South—I don't know what it is. But, you don't necessarily look at a Hispanic person or Black person and say 'Oh, they are really racist.' You know? I don't know. . . . The progress is just really slow with racism. . . . I don't see it going away anytime soon. For any culture.

Similarly, Elizabeth explained that she felt embittered about the guilt she believed Whites were supposed to feel for racism. Like several other tutors, she explained that this guilt was undeserved because Whites had no control over being born members of the dominant group. She also thought it was unfair that she had to feel embarrassed about her culture and race because of events, particularly slavery, that took place long before she was born. These young women resented bearing the responsibility of racism as White people and strove to share the burden with people of color by pointing out that "they are racist too." As they did this, they unknowingly gave more evidence for the argument made by Helms (1990), Frankenberg (1993), Terry (1981), and other race scholars that recognizing one's own race and societal racism is nearly always a choice for Whites, never a de facto burden of being born to the dominant culture.

The Invisibility of One's Own Racism

While all women easily shared stories about what they considered to be the racism of others, they also pointedly denied that they, themselves, were racist. Indeed, the stories they told about the racism of others seemed intended to highlight their own contrasting, nonracist qualities. Even when tutors admitted to small prejudices, they still firmly believed that they were much further along in their "open-mindedness" and racial tolerance than most people. However, as I outlined earlier, all women showed signs of racism, ranging from deficit thinking to beliefs in racial separation.

A major contributing factor to the reluctance of these women to name their own racism, no matter what negative things they said about people of color, was the fact that they thought of themselves as good people. In their minds, good people could not be racist because racism necessarily suggested hate. Elizabeth's words best illustrate this perspective. In describing the racism prevalent in the hometown of her boyfriend, she explained that her mother was from the same small town and emphasized, "My mom is probably the best person I have ever met in my entire life, a saint, and she is from there. And she is not at all racist, closed minded. So I don't let that be an excuse." Later, when I asked Elizabeth if she could be racist, she reeled back in horror, gasped, and exclaimed, "No. Absolutely not. I think *racism* is a bad thing." She clarified, "It's not like I'm a bad person. I *know* I'm not a bad person. I *know* I have a good heart. I think I have a better heart than a lot of people I see." For all these reasons, tutors were very reluctant to admit to their own racism. While Elizabeth realized she was not perfect, she did believe, like the others, that she was much further along than most people in being a tolerant, "open-minded," good person. Moreover, she and many other tutors explicitly and subtly expressed their thoughts that all teachers should have racial ideologies as advanced as their own.

In analyzing our discussions about racism, it became clear that all the tutors but Megan associated racism with others and not themselves. They expressed disgust, anger, and embarrassment at the racism of others, but they usually tolerated it. Even Rachel and Becky, who explicitly called the men they dated "racist," still continued dating them. Although racism made them mad, it did not cause them to change their lives. Only Elizabeth seemed very concerned about the effects another's racism could have on her life; although she, like the others, seemed most concerned with surface indicators of racism, particularly language, rather than deeper racist ideologies. Becky, Elizabeth, and Rachel specifically wanted the men they were dating to stop *talking* in racist ways; they did not mind racism as much if it was not verbalized. Indeed, in these early interviews, only Claire and Megan mentioned that an individual could be racist even if she or he did not outwardly show it. This acceptance of unspoken, passive racism is directly linked to the color-evasive era we live in today (Frankenberg, 1993; Omi & Winant, 1986, 1994).

Several women also showed clear signs of color-blindness as described by Frankenberg (1993), L. Bell (2002), and Bonilla-Silva (2003). Amy's comment that most White people "could care less where you're from and what color you are" indicates this ideology, as do the words of Claire, Elizabeth, and Rachel that their goals were to "treat everybody the same," and, thus, help all children succeed. As multicultural educators such as Delpit (1995),

Ladson-Billings (1994), and Grant and Sleeter (2003) all point out, treating all children "the same" assumes that all children are exactly alike; in reality, this ideology assumes that all children are White. Color-blindness would be more aptly described as vision filtered by a White lens. Because so many women specifically used the term "color-blind," I asked if they had learned this term in their education classes. They responded that they had simply picked up the term through the media, their families, and other natural venues of life rather than through their classes. This makes sense because color-blind or color-evasive language is the dominant language of race today (Frankenberg, 1993).

Backlash

While most of the tutors generally tolerated the prejudices and racism of the Whites they knew, most of them strongly resented what they perceived to be the racism and privileges of people of color. In our conversations, Ashley, Amy, Becky, Claire, Gen, Elizabeth, Michelle, and Rachel all shared clear feelings of resentment toward people of color that seemed to be rationalized in two distinct ways. First, they resented that people of color never seemed to be portrayed as racist, although they felt that they often behaved in racist ways. Second, they resented the guilt they felt obligated to bear as penance for the sins of the White race. Because they were born in the late-twentieth century, they did not see the connections between themselves and the plights of people of color. In addition to influencing the ways we all talk about race, color-blindness has influenced school curricula as well. No young woman I talked with had had much, if any, school coursework on the history of diversity in the United States before entering college. For some of them, the SLA course was their first experience with critical attention to diversity, and that was not the main purpose of the course.

It was likely because of their ignorance regarding the history of different races in the United States that so many tutors lamented the choices people of color seemed to have made regarding housing and schooling, among other things, without seeing the larger, White-dominated societal role in these decisions. Michelle, for example, expressed bewilderment and dismay as to why people of color would choose to live on the east side of town. She likewise thought it was nonsensical to locate a historically Black college in this neighborhood of color because, in her mind, it was too far from downtown (two miles) for convenience. Michelle had no knowledge of the United States's history of compulsory racial residential segregation or of historically Black colleges and universities. The roots of this particular college predated the university that tutors attended by eight years. The "color line" in our town had originally been drawn in the Jim Crow era. People of color could not receive utility hookups if they lived on the west side of the highway that legally segregated the town until the late 1960s. Michelle and the other tutors were unaware of this history. Leonardo (2002, p. 34) calls this ignorance the result of a "pedagogy of amnesia." This pedagogy is informally taught through schools, the government, the popular media, and the stories handed down through family generations.

This ignorance and the angry feelings of resentment that often accompany it vividly illustrate the notion of "backlash" presented by Omi and Winant in 1994 and further articulated by Winant in 1997. Winant (1997, p. 42) argues that White resentment toward people of color and policies, such as affirmative action, that seem to privilege people of color are "currently at hysterical levels" because "They represent Whiteness as a *disadvantage*, something which has few precedents in U.S. racial history." Indeed, several women expressed the notion that as White people, they felt unfairly disadvantaged in the United States. Claire and Elizabeth, for example, shared particularly strong opinions about the disadvantages of Whiteness. Claire believed that our university focused more attention on recruiting and retaining people of color than it did on Whites. In fact, she said some of her White friends joked about applying to the university with fictional Latina/o last names in order to have a better chance of getting accepted. She concluded this story by saying, "It sounds really bad, but it seems like [our university] is really focusing on that and I don't think that there's . . . I don't think that there's any White *privilege*," virtually spitting out the word "privilege" to highlight the ridiculousness of it.

Elizabeth's concerns were similar. She felt that cultures of color were privileged over the more neutral, White, American culture to an unacceptably extreme degree. She articulated her frustrations by explaining that

> These children [of color], it seems like sometimes they have made such a big deal about preserving their culture and everything, which I think is important—but, if they are growing up in America, then they should also be familiar with American . . . customs, or . . . the heritage of America, or the history. I think they should know that. That's almost *depriving* a child if they are going to grow up here, if you don't . . . incorporate this in with their culture too.

The more we talked, the more it became clear that Elizabeth considered White-dominated American culture and White-dominated American school curricula the necessary, neutral foundations upon which people of color should add their own peripheral histories and perspectives. This kind of approach to multicultural education in the United States is the most common and the least successful (Banks & Banks, 2003). Just as Omi and Winant (1994) suggest, Claire and Elizabeth felt that these attempts to displace White privilege were divisive rather than unifying. That is, they felt that, as White people, they were unfairly disadvantaged by more multicultural approaches to education. However, their concerns were unfounded. Claire did not realize that Latinas/os made up less than 14 percent of our university population while Whites accounted for nearly 65 percent the semester we met. Moreover, the dominance of the White perspective in schools of education and elementary and secondary schools was invisible to Elizabeth because it is so much the norm in our society. The resentment that these young women felt toward people of color and the policies that they felt benefited them seemed firmly linked to both their lack of historical knowledge regarding ethnic and racial groups in the United States, including Whites, and the invisibility of their own privileges.

Negative White Identity

In addition to this resentment of people of color, the more we talked, the more it became evident that all the women but Megan associated Whiteness with many more negative than positive qualities. The worst of these qualities was racism. Indeed, they seemed to unwittingly share the belief of many race scholars that Whiteness is necessarily linked with racism (Helms, 1990; Ignatiev, 1995, 1997; Ignatiev & Garvey, 1996; Roediger, 1991/1999, 1999). Thus, because they rejected racism, they felt they should reject Whiteness as well. Although they found it hard to articulate, most women associated White identity with shame for all the crimes of oppression Whites have committed against people of color. Gen's words clearly illustrate this association.

> In history, White people have oppressed the Hispanics and the African Americans, and we used them as slaves. . . . As a culture and in American history, we were *horrible*. I mean we were horrible to the Indians, horrible to the African Americans, horrible to the Hispanics, kicking everybody off their land. Who said that this was our land to begin with? So maybe that's part of why I don't *grasp* a White identity. Because it just—it makes me so mad to think this is what it means—this is part of our history. . . . I really don't see anything of our history that I could be proud of. . . . And as much as we tried to change, now we are damned.

These words clearly express the shame and guilt most of the women attached to the White label. Gen felt sickened by the crimes of White Americans and preferred to reject White identity rather than embrace it. Her words also express the frustration of Whites who feel that they are still "damned," despite the passing of time and the changing of generations. Like the others, she felt that people of color seemed encouraged to enjoy their cultural heritage, their sense of community, and their shared histories, while White people were only encouraged to feel guilty. Gen spoke for many when she said she wished the United States would just move past racism and give White people a break. So did Elizabeth, when she expressed her wish that we could all just go back to simpler times when people were happy with what they had, before racial issues became "such a big deal." Without realizing it, Elizabeth was longing back to the days of essentialist racism, when the advantages of Whiteness were clearly delineated and undeniable. Having a negative White identity, at that time, would have been preposterous.

Helms (1990) argues that, while racism is a fundamental aspect of Whiteness, it leads to a negative White identity that is psychologically unhealthy. Specifically, she suggests that "The greater the extent that racism exists and is denied, the less possible it is to develop a positive White identity" (p. 49). Indeed, conversations with the tutors supported this hypothesis in that the only one who seemed to have a positive White identity was Megan. She was the only tutor I spoke with who felt comfortable acknowledging her own racism as an inevitable consequence of living in a racist society. All the other women simultaneously revealed racist qualities and denied their own racism. They also longed for a positive White identity, but lamented the fact that a negative White identity seemed to be the only kind of cultural or racial self available to them. These contradictions fanned the flames of their resentment toward people of color, who seemed to have the luxuries of strong racial identities, clear communities, and defined histories.

Helms (1990) and Tatum (1999), among others, argue that a positive White identity is necessary for psychological health and antiracist behavior. Holding one's tongue when it comes to racist words is not enough to generate this positive White identity. Rather, as Tatum (1999) notes, silence regarding racism must still be recognized as a form of "passive racism." Passive racism is still racism. I find Tatum's "moving walkway" metaphor to be a very helpful tool for better understanding this type of racism. She explains that

> I sometimes visualize the ongoing cycle of racism as a moving walkway at the airport. Active racist behavior is equivalent to walking fast on the conveyor belt. The person engaged in active

racist behavior has identified with the ideology of White supremacy and is moving with it. Passive racist behavior is equivalent to standing still on the walkway. No overt effort is being made, but the conveyor belt moves the bystanders along to the same destination as those who are actively walking. Some of the bystanders may feel the motion of the conveyor belt, see the active racists ahead of them, and choose to turn around, unwilling to go to the same destination as the White supremacists. But unless they are walking actively in the opposite direction at a speed faster than the conveyor belt—unless they are actively antiracist—they'll find themselves carried along with the others. (pp. 11–12)

Most of the tutors were content to stand still on the conveyer belt. They assumed that, by not running forward, they were not being influenced by racism. Megan did not seem to be forcefully walking in the opposite direction, but she realized that the conveyor belt existed.

Helms (1990) notes that, "In order to develop a healthy White identity, defined in part as a nonracist identity, virtually every White person in the United States must overcome [some] aspects of racism" (p. 49). To do this,

He or she must accept his or her own Whiteness, the cultural implications of being White, and define a view of Self as a racial being that does not depend on the perceived superiority of one racial group over another. . . . Thus, the evolution of a positive White racial identity consists of two processes, the abandonment of racism and the development of a nonracist White identity. (p. 49)

At the beginning of our semester together, only Megan held this understanding of Whiteness and racism. Although all the other women claimed to be nonracist, they revealed racism in many different ways. Most made comments that would be considered actively racist by just about anyone. Their inconsistent beliefs and behaviors regarding racism likely contributed to their negative White identities.

Conclusions

Color-blindness and racism together create a disturbing, destructive, and yet fragile web of partial truths and downright lies. Color-blind racism might be the only construct that allows Whites to make derogatory comments about people of color, to avoid people of color, to misjudge them, and to work in subtle and explicit ways to disenfranchise them without requiring Whites to ever think of themselves as "racist." When most people tell a lie, steal something, or commit an immoral act, they know they have done it, even if they deny it. In contrast, Whites can say and do almost anything against people of color and not realize they have done it, let alone feel remorse. "Racism" has such a negative connotation that few people are willing to assign themselves this label, no matter what they say or do. I often wonder if "murderer" is the only appellation with a worse connotation.

However as the tutors show, their negative thoughts about people of color and English-language learners did have negative consequences. While they continued to think of themselves as individual "good people," they had a hard time associating themselves with Whiteness. For tutors, Whiteness was a category shaped almost entirely by negative, racist actions. It was as if every negative comment they shared about people of color hurt Whites as a group, but not them as individuals. Understanding racism as a system that advantages Whites and disadvantages people of color is tremendously useful in that it rejects color-blindness and accounts for the systematic, institutionalized nature of racial inequality and the passive ways it is reproduced. All members of society contribute to this reproduction of inequality simply by going about "business as usual" (Tatum, 1999 p. 11). In this way, all members of society are responsible for racism, just as we are all influenced by it. With this understanding of racism, everyone is charged with dealing with it, not just people of color because they are unfairly victimized by the system, but Whites because they are unfairly advantaged by it. This systemic understanding of racism encourages us to examine not just the actions of the Ku Klux Klan and "those other racist teachers," but our own actions and how they contribute to both equity and inequity. We must then ask ourselves if we are satisfied with what we discover.

CHAPTER 4

Looking in the Mirror:
Confronting Racism with Tutors

As the weeks went by and the tutors and I got to know each other better, I began to realize that the racism the women revealed to me and to themselves, as discussed in the previous chapter, troubled them deeply. This unease seemed to be related, at least in part, to the connections they made between racism and evil and their positive views of themselves versus their negative views of Whiteness. Sharing Tatum's (1999) definitions of active and passive racism might have helped them accept the notion that their own racism was passive, rather than simply "evil." Likewise, sharing Helms's (1990, p. 49) statement that White identity "is closely intertwined with the development and progress of racism" might have given them some food for thought about the inevitability of passive racism in their lives. Before these tools could be helpful to the tutors, however, it seemed to me that they first needed to acknowledge the ways that they were influenced by and reproducing racism. That is, they needed to acknowledge their own racism as those privileged by the "system of advantage based on race" (Tatum, 1999, p. 7). Although many of them did agree that "small prejudices" floated around in their minds sometimes, I did not consider these minor confessions to be true acknowledgments of racism because they did not challenge their nonracist self-images. In addition, because the women generally thought of small prejudices as inconsequential, they felt no dire sense of responsibility for racism. Instead, they thought of themselves as removed from racism altogether.

However, as Helms (1990) suggests, these denials did have consequences, the most obvious of which was a negative White identity. The second consequence was even more detrimental. While the women shared with me their deficit thoughts, their low expectations, and their other racist assumptions about the English-language learners of color they tutored, they also spent at least 10 hours working one-on-one with the children. Their racism necessarily accompanied them to their tutoring sessions and affected their relationships with the children in subtle and obvious ways. Michelle offers a good example of the inconsistencies that came of this. While she outwardly bombarded the child she tutored with praise, she inwardly considered Valerie's language skills extremely deficient. Her praise was insincere and demeaning; it also gave Valerie the message that her tutor was very proud of her when, in fact, she was not. Additionally, Elizabeth, the young woman from the "White suburban Beverly Hills," who tutored the same child I did, was so afraid to ask Martin any personal questions that she never created a comfortable learning environment, which is the first step for successful tutoring. Moreover, she tried to keep Martin reading at the second-grade level when he was able to read at the fourth-grade level. Similarly, Rachel, the woman with the *chai* pendant, quickly misjudged the skills of two children she had trouble tutoring. She reported both these children to their teacher, labeling them disruptive and apathetic. Their developing English skills likely kept these children from full participation. Finally, the young woman from the Rio Grande Valley, Ashley, clearly lacked enthusiasm working with Latina/o children, which noticeably transferred to her tutoring sessions. When I observed her, she patiently, but indifferently, tried to pass the time as painlessly as possible. In her journals, she pondered why the children seemed so listless, as though they did not want to be there at all. It seemed to me that Ashley, rather than the children, set the tone for these interactions. Although I liked all these young women very much, and I felt that they were doing their best at the time, I also saw some serious problems that seemed to be linked to their unacknowledged racism. Getting them to admit their own racism in a meaningful way thus comprised the next part of my work with them.

Before I describe the intervention I undertook with these tutors, I must first describe some of the factors that led to it and helped frame it. As I have already detailed, the more I talked with them, observed them, and read their journals, the more I became concerned about the unacknowledged racism that was influencing their interactions with the children. However, I was uncertain as to what I was going to do about this, and how I was going to frame the intervention. I had planned to share the written interview transcriptions with each individual tutor all along, but I was uncertain as to how I would actually confront racism when it came time to do so. I hoped that the tutors would lead me to this decision, and, eventually, they did. The way this happened is discussed below.

A Lesson from Which to Learn

During the semester, I was meeting with nine different women at times that were convenient for them. I was also observing them at times that were, again, convenient for them, and reading the journals they and their classmates submitted for class. I was also observing and teaching all SLA students during our class twice each week, keeping a journal of the whole experience, and tutoring Martin at Willow Elementary each week. Through all these different experiences, I was learning a lot about the Whiteness and racism of SLA students and what I learned constantly influenced my thoughts about the class, the tutoring situation, the young women, and the need for intervention. The strongest example I can give of how my interactions with some women influenced the way I constructed the intervention is to recount my interview with Amy and Michelle.

Amy, the sensitive young woman from San Antonio, and Michelle, the wealthy young woman whose family had sponsored a Russian immigrant family when she grew up, were good friends and tutored in the same school at the same time. Because it was so convenient, we agreed that I would observe each of them on the same day, and then meet with them together afterwards. All other interviews were with individuals. As I recounted earlier, during Michelle's lesson, I observed her overwhelm Valerie with praise, hugs, and warm affection while they sat together; yet the moment Valerie got up to talk with another tutor, Michelle turned around and complained to me about her "poor English." The disrespect and contempt Michelle showed for the child stunned me. I did not know how to react except to ask Michelle to explain her thoughts to me. Immediately after this exchange, I had a half-hour observation with Amy which, fortunately, was uneventful.

I met with both tutors immediately after Amy's observation in an empty room at the school. At this moment, I was still struggling with my teacher-researcher role in light of Michelle's comments and actions. Personally, I was devastated by Michelle's behavior with Valerie; I considered pulling her out of her tutoring situation altogether. However, as a teacher educator, I (usually) tend to side with the perspective of Melnick and

Zeichner (1998), that it is our responsibility to help shape good teachers. Thus, I felt it was my duty to help Michelle become a better tutor for Valerie because she spent time with her every week and because she would likely work with second-language learners again someday. Moreover, as a teacher and a researcher, it was very important for me not to disrupt our trusting relationship. I could not harshly confront Michelle and still stay within my own teaching and research philosophy. So, under the burden of this dilemma, I decided to let Amy and Michelle take control of our interview and direct it however they wanted. As their instructor, I would question them and negotiate meaning with them, as I tried to move them to a more complex understanding of what had gone on in their lessons (Ivek, 1994; Freire, 1970/2000; Vygotsky, 1978).

By meeting with me as a pair, Michelle and Amy gained a great deal of confidence. As one of them would talk, the other would voice her agreement. Sometimes they finished each other's sentences. Perhaps because of our previous discussions about Whiteness, racism, and Valerie, Michelle felt very comfortable talking about her perceptions of Valerie and Mayan Elementary. She talked a lot about Valerie's "poor English," and suggested that "her grammar was bad today" because "she had a long weekend and she was with [her family] a lot, and yesterday was her first day back; [so her family's influence] is still rubbing off on her a little more." Michelle explained that it was her job to model "correct English" for Valerie to counteract the "slang" her parents spoke at home. She suggested that Valerie "should always be trying to improve," so she would sound less like a "street Mexican" and more like Michelle. These thoughts matched the role model and savior personas Michelle had constructed for herself. Amy agreed with Michelle's comments, adding that it was "sad" but true that we are all necessarily judged on our language skill. Michelle added, "That talk is *fine* for the streets, but not for the school. Not for when you're writing, doing vocabulary in *English*." As these comments indicate, both women thought of English as a more sophisticated, more formal version of language than the children's home languages, something that has been noted in the literature on English-language acquisition (Cummins, 1994). As they discussed the deficiencies of the children, both women offered support and respect for one another's comments, further distancing themselves from the children.

We then talked a bit about different English dialects and ways to model standard English while valuing the home language (Fillmore, 1989; Solomon & Rhodes, 1995). I also gave Michelle some advice for contributing less to her lessons with Valerie and encouraging Valerie to contribute more. At this point, I was not comfortable "confronting" the racism the two young women had shown because I had not done that with any other tutor. So, I thanked them for being so honest and then asked if there was anything else they wanted to say. They got very quiet and looked at each other. Finally, Michelle said, "You can ask us anything for your study. We can be your guinea pigs." We all paused for a moment to take in the connotations of that comment, and then Amy added, "I feel like we're being so racist." I was so surprised that they brought up this topic that I did not know how to react. Consequently, I directed the conversation back to Amy and Michelle and asked them to explain what they meant. Michelle responded by mimicking herself saying, "That's Mexican English." Hearing this remark, Amy quickly comforted her by saying that, "[Earlier,] I felt like I was coming off as the biggest racist, close-minded person, but I think it's just because these are things, like we said last time, you don't talk about." Michelle quickly agreed and added that she lately had been "analyzing [racism] a lot." They seemed very anxious to talk about what this racism in their own words could mean. As I listened, they opened up more about their "honest," very negative, feelings about the school and the children.

When Michelle invited me to ask her anything, she was clearly signaling a willingness to open up a critical discussion. She and Amy looked to me for guidance. However, because this was such unchartered water for all three of us, I did not know how to guide them through a critical discussion of their own racism. This lack of action on my part gave Amy and Michelle the message that the goal was to talk about their feelings more honestly, but not more critically. As we left Mayan Elementary together, Michelle commented on the "dirty," "poor," "trashy" nature of the neighborhood, while she and Amy both laughed about the need to keep their car doors locked. As they bid me goodbye, Michelle sang out, "We are the honest ones!"

By not having a plan of action with which to further examine the racism Amy and Michelle brought up, I stumbled at this moment. The two women consequently filled in for me, supporting each other through their own analyses of the situation. Being together also gave them the confidence to massage each other's racist thoughts and comments, moving their racism from a negative place to a positive place. That is, after one woman dared to express her own racism, her friend dismissed her insights as not racist and not important. Thus, the racist thoughts no longer seemed racist at all. In Michelle's words, they just seemed "honest." These two young women actually grew emboldened by their denials of racism and their open embrace of deficit thinking. They seemed to come to a new understanding that freed them from their guilty thoughts. Titone (1998) argues that all attempts at antiracist education must be guided by a strong leader if they are to be successful. She suggests that leaders of antiracist efforts must know their own positionality well; they must encourage a loving, trusting environment that is capable of withstanding strong emotions; and they must know how to take action and maintain leadership throughout the process. Because of my lack of experience with antiracist education, I faltered in this third requirement for successful antiracist teaching. This break in guidance allowed Amy and Michelle to move our discussion in a more comfortable, less threatening direction.

The language that characterized the new direction of our conversation was safe and self-congratulating. It enabled Amy and Michelle to reassure each other and draw attention away from their racism. Delgado (1995b, p. 65) describes this kind of supportive dominant group talk as talk that provides a "form of shared reality in which [the group's] own superior position is seen as natural." Through this talk, the women reaffirmed, rather than challenged, their racist thoughts. McIntyre (1997) found the same kind of discourse in her study of the identities of White student teachers and labeled it "White talk." She described this kind of discourse as counterproductive to the examination of racism. In her words, it is:

> Talk that serves to insulate White people from examining their/ our individual and collective role(s) in the perpetuation of racism. It is a result of Whites talking uncritically with/to other Whites, all the while, resisting critique and massaging each other's racist attitudes, beliefs, and actions. (pp. 45–46)

The women McIntyre (1997) studied had trouble moving beyond the dominant storytelling of White talk. Instead of digging deeper into their own hearts and confronting the weight of their own racism, they dismissed one another's racism and reassured one another's goodness. They acted as caring friends who, naturally enough, did not want one another to feel bad. Indeed, that is just what Amy and Michelle did. As I left the two tutors that day, I got the awful feeling that I had caused more harm than good by not leading them to confront their own racism. Indeed, they now seemed to be reveling in their racism rather than trying to deconstruct it or take responsibility for it.

As I drove away from Mayan Elementary that day, I vowed to myself that I would not contribute to White talk (McIntyre, 1997) or dominant storytelling (Delgado, 1995b) again when I met with tutors. The first step in accomplishing this was not to meet any other tutors in a group. That format seemed to exacerbate this kind of storytelling. The second step was to firmly but gently confront the racism revealed in our conversations about race.

Because of my teaching and research philosophy, these firm confrontations had to be couched in trusting, comfortable, reciprocal conversations where tutors did not feel that I was attacking them (Brown, 1994a, 1994b; Krashen & Terrell, 1983; Henry, 1998; Horwitz, Horwitz, & Cope, 1986; Frankenberg, 1993; Titone, 1998; Wink, 2000). Moreover, due to my experience with Amy and Michelle, I knew that my leadership had to be unwavering (Titone, 1998). I was certainly a little nervous about this endeavor, but I felt strongly that it had to be done.

The work of George and Louise Spindler (see Spindler & Spindler, 1982, 1990, 1993, 1994; Spindler, 1997, 1999) inspired the intervention strategy I adopted. The Spindlers worked one-on-one with teachers to help them better "see" the borders of their own culture and the ways that their culture influenced their teaching. The Spindlers' (1987) work with Roger Harker is most well known. Roger was a popular teacher who, nonetheless, marginalized his students of color. The Spindlers observed Roger teaching and then shared insights with him about how he was only teaching to the children in class who shared his culture. Through numerous weekly observations, frank discussions, and the sharing of observational data with Roger, the Spindlers sought to make him aware of his ethnocentrism and the ways it affected his students. In their work, the Spindlers sought to bring "cultural knowledge used by the individual . . . into full awareness so it can be dealt with as potential bias in interpersonal relations" (Spindler, 1999, p. 466). In my own version of intervention, I focused specifically on the ways that racism and White privilege influenced tutors as members of the dominant White American culture. I then worked with tutors one on one to help them recognize these influences on their work with the English-language learning children of color they tutored.

Gentle Confrontations

The next time I met with tutors, I gently called attention to the racism I observed in their words. I also gave all women copies of their own interview transcriptions and asked them to review them carefully for racism or anything else that made a strong impression on them. My goal was to help them become aware of their racism by examining their own spoken and, later, written words. Because all women were individuals, different aspects of this critical intervention affected them differently. Gen, Ashley, and especially Elizabeth were strongly moved by our firm discussions of racism. After our very powerful interviews, their transcriptions and our subsequent conversations seemed to reinforce what they learned about themselves. Most other tutors, in contrast, were not strongly moved by the racism they "heard" in their own words while we were talking. However, nearly all of them were stunned by the impressions they made in the transcriptions. Nearly all women were strongly affected by one form of intervention or the other. Because this critical intervention appeared to be so successful, in the following section, I will outline the intervention experience of each tutor. Because the firm conversations about race came first, I will begin with a retelling of my conversations with Elizabeth, Gen, and Ashley. I will then discuss the effects reading the transcriptions had on other tutors.

Hearing Racism

Through our critical discussions of racism, Elizabeth, Ashley, and Gen revealed their racism, admitted it, and took responsibility for it in what seemed to me to be a sincere fashion. There is no way to measure the "validity" of the assessment of sincerity. I can only emphasize that, as I got to know these young women over the course of the semester, their tears, their words, and their actions indicated to me that these conversations about racism made a very strong impression on them. It was not easy, but each of them seemed strongly affected by the process they went through to realize their own racism. Moreover, at the end of these conversations on racism, each of them vowed to work toward an antiracist White identity (Helms, 1990; Tatum, 1999; Titone, 1998). Because these conversations were so powerful, I think it is important and useful to retell them here in story form, similar to the ways they first unfolded. Because Elizabeth's problem-solving process was so clear, and because Ashley and Gen seemed to follow a similar process, I present my conversation with Elizabeth in great detail and then follow with more condensed versions of the conversations with Ashley and Gen.

Elizabeth

Because I met with Elizabeth just 24 hours after I met with Amy and Michelle, my goals for our conversation were very clear. I wanted her to be able to admit her own racism in a sincere fashion and then to take responsibility for it. For this, our second meeting, we decided to meet at my house. At the end of our first meeting in a local coffee shop, she had confessed that she did not feel comfortable talking about issues of race in a public place. The change of venue made a tangible difference. While Elizabeth had spoken hesitantly at the coffee shop, as she walked through my front door, words poured out of her mouth. She was very anxious to express her frustrations with the myriad issues of multiculturalism. On the one hand, she was a supporter of diversity and felt that all cultures should be valued. On the other hand, she felt that traditional White American culture was being usurped by cultures that, in her mind, should be more peripheral.

The apparent ethnocentricity of marginalized cultures vexed her; she felt that people of color wanted too much attention.

As she freely expressed her frustrations, like Amy and Michelle, Elizabeth also began to hear the "politically *in*correct" sounds of her words, and she realized that she might, in her words, "sound racist" or "sound bad." The fear that she might be incriminating herself moved her to pause in her catharsis and try to better explain her intentions. She emphasized that, although she was frustrated by people of color and all the unfair privileges they seemed to have in society, "I would be willing to put my personal opinions aside [if] I'm going to be teaching children [of color]. I want to do it the right way." This comment was Elizabeth's attempt to repair her image as a giving, loving person who would certainly benefit the lives of all children, regardless of their race, home language, ethnicity, etc. With her self-image intact, she sought to move on with the conversation.

However, rather than comfort Elizabeth by voicing my agreement with her plans to somehow put her feelings aside or condone her words with silence, I stopped her here with a question. I asked her if she really thought she could put her personal feelings aside. Without hesitating even a moment, Elizabeth answered, "Yes." However, she had a very hard time explaining how this would be possible. Finally, she tried again to explain her contradicting feelings,

> I think that emphasis is put on making *less* of a deal about White . . . culture, heritage or—because, it's like, you have to be *careful* what you say. Not just about racism though. Because, I wouldn't—I would try not to—you might think everything I've said is racist, but, you know, I wouldn't call someone a derogatory name or something. But even if you are not saying that, it's . . . you have to . . . you're going to have to listen to this tape 30 times to understand me!

Trying to speak honestly, somewhat within and somewhat outside the limitations of political correctness, left Elizabeth tongue-tied. She had a very hard time expressing her feelings, but her frustrations certainly came through. She was trying to explain that, while she was against politically correct language and so much attention to diversity, she was still against racism. However, the racism that tinted her own words as she said this added to her frustration.

No one else was around to comfort Elizabeth and assuage her fears that she might be racist with the sanctuary offered by White talk. Moreover, rather than alleviating her anxiety by allowing her to move on in her invective, or comforting her with stories of my own racism, I listened carefully and then I called her on her own contradictions. Again, I pointed to her own words. This time, I asked her to explain why she said, "You might think everything I've said is racist." This question flustered her; she clearly wanted to move past this topic. However, she gathered her courage, thought a few moments, and then explained that her words could be interpreted as racist because they were perforated with stereotypes. In a sympathetic manner, I told her that it sounded to me that she "wished" she were happy about cultural diversity, but, in all honesty, she really wasn't. Ashamedly, she agreed with this assessment.

We continued to negotiate why Elizabeth thought that she might sound racist, and I drew her attention to her earlier comment that "I would be willing to put my personal opinions aside" when she worked with children of color. I asked her, "What are those personal feelings that you have to put aside?" She answered that she had not asked the child she tutored, Martin, any personal questions because she had, perhaps unconsciously, expected him to have a "hard family life" he would be too embarrassed to talk about. She explained that these were probably negative expectations on her part because, she, herself, certainly would not mind if anybody asked her about her own home life.

As Elizabeth acknowledged the negative assumptions she had made about Martin, she seemed to catch a glimpse of her own racism in action. This sighting stunned and appalled her. For a moment, she could not believe herself. In a critically self-reflective manner, she recounted to me that the professor who taught her multicultural education class constantly reminded his students not to judge the children they tutored. She emphasized that she "totally" agreed with this philosophy in her mind and in her heart. However, at this moment, she realized how much she had been judging Martin. She told me, "I sit here and I listen to myself and it's freaking me out!"

Given her last comment, I asked her if she was able to admit that she might be racist. Quickly and passionately she exclaimed,

> No. Absolutely not. Because, I don't . . . when I think of someone being racist—all my life—that means you look at someone and you think that they are not as good as you are because of their heritage or—and I don't *consciously* do that. You know, I think *racism* is a bad thing. And that's just not the way I was raised—to look at someone and judge them like that. So I wouldn't say—I would never want to admit that I'm racist, but, now that I'm talking about how I—*totally*—Martin—I associated him with hard times and . . . all that, I see that that is probably racist. You know, and some other things are probably racist, but [sigh] I don't know . . . I guess

I am, subconsciously, but I don't mean to be. You know, I don't not like someone because of it. You know what I mean? But it *sucks*! Because it makes you feel bad! A bad person. Like, I shouldn't be teaching kids. You know, I'm going to judge them.

As this passage indicates, Elizabeth called herself on the racism she heard in her own words—even the racism in her own denials. She realized how racism had affected her judgment of Martin, and she also realized that it could affect her judgment of other children. As she reflected on the ways she had judged Martin, she objectified her world and became critical of it. However, she still tried to deny some aspects of her role in perpetuating racism. While she reluctantly admitted that she could cause harm to children because of her racism, she called her racism "subconscious," and tried to rationalize it as something she had no control over.

Elizabeth also emphasized that describing herself as racist would make her feel terrible, like "a bad person [who] shouldn't be teaching kids." This sudden consciousness was an awful blow to her; after all, she had wanted to be a teacher her whole life. Recognizing her racism automatically chipped away at some of her White privilege. Although she wanted to be a good teacher for all children, her desires alone could not guarantee her success. To make herself feel better, she once again sought to deflect her responsibility for racism. In restarting our conversation, she tried to explain that, although she showed some signs of racism, she could not help it because she was a member of a racist society. Specifically, she explained that, "It's such a subconscious . . . thing that I guess I—everyone—not everyone— but, most people—White people—or American culture people have [it]." This was the first time Elizabeth made a connection between herself and other Whites as members of a group. Even though this was a connection in racism, for a moment, this group identity comforted her because it deflected her own personal responsibilities.

While Elizabeth had made some profound realizations in our conversation thus far, she also tried to keep the consequences of these realizations at bay. That is, she did not want her newfound consciousness to change her life. She wanted everything to continue on as it had before. Thus, she conjured a quick solution that might counteract her racism. She explained,

I will just have to really be aware, I guess. I just—I don't see myself treating a child in a negative way or judging. I mean, it may be judging, but I would *never* portray it, I don't think. Definitely not on purpose, but . . .

As she heard herself talk, Elizabeth again became very critical of her own words. She realized that she was not offering a true solution. She claimed she would never judge a child, yet she had just witnessed herself doing this. Then she claimed she would never portray this judgment; but, at the same time, she realized she might. Finally she resolved that, if nothing else, at least it would not be on purpose.

Again, I called Elizabeth on her contradictions. I asked her, "If you think you have some negative assumptions about a child's background and you're working with that child, do you think it could come through in some way?" Reflecting on this question, Elizabeth paused and then said, "Martin could think that because I'm not asking about his family when I'm trying to be careful . . . I don't know if it'll go through or not, but . . . I don't [know]." The weight of this admission frightened her. She did not want to hurt a child, purposely or not. So, once again, she tried to skirt the consequences of her racism. This time, she contrasted her own more passive, more unintentional racism with the active, intentional racism of other White teachers. Specifically, she said,

> I think that there are people, there are teachers that are *really*— they don't think that children of color or whatever should be treated the same. They don't think that they are worthwhile of an *education* or whatever. I think *that* is bad. But *I* think that everyone is worthwhile of an education and everyone's worthwhile of, you know . . . of . . . so I don't think it would come through . . . as much, you know? I mean, I would not *ever* do anything to make a child feel bad about themselves or feel different, you know? And if I do, then . . . huh!

Although Elizabeth kept trying to deny her role in the perpetuation of racism and the damage this caused children, she was nevertheless very critical of herself. Her final comment, "And if I do, then . . . huh!" expressed the helplessness she felt coming to this conclusion. Even though she did not want to be racist, at this moment, she realized that she might be. As a kind of last-ditch effort to deny the effects this could have on her teaching, she put her head down and said, "I think kids are so generally pure and the best thing we have."

Because Elizabeth finally acknowledged that both her good heart and her racism could coexist in her teacher persona, I sought to draw attention to the challenges children of color and English-language learners face in schools all over the United States. Specifically, I asked her why she thought these children so often struggle in school. She suggested that some teachers and schools treated children badly and, after thinking about it more, she said that it might be because "White teachers are culturally constructed to be racist." Believing we had finally reached the end of our journey,

I asked her how she felt coming to that conclusion. Miserably, she looked at me and asked, "So what you are getting at is that minority teachers should teach minority children, right?" Because I do believe that more teachers of color would benefit the field of education, but that many White teachers can learn to become better teachers for children of color, I told her, "Oh, no. I'm not saying that." Curious to know what had generated this question, I asked her, "Why are you saying that?" She answered,

> Because I just feel like that's what we are getting at. Because I know that whatever I've said that is racist is not my fault. You know? It's a society thing. Like you said, American culture is racist. It's not like I'm a bad person. I *know* I'm not a bad person. I *know* I have a good heart. I think I have a better heart than a lot of people I see. So, what I am is, I guess, being a product of society or American culture.

This was Elizabeth's last-ditch effort to reject the responsibility that was quickly falling on her shoulders. These denials were typical examples of White talk (McIntyre, 1997). However, because she had no one to agree with her on this, her excuses did not hold water. Rather, her defenses started to crumble.

Although I agree with Elizabeth that racism is a part of our society, I also asked her that, even if our racism comes from society, "Isn't it still a bad thing, aren't we still responsible for it?" At these questions, she finally capitulated. Very passionately, and very insightfully, she said,

> It's a big deal, but I don't think it's made a big deal because I have *never* even thought about it like this. I don't think people realize—reading all those articles and stuff about it—and White people say in class that they know people who are racist. You would think they are racist: they don't like Black people; they want segregation, blah, blah, blah. You hear them, but you don't really think about that you have the views inside you, whether you put them there or not. But as for me, it's a *very* big issue. I mean it is huge. I mean . . . humongous.

As she finished this statement, Elizabeth started sobbing. It seemed to me that she had finally seen the whole picture. Rather than just the "tip of the iceberg," she glimpsed the hulking, colossal entity that is White racism. It is so colossal, in fact, that it permeates even the best of us, despite our intentions. The enormity of it, as well as the largely superficial attention it gets from White Americans and the dominant American culture, overwhelmed Elizabeth. Her comment that "It's a big deal, but I don't think it's made a big deal," was extremely insightful. Nothing in her home life, her teacher education, her work with children, or her experience with American culture had prepared her to deal with her own racism. All these aspects of American life had distanced her from it. As she said, "It's a very big issue . . . it is huge." As Elizabeth cried, I hugged her and told her that I, too, had gone through a similar process when I admitted my own racism for the first time. She cried quietly for several minutes. As she collected herself, she attempted a laugh and said, "I never thought I would be crying over racism!" White Americans almost never respond so passionately to racism in the abstract. Recognizing racism in one's self is what triggers this kind of emotion. This recognition implicates all of us White folks in the perpetuation of racism. Rather than pointing to "those other teachers," grandparents from another generation, or even the Ku Klux Klan to illustrate racism, with this recognition, we Whites have to point to ourselves. This acceptance of responsibility and blame for racism is what upset Elizabeth so deeply.

At this point in our discussion, it was clear that Elizabeth had finally grasped the severity of the situation. She was devastated by her own contributions to the reproduction of racism. In trying to express her feelings, she explained that

> I mean, you look at people horribly your whole life for being racist and calling people names, whatever, but, realizing it's in you . . . it's just . . . [long pause] I mean, it's very shocking . . . [long pause] and it's frightening because you don't want to inflict it on others, especially kids.

At this moment, Elizabeth felt devastated. She also felt very unsure of herself, as if the rug had been pulled out from under her. Although she stated several times her resolve that she was "a good person" who "consciously" worked toward the successes of all children, she also now realized how she could work against the progress of students like Martin who were different from herself in terms of race, ethnicity, economic class, and language. Rather than looking outward at the "deficits" of the English-language learners of color she tutored, she turned her perspective inward and began to focus on her own contributions to the challenges facing these children in school. This new perspective was a very powerful one as it gave Elizabeth the ability to make changes in her own actions (Freire, 1970/2000).

Ashley

Just as the conversation with Elizabeth started with a flood of information about the topic of her choice, my conversation with Ashley started when she talked at length about the children she tutored and the progress she seemed to be making with them. Despite positive developments, she still hoped not to teach Latina/o children. As the semester progressed, she changed her mind about wanting to work with White children from high-income backgrounds and, at one point, planned to work as a missionary in Australia. At that time, she said that American children no longer interested her. I felt that this topic was an excellent starting point for a gentle confrontation of racism. The more we talked, the more Ashley began to hear the racism in her own words. We talked about Mexico and she rolled her eyes to indicate her dislike of the topic. In response, I invited her to explain her feelings. Knowing what I was getting at, she reluctantly explained that her aversion to Mexico and Tex-Mex came with her move to our southwestern American town. I asked if the racism of her new friends or the dominant culture had any influence on her feelings. At first, she was hesitant to agree with this assessment. However, when I told her my thoughts that all White Americans are racist, she immediately agreed, saying,

> Yeah, we are. . . . I don't know. I just—I know I am! I know I am. I mean, I'm not going to deny it when I know it's true. I know I looked down upon the whole Tex-Mex thing. That's probably wrong, but, you know, and I've noticed since I've come here all my friends are White. I've noticed that.

Being able to admit her racism seemed to bring relief to Ashley. Unlike Elizabeth, she did not need to be cajoled to make this recognition. She recognized her racism and seemed to be waiting for a safe moment to explicitly name it. Like Elizabeth, as our conversation continued, she insightfully assessed racism as "a big deal" that is not made a big deal in the United States. She also went on to explain that just "living life" and "going with the flow" naturally exacerbated racism and promoted distance between herself and people of color. Without realizing it, she was defining racism in virtually the same manner as Tatum (1999).

Admitting her racism enabled Ashley to critically discuss it and the effects it could have on children. Although, like Elizabeth and several others, she rationalized that, "I really work hard not to put across anything . . . because I know it's not them; it's not their fault," she also began to ponder the impact her racism could have on children. At one point, she specifically asked me, "Do I show prejudices in my journal?" I thought for a while and then told her that her journals were very methodical and technical, without much emotion or detail. Because our conversations were so rich, and she voiced her prejudices and racism so plainly, I found it odd that such thoughts were omitted in her journal. I told her that I thought she might have been purposely omitting any personal feelings because she did not want to see her racism in writing. After talking with Ashley and analyzing the tape of our conversations, I realized that I should have also told her that her lack of enthusiasm was apparent in the tutoring session. I wrote these comments on the transcriptions that I later gave her.

In our first conversation about Whiteness and personal background, Ashley had been the only tutor who admitted that she might be racist. She had brought up the notion, but then quickly dismissed it. In this more explicit discussion of racism, she did not deny her own racism, nor did she become horrified by it. In fact, it did not seem to surprise her. While Elizabeth glimpsed her racism for the first time only in our second interview, Ashley had seen this first "tip of the iceberg" on her own, prior to our first meeting. By the time of our second interview, she seemed resigned to the idea that she might be racist. Indeed, when I explicitly pointed out her racism, she seemed to accept it with a sense of relief. Just as it did with Elizabeth, this piece of knowledge seemed to help Ashley better understand herself and her own limitations as a teacher.

Gen

My conversation with Gen also started with a flood of information. She was excited to tell me that she had just received a good grade on a test where she had written a short essay about institutional racism. However, the more we talked about the concept, the more I realized that she did not understand it very well. Thus, I invited her to give me some examples of it so we could together negotiate a better way of explaining it. Gen explained that institutional racism occurred when people of color had a hard time succeeding in education. When I asked her to name some of these difficulties, she could only point to deficits in intelligence, confidence, home life, and motivation. As she gave these examples, I wrote them down. Next, I asked her to focus more explicitly on the institution and the effect it could have on educational success. Again, she gave similar examples that placed blame on the person, rather than the institution. Because she had had so many troubles in school herself, I asked her what had "helped" her to drop out of school. She laughed at this use of the word "help," and said "teachers." I then told her that this was the first example she had given of institutional racism.

Drawing her attention to the list of individual qualities she generated, I pointed out that these were all examples of deficit thinking because, in essence, they "blamed the victim." As I said this, I drew a circle around her comments and wrote the phrase "deficit thinking" next to them. I then explained that this kind of thinking is a kind of racism. Gen was shocked, and immediately exclaimed, "Really? I don't mean to be that way. I'm still learning." We then talked more about the effects her teachers and her school had had on her as a high school student. However, in trying to describe her experiences with racism, Gen could only give examples of the ways in which White people were discriminated against. After listening to her talk for several minutes, I asked her, "Did you notice that the few times that you have talked about discrimination, you have talked about discrimination against White people? Can you think of discrimination that goes on against people of color?" Again, Gen was surprised by this question. She then opened up a discussion of the Ku Klux Klan and contrasted the values it embraced with her own upbringing. Like the other tutors, Gen expressed disgust at racism. She also pointed out the many destructive and oppressive actions of White people throughout history and said that it was hard for her to construct a White identity for herself because she associated it with so much negativity.

In talking about the evils of Whiteness and racism Gen found an uncomfortable connection with herself. She wrapped up our conversation by stating,

> I don't want to be the one to do—I don't want to be discriminating. I don't want to be prejudiced. You know, I don't want to be racist. And—I don't want to do this either! [Points to the term "deficit thinking" on the sheet of paper.]

Like Elizabeth, Gen found a common identity with Whites through racism and it shook her. She adamantly did not want to be racist and vowed to do whatever it took to get past it. Although they were very different from each other, Elizabeth, Ashley, and Gen appeared to be strongly influenced by these critical, unyielding conversations about race. In these conversations, all three tutors acknowledged their own racism and claimed to want to work toward an antiracist White identity.

Seeing Racism

While Elizabeth, Ashley, and Gen were very sensitive to the racism in their own words during our conversations, other tutors needed to "see" the racism in their printed words before they could believe it. A few days after our second interview, I gave each tutor the verbatim transcriptions of our first meeting and the summarized transcriptions of our second meeting. Tutors received only their own interview transcriptions. I asked them to examine these transcriptions for any indication of their own racism or anything else that might surprise them, and then to call me when they were ready to talk about them. Most were very curious about this activity, as they were anxious to see how their words made them sound to other people. The sharing of transcriptions proved to be a very powerful method of critical intervention. For Elizabeth,

Ashley, and Gen, the transcriptions seemed to reinforce what they had learned in our second interviews. However, for Rachel, Claire, Megan, and Michelle, the transcriptions had a strong eye-opening effect. These young women were intensely moved by what they read in their transcriptions and our consequent discussions. At the same time, Becky and Amy seemed much less affected by this attempt at intervention. Because each conversation was unique, I will discuss each of them below.

Rachel

After the tutors had examined the transcriptions for a few weeks, I asked them, in our next meeting, to talk about their transcriptions and comment on what had surprised them the most. Each noticed something different in her own printed words. Rachel, for example, noticed right away the low expectations she had constructed for just about everything regarding the children she tutored and the school they attended. She said many times that she was "surprised" at her low expectations because she seriously thought that she had no preconceived notions, no prejudices, and no racism. Moreover, she was very surprised that she "sounded like a snob" when she talked about how nice the neighborhood surrounding Smith Elementary seemed. She explained that

> Why wouldn't I think it's nice? You know, the demographics of the school . . . and here I am saying "It's really nice"; "But it's really nice"; "The neighborhood seems really quiet and peaceful," or whatever. Well, why wouldn't you think that? I sound like a snob! Some people would associate the demographics to be lower SES [socioeconomic status] and mean not nice.

When talking about their own upbringing, several women had admonished "the snobs" they grew up with for their racist, elitist behaviors. Rachel, in particular, had talked at length about how uncomfortable these "snobs" had made her feel in high school. Seeing elitism in her own words made a strong impact on her. To make sure she was seeing a strong connection between herself and the snobbery she rejected, I gently commented that she must be "one of those people" who associate low SES with "not nice" because she had those same elitist, racist thoughts. Rachel was a little stunned by my words but admitted, "I did [have those thoughts]." She paused a moment, her voice softened, and she said once again, "I guess I did." It seemed that both her words and mine made a strong impression on her.

Like Elizabeth, Rachel felt very uncomfortable at this admission. To deflect the blame for this obvious example of deficit thinking, she changed the subject to the negative image the principal had given of the school when she visited the SLA class to recruit volunteers. Rachel reminded me that the principal described

Smith Elementary as serving a low SES population of primarily Spanish-speaking children. It is interesting that Rachel interpreted this information as negative. This strange interpretation of demographic information reminds me of the anger with which some students in my multicultural education classes have responded to United States Census data. Some students have suggested that the Census perpetuates racism and inequality by simply publishing data about race. It seems that information about education, income, and even population numbers is automatically perceived by some as negative when it is connected to race. Those holding this strange perspective likely have negative beliefs about people of color, as well as strong attachments to color-blindness. To those of this mindset, any reference to race or ethnicity is considered negative.

After recounting the principal's visit to me, Rachel added, "It's a shame when parents do not care about education." At this point, I pulled Rachel back to her own comments. I asked her if she realized she had very low expectations for the children and families served by Smith, as well as Smith itself. Her very words were revealing these low expectations. She was reluctant to admit this, but the more she thought about it, the more it seemed hard to deny. Finally, she said,

> I know we talked about my expectations and I said that I had none, but I guess now I see that, maybe, I did have some and I really didn't know what to expect; but, I think my expectations were really low.

Although she admitted these low expectations, Rachel again felt very uncomfortable. Just as Elizabeth had done earlier, Rachel then contrasted her own "open mind" with the close-mindedness of her more actively racist friend, Alicia. Specifically, she said, "I don't think that I'm a terrible person;" she then described Alicia as "disgraceful." As we talked more about how racism affected her personally, she explained her thoughts that, "I'm sure it affects me. But, I don't think it *negatively* affects me . . . I don't look down upon people for their beliefs or their culture or their race." This comment was virtually identical to the comment Elizabeth had made earlier, at the same point in our discussion about racism, that "[I] think that there are . . . teachers that . . . don't think that children of color or whatever should be treated the same. . . . I think *that* is bad. But *I* think that everyone is worthwhile of an education. . . ."

Rather than support Rachel with White talk, I pulled her attention back to her own transcriptions and the comments she had just made about her own low expectations. "So," I told her, "You do look down upon these children." Rachel sat in stunned silence for a moment after this comment. This part of our conversation had affected her very deeply, and the connotations of it were still sinking in. We talked for nearly two hours and, although she denied her racism for the last half-hour or so of our conversation, she kept thinking about it. When we met again three weeks later, she talked at length about how disappointed she was with herself for her low expectations and her racism. She said she could not stop thinking about it.

Claire

When I asked Claire what she saw in her transcriptions, she immediately said, "I'm racist. That's probably about all I have to say! I am definitely, definitely racist." As she said this, she laughed in a kind of shocked, embarrassed way. Although she was ready to admit her racism, she was certainly not happy about it. She explained that she particularly noticed how much she stereotyped people of color. Moreover, like Rachel, she thought she sounded elitist and called herself "snotty." Perhaps because Claire had gone to school with many Latina/o friends, it was rather easy for her to talk about race and racism. She was critical of herself, but not devastated. She told me, "I don't know. I think—I think I kind of sound defensive and I don't want to be racist, but I am. I really think [I am]."

Although Claire was very self-critical, she also wanted to be comforted. Thus, she sought to generate some White talk by explaining how people of color in her high school had "looked *down* at us in a sense." Rather than comfort her, however, I gently asked her "Okay. Are you being defensive now?" She laughed and responded, "Probably!" We then went on to talk about her impressions of the way she sounded in person as compared to how she sounded on paper. She explained,

> I think I sounded—I think if I handed this to . . . just some stranger on the street, Black or Hispanic, not knowing what this project is or anything, I think they would [say], "Uh huh, she's racist." I do. [She laughs at herself here.] And it just made me think a lot more, definitely.

I agreed with Claire and told her that even though we can always say, "That's not what I meant," our feelings still rise to the surface in some manner. She readily agreed and pointed to her transcriptions saying, "It's black and white! Right here! Completely."

Because Claire seemed to be sincerely admitting her racism, and taking responsibility for it, I asked her what she planned to do with this new consciousness. She explained that she was going to "really try to stop" the comments she made about people of other races. She also said she was going to voice her disapproval for the racist comments she heard from others around her. I reminded her that comments are just the surface indicator of the racism that lies deeper down within us. Again, she readily agreed. She told me that she planned to critically reflect on her thoughts and actions, in addition to her words. At the end of our conversation, Claire commented that, "I think White people kind of don't—not necessarily don't care—but we're just lazy and don't want to do something against it." Although she didn't explicitly articulate it, Claire was drawing a connection to the privileges of White people and the luxury they/we have of not opposing racism if they/we do not feel like it (Frankenberg, 1993; Scheurich, 1993; Terry, 1981). These comments give more credence to the "moving sidewalk" metaphor offered by Tatum (1999).

Michelle

Since my previous meeting with Michelle and Amy had prompted the firm intervention I was now taking with tutors, I was very anxious to see how this new approach would work with Michelle. Moreover, since our last conversation had been waylaid by White talk, I was curious to discover how this new conversation style, with its emphasis on confrontation, admission, and responsibility, would play out. Because I had changed tactics since we last met, I expected our conversation to have some uncomfortable stops and starts. However, Michelle was as chatty as usual and we had a very easy time talking.

The first thing Michelle had noticed in her transcriptions was how often she said "like." Rather than just being self-conscious, she saw this as a connection between herself and the children she tutored. As she explained, "I kept saying 'like,' and I was thinking how I was talking about how the students were speaking in slang and I was thinking, 'Wow. I really spoke in slang.' 'Like' could be considered a slang word, couldn't it?" She realized that, just as she had judged the children by their language, the outside world readily judged her. In fact, because the verbatim quotations of tutors were peppered with fillers such as "like" and "uhm," many of them asked me to take them out so they would not "sound stupid." A friend of mine who read an early draft of this book also said the fillers made tutors sound silly, young, and not very intelligent. After much reflection, I decided to take out the fillers so I did not misrepresent the women I spoke with as I decontextualized their comments. They were not stupid and it would have been a mistake to portray them as such. By reading her own verbatim comments, Michelle got a glimpse of the misperceptions she had of the children she tutored. I thought this was a very strong connection.

Like several others, it had been very important for Michelle to consider herself a role model who was capable of "saving" the children she tutored. So, I was not surprised when she moved the conversation to this topic. She explained that she had a hard time being a role model for Valerie and Cristobal, especially regarding their language use. She wanted to be a model for standard English, but she did not see the children following her example. At this point, I tried to help her deconstruct the notion of role model. I asked her why she thought Cristobal and Valerie would want to talk like her or otherwise model themselves after her. Perhaps because we had just talked about this in class, using chapters from Lisa Delpit's book *Other People's Children* (1995) as our guide, this was an easy subject for Michelle to discuss. She explained that

> [It's hard to be a role model,] especially with those kinds of people that we are the extreme opposite from. We don't speak their language like they do. And we don't have big families. I mean, I don't know if Cristobal and Valerie were telling me the truth, but Valerie has eight brothers and sisters, four dogs, and three cats. I live in a house with my mom and dad! I'm the only child. We don't have any pets! And so I'm minus eight brothers and sisters and minus four dogs and cats. So I feel like I lead a different life from her. You know what I'm saying? My *upbringing* was so different from hers. She has sisters that have kids!

Michelle concluded that, although they were so different, she could at least encourage the children to try hard in their studies. She seemed, to me, to be deconstructing her role model persona and examining her own positionality with a critical eye.

As we continued talking, Michelle went on to say that she thought she might sound racist and like a bad person in the transcriptions. She explained that she had opened up about her honest feelings because I had repeatedly told her that I wanted her to share her true feelings, not political correctness. At this point, she seemed a bit wary about my intentions. I reassured her that I did want her to be honest, but that I also planned to analyze the racism that came through in her honesty through the critical perspective I was taking. Then, just as Elizabeth, Ashley, and Rachel had done, she said, "I can hold things back when I need to and, luckily, most people don't notice." However, as she said this, she realized that she was, essentially, admitting her own racism. As she heard the weight of her words, she said, "I think that with this study, that's what you're talking about."

I asked Michelle to explain to me where, in her transcriptions, she thought she sounded racist. She thought a bit and then said,

> When I was talking about the Mexicans, street Mexicans, homeless, gangs, I did. The sag style, the saggy pants, I did feel like I

was being a little racist; but, I felt like I was being more honest than racist.

This final comment seemed a natural follow-up to her comment, in our previous interview, that "We are the honest ones!" Because I had allowed this previous comment to go by without confrontation, and because Amy and Michelle had successfully engaged in White talk when we last met, it was only natural that Michelle would expect our present conversation to take the same tone. However, this time, I did gently confront her. I asked her, "Can you be both [honest and racist]?" Thoughtfully, she answered,

> I don't know. Without offending someone? I don't think you can. I'm not offending *you*, I don't think because this is business—not for business, but for your study. But, if I was telling this stuff to Cristobal's mom, I think that I would offend her. If I was honest and racist at the same time.

While Michelle seemed to catch a glimmer of her own racism here, I felt it was important to explicitly point it out. Gently, I told her, "If that's honesty, then you must be racist—if you can see it." Michelle just stared at me in silence. After a few moments, I asked her how this made her feel. Words never failed Michelle. Passionately, she stated:

> It makes me feel . . . we are hiding so much from the world today. People—I don't think racist people should be *so* racist, but I feel people are holding so much back and saying that behind people's backs and behind closed doors that they—it's not serving any— it's not correct—it's *not right*. You know what I'm saying? We are just closing ourselves off so much to the world.

By naming her racism, Michelle seemed to realize the pervasiveness of racism in our society. Once she admitted that the negative thoughts in her heart were racist, she suddenly saw racism everywhere. Rather than believing that most people were not racist, at this moment, she seemed to suddenly believe that nearly all people were racist. She realized that by denying racism, we Whites are "closing ourselves off so much to the world." That is, we are avoiding the problem as we contribute to it.

While Michelle did admit her racism here, she had not yet taken responsibility for it. Therefore, I asked her whether she thought that racism could be considered a good thing, since it clearly influenced all of us White people. Immediately, she responded with the words, "No. Especially if you're going to be a teacher. I don't want to present that to my classroom."

However, like Elizabeth, Ashley, and Rachel, she immediately followed this acceptance of responsibility with more denial. She said,

> But, if I can keep that a bit more in my home life. I mean, people have it; but if I can just not let it affect what I do, then I think it's okay to have those feelings because everybody does. Not okay. But, I think everybody has them.

Just as I had done with the others, I drew Michelle's attention to the notion that her true feelings would come out one way or another with the children she taught. To help her make a personal connection, I then asked her if she had ever felt anti-Semitism, despite someone's best intentions. She gave an example of a time she helped a Christian family decorate a Christmas tree. While this family was verbally supportive of her Judaism, they nevertheless teased her and put her down for not knowing the traditions of Christmas. I commented that this seemed like a good example of passive anti-Semitism, similar to the passive racism we were discussing.

This example made a very strong connection for Michelle. Immediately, she brought up Cristobal, saying, "Now I see it. I'm correcting him in my own mind, but I'm showing him, '*I disapprove of the way that you are speaking*.' And I say it like, 'I said it right and you said it wrong.'" I reminded her that, according to Delpit (1995), when she disapproved of his language, she disapproved of his family and friends as well. Michelle seemed shocked at herself here. I asked her if this realization made her feel bad, and she readily answered, "It does. It makes me feel worse." Michelle digested this for a moment and then said that she just wanted to "model correct English" for the kids she tutored. She also added that, "I want to instill in him good values so he knows—not good values, but . . ." I pointed out the deficit thinking in this statement, but she had already noticed it. That is what caused her to stop mid-sentence.

To help Michelle feel that she was not alone in coming to this recognition of racism and responsibility, I told her a little bit about what some of the other tutors had been through, carefully shielding their identities. I also told her that coming to terms with racism and Whiteness was often an upsetting, threatening experience. She admitted that she did feel bad and overwhelmed, to an extent; "But," she explained,

> I feel like you are teaching me and you are making me more aware of ways I can help the way I feel. And ways I can work with my racism. And I feel like [the multicultural education professor] too, with his class, has shown us ways to help our classroom . . . Yes, I know, especially growing up the way I did; but there is a way that I can work on it . . . I feel that I can adjust myself better now

if I just know how to do a better job of it in the future . . . I try.
I'm learning.

These final comments seemed, to me, to be a sincere admission of racism
and responsibility. At this point, Michelle was not looking for an easy
solution. Rather, she was critically examining her own role in the reproduction of racism. Just as she said, there are "ways I can work with my racism." Acknowledging one's own racism, realizing the effects it can have on
children of color, critically reflecting on this situation, and then actively
working to change it; comprise ways of working with one's own racism
and consequently changing the world (Helms, 1990; Tatum, 1999). These
last comments from Michelle give evidence for the empowerment that
comes with admitting, and taking responsibility for, one's own racism.

Megan

Because Megan had already come to terms with her own racism through
an African-American culture class she had taken earlier, she had an easy
time talking about the racism she found in her transcriptions. Indeed, she
was happy to talk about it and explained that she really appreciated our
conversations because they gave her a chance to further explore racism in
a safe setting. As she said, "You're not going to argue with me or get upset
about what I say. It's kind of a more . . . calm environment to talk about it."
That said, I asked Megan if anything surprised her in her transcriptions.
She answered that she was very surprised to see that she had said, "wealthier children naturally have a better chance for education because they go
to good schools and they have *good families*"; she read this directly from
the summary of our second interview. She explained that, "That's not—I
shouldn't have said that. That's not what I meant." I told her my perspective that even if comments such as those are not what we truly feel, they are
what "come out." These kinds of comments indicate how strongly we are
influenced by racism, despite our best intentions. Megan readily agreed,
and added, "Yeah, when I read that, I [thought] 'Oh, no!'"

Megan then scanned through her transcriptions again and pointed out her
comments about putting her own future children in a small-town, suburban
school. On her transcriptions, I had written the comment that I wish we had
talked more about this connection between small town-life and racism. Megan
had thought about my comment and told me that she still felt strongly about
raising her own children in a small, ethnically homogenous town because

it's just when I'm married—for my own children—I want them—
that's the environment I want them to grow up in. Just a safe place
with good schools—but, I know that's bad, [considering] what I just

got through talking about. I want them to experience diversity; but still, I want them to be safe.

Although Megan was much further along than other tutors in her grasp of racism, Whiteness, and the responsibilities that go along with these two entities, she also showed some of the same signs of racism they did. Here, Megan associated diversity with danger. Although she was supportive of diversity in theory, it was not so important to her in her everyday life.

I drew attention to Megan's inconsistencies here, inconsistencies that she noticed herself and even pointed out. I also made a connection to our class readings by Lisa Delpit (1995), telling her that so many educators are concerned about the plights of "other people's children" and enjoy working with them; however, they prefer to put their own children in a different situation. Gently, I told her, "I think you're buying into that when you say this." Megan reflected on this thoughtfully for a few moments. Finally, she said that her family has a long, small-town history that is important for her to maintain. I told her that while this part of her point made sense, she had to also realize she was associating a homogenous White community with—and then she cut in and said "a safe place." It was clear that, with a little prompting, Megan could critically assess her own passive acceptance of racism.

Because it was so easy to talk to Megan about racism, I asked her whether our conversations had made her think any more about her own racism. Enthusiastically, she agreed, answering, "Yes it has because before I didn't really spend time thinking about it after [the African American culture] class. I was aware of it, but this has made me think about it a lot more. And I want to start working with it again." I asked her if she had noticed our conversations influencing her thoughts when she was tutoring or writing in her journal and, again, she readily agreed, saying,

> Yeah, definitely. I guess just more awareness. Just trying to think—think outside the box—think outside myself. How things could look, or just look back at the [journals] because right after my tutoring session I'll write down what happened and just kind of look back and think of what I said to the student and think, "Was that what I meant to say? Is that what I meant to project?"

Like the other tutors for whom these conversations were successful interrogations of racism and Whiteness, Megan turned her analysis inward and began to critique her own role in perpetuating racism. Like the others, she seemed to feel empowered by this new sense of control. She wanted to keep working on it and keep moving toward an antiracist identity (Helms, 1990; Titone, 1998; Tatum, 1999). Because her journey had started before we met, she was already rather far along.

Becky

Like Rachel, Becky thought of herself as an actively antiracist individual when she volunteered to talk with me. She claimed that all of her friends were Latinas, and mentioned that she had dated African Americans in the past. She also emphasized that she actively confronted the racism of the White man she was presently dating whenever he said anything offensive. Many times when we talked about antiracist endeavors, Becky would get very excited; claiming to even "get goosebumps just thinking about it."

For this, our third interview, I met Becky just after my own tutoring session at Willow Elementary. That day at Willow, I had suddenly seen for myself what many of the SLA students had been writing about in their journals: the director of the tutoring program seemed to value the tutors more than she did the children. Moreover, I was getting the impression that the language-learning environment in the school was subtractive, rather than additive (Collier, 1995; Lambert, 1974; Trueba, 1988, 1998). That is, students were made to feel ashamed of their home languages, cultures, and families. The culture of this tutoring program supported the erasure of the students' home cultures and languages. Several SLA students had written astutely about this in their journals and this day the child I tutored, Martin, had expressed his own nervousness about speaking Spanish in the classroom. This was stunning to me because Willow Elementary had a well-respected bilingual language program.

After listening to my story, Becky became very excited and reciprocated with a story of her own. She said that she, too, had experienced racism recently. "We've been talking about racism and everything," she explained. "So I don't normally, consciously dwell on it, but it's *more* in my brain now because we've been discussing it." She then explained that, while riding a city bus, an African American woman she sat down next to openly voiced her dislike of White people and even moved away from Becky to sit next to another African American. Becky was very surprised by this and explained that "I don't really ever feel discriminated against, but I did feel it from her and I was just—she has all this pent-up anger and she's taking it out on everybody." I asked her if she could see where this anger might be coming from and she said,

Well I guess in 1965 some White people were mean to her [the woman had said this]. So maybe even one person hurt her—a White person—and so she's going to be angry at all White people. So, that's my impression because she didn't even know me and I don't think I did anything wrong.

Here, Becky was clearly painting herself as a victim of "reverse" racism. Rather than making her more aware of her role in racism, our conversations seemed to have contributed to her new embrace of victimization. She thought of racism as irrational hatred against anyone, rather than a system of advantage.

Because Becky was moving our conversation away from her own racism, I pulled her back to it by asking her if she had seen anything in her transcriptions that surprised her. Without hesitating, she responded that, "I wasn't really surprised about anything." I prodded her some more and she admitted that

> Well, I know that I have racist . . . ideas, so it didn't surprise me. I pretty much admitted it, so it wasn't such a shock to me when I read it because that's what I said. So, it was kind of straightforward. It wasn't like there [was some] hidden, deep racism in there I didn't know about before. And, I wasn't like "Augh" because I know. So, I wasn't really surprised.

Concerned that Becky was only admitting to what she considered innocuous forms of racism, and concerned that she had not seen all the racism I had seen in her transcriptions, I prompted her further, first by explaining that most other tutors I spoke with had had very strong reactions to their transcriptions. Dutifully, she thought a little more and then commented that she was surprised to learn that there were more White people than people of color on public assistance. We had talked about this in our second meeting. "But," she said, "other than that, I didn't really see anything shocking to me." She then paused a moment, laughed, and nervously asked me, "Did you?"

I took this invitation as an opportunity to share with Becky some of the comments that I had marked as racist. I scanned through her transcriptions, looking for her early comments about her worst teacher in elementary school. Describing her, she had said, "I had a Black teacher, not that that necessarily had anything to do with it." I told her that, with these words, she was indicating that this teacher's race negatively affected her teaching ability, despite her comments to the contrary. If she truly thought this teacher's race had nothing to do with her teaching ability, she would not have mentioned it. Becky listened, but immediately defended her comments by explaining,

> Well, I think because she was the only Black teacher in the school . . . And I don't think I'm stereotyping her because she is a Black person—but, she seemed to be really irritable, and not very open and friendly. And we were pretty much all White children; and, like I said, she was the only Black teacher in the school. And I don't know if she had any bitterness or something was bothering

her, but, no, I've seen other Black teachers who are better—open and fun and creative with their children and don't just have to sit at a desk and read all day and not interact with them. So that's why I said—what did I write exactly? "Had a Black teacher, not that that necessarily had anything to do with it." Yeah.

At this point in the semester, I had quite a bit of experience gently but firmly confronting racism, so I was ready to do this with Becky. I told her that just phrasing her comments in such a manner indicated that she was associating her teacher's race with problems. When I asked her if she saw this, she again shook her head and said,

> No. I really don't. No. I just wanted to say what her race was. But I don't think that it has . . . I just think she was a poor teacher. And maybe because she was Black in an all-White school she had issues with her peers or other things like that. But, I don't necessarily—I don't know. That's why I said I don't know if it has anything to do with it or not. Because, there are some White teachers that suck, that are just absolutely horrible.

I pressed on and said that if she did have a horrible White teacher, she probably would not associate her problems with her race. Becky grudgingly agreed, stating, "Probably not."

Because Becky was resistant to recognizing the racism in her own words, I pulled her attention to another passage from the transcriptions that I mentioned earlier in this book:

> Becky: *In public school I saw catfights between girls in the hallway, and boys would always try and touch you and kiss you.*
>
> Sherry: *Even in a middle-class or upper-middle-class school?*
>
> Becky: *Well, they bussed people in. So I would—see, they started to bus people in. . . . These Puerto Rican girls would go at in the hallway and there was a Black boy that liked me and he would try and touch me and kiss me. And I think that kids in public school—they don't all come from the same, the same values as others. You know there's a lot of peer pressure and aggression and in the private school I felt safer because they all came—pretty much came from the same background as I did.*

I told Becky that I saw her reference to people who were "bussed in" as a reference to people of color and that all the trouble she had mentioned in her school seemed to be caused by people of color, people she described as having deficient values. She admitted that the Puerto Rican girls did "shock" her, emphasizing that she could not remember whether they were actually "bussed in" or not. I told her that "I'm just going on what you said here," to again draw her attention to the power of her words. She laughed and said, "But it did scare me."

This was an excellent opportunity to open up a discussion about all the fear that permeated Becky's comments about people of color. She had used terms such as "afraid" and "scary" in our discussions of people of color more than any other tutor. I drew her attention to this fear, pointing out several examples. Rather than deny it, Becky sought to give more evidence for her perspective. She said that even her Latina friends were afraid to go to the east side of town. She surmised that this was simply a fear of the unknown, emphasizing that it had nothing to do with race. She then brought up the notion that, as a woman, she was especially vulnerable in unfamiliar settings. She talked at length about the African American and Latino men who had sexually harassed her over the years. As a woman who also has dealt with my share of sexual harassment, although primarily from White men, I felt it was important to acknowledge the fear and anger this kind of victimization generates. However, I also pointed out to Becky that her pervasive fear of people of color was another way that racism had influenced her life.

Because Becky was still denying her role in racism, I again looked to her transcriptions, pointing to her comment that people of color were not in her branch of the military because "If you had a higher intellect you'd be put into a field like administration, medical—I was put in medical." She immediately defended herself by saying, "I think I was misquoted." To this, I answered that I had double-checked this comment and was sure that was exactly what she had said. "No," she clarified, "I think I misspoke." She then went on to say that she would never believe that Whites were intellectually superior to people of color. I told her that, despite her intentions, those were still the beliefs that rose to the surface when she talked about people of color. I even shared with her that other tutors were having the same experience, so she would know that she was not alone. However, she persistently refused to name the racism influencing her beliefs, clarifying that

> I probably meant it was my education. How smart I became from my education. So that's what I probably meant. Not just—I would *never* think that a person of Hispanic or Black background didn't have the capability that I did or weren't as naturally intellectual as I am. I would never think that. That's ridiculous.

She then explained that in her journals she had written many times that her Latino tutee "had a lot of potential." Like the African American men she dated in the past and her Latina friends, she used this journal comment as evidence for her lack of racism. Trying hard to remove herself from her recorded words, Becky emphasized, "You are thinking that I think that they may not naturally have the same [intellect], but I don't. No. That would be so silly." By continuously emphasizing that she would never think less of people of color, Becky completely avoided an inward glance at her own racism.

As our conversation wound around, I finally asked Becky if she could imagine the ways in which her negative thoughts, like those I pointed out in her transcriptions, could affect the children she taught. Like several others, she rejected the notion that she could inadvertently hurt the children she tutored. Specifically, she said,

> You know, I try *not to*. I try to be very careful because I may—on the whole, I'm not as racist as a lot of people. I think that I have a lot more open-mindedness than—because I had Black friends and went to the prom with a Black guy. I wasn't afraid to do that, you know? I think I'm a lot more open-minded.

Unlike Rachel, Elizabeth, Michelle, and Ashley, Becky never swayed on this point. By emphasizing that she had dated people of color, she was also emphasizing that she did not have a fear of people of color, or any serious racism, despite the fear and the racism that colored her words. Becky and I went on to talk more about racial and cultural differences, the child she tutored, and her own background growing up in Connecticut. In our fifty-minute conversation, she never admitted her own racism on more than a superficial level, and she never took responsibility for it. Her perspective never shifted inward. Moreover, she never once recognized the skewed perspective her color-blind "eyeglasses" (Delgado, 1995b) had given her.

Amy

Amy's denial was different from Becky's. She did not describe herself as an outspoken antiracist. Rather, she admitted that she had never much thought about Whiteness or racism, so these concepts were somewhat difficult for her to discuss. She also admitted that in this, our third interview, she could still not define Whiteness in an articulate manner. When she examined her transcriptions, the only comments that made an impression on her were those that indicated she judged the children she tutored too quickly. In her words,

> I think I was too quick to say, "No I can't [relate to them]," just because of the two different backgrounds that we have. I think that you can—now, I think that you can relate to them through other things. So, just because your *backgrounds* are different, or you don't necessarily speak their first language, you can find other things to relate to them. I think I was too quick to judge them.

I asked Amy how she felt when she realized this, and she explained,

> It makes me feel almost *bad* that I jumped to all these conclu-
> sions before I knew anything about the situation or the situation
> that the children are in and who they are and . . . that just doesn't
> make me feel like a great person because of it.

She then drew a connection between the language skills of the children
she tutored and her own experiences in speech class as an elementary
student, explaining that she could remember that "It's so frustrating when
you can't pronounce something the way that it should be." She then talked
about the writing skill of one child and, again, thought she had judged
him too quickly. She said, "I should have been more open-minded and not
just looked at—'Oh he has bad handwriting and his sentences are a little
choppy so he's not going to [succeed].'"

In addition to quickly judging the children she tutored, Amy also regret-
ted quickly judging Mayan Elementary. As she said, "I felt kind of bad that
I was thinking, 'Oh this is such a bad place. Bad things are going to happen,' when, every time I've been there, I've never seen anything." A very
sensitive person, Amy realized that she had been relying on stereotypes
and "stock" stories (Delgado, 1995b, p. 66) to make sense of the east side
of town. Because she was being so reflective, I asked her what else she had
noticed in her transcriptions. She said that nothing else really surprised
her. Wanting her to take another look, I reminded her that, during our
last meeting, she had said that she thought she sounded, "like the biggest
racist." I asked her if anything in her transcriptions made her think more
about this comment. She answered that she got this impression mostly
from reflecting on our second interview. I asked her to pull out that set of
transcriptions and she told me that she had never received them from me.
Mortified, I raced to my computer, printed out the transcriptions, and left
Amy alone to review them for several minutes.

After she read this second set of transcriptions, she explained her feelings that

> Just because you have a racist thought in your mind, you are not
> necessarily a racist person. You have the potential to maybe act on
> the thoughts that cross your mind . . . I don't think that just because
> somebody, every once in a while, has those thoughts . . . that they
> should be considered a racist person.

Clearly, Amy still defined racism as active hatred, rather than passive
acceptance of the status quo (Tatum, 1999). She added that, "If you realize that [racist thoughts] are in there and you can do something about

it . . . then, I don't think you should really be considered a racist person because you're trying to improve the way that you are thinking." I countered this rationale by asking Amy if racism could still affect her teaching, even though she was trying to "work on it." She answered that, "I just think now I'm more conscious of it so it's not—or at least I'm going to try—[so it's] not something that I do."

Because of the manner in which she said this, I thought of this answer as a kind of easy solution that did not really get to the heart of the matter. Thus, I pressed Amy further. She responded by articulating the same thought in more detail. Specifically, she stated that

> Me, personally, I'm becoming *aware* of how the thoughts that I have could affect my teaching—that by the time I become a teacher, I will have just gotten to the point that I—*in my own life* and in the way I think—that it wouldn't be an issue anymore.

She went on to emphasize that she needed to become more "aware, so I don't become this extreme racist person." As she said this, I drew a line on a piece of paper, and labeled one end "extreme racism" and the other end "antiracism." I suggested that, rather than not becoming an extreme racist, she could move the opposite direction and try to become an active antiracist (Tatum, 1999). Amy listened to me patiently, but in our hour together, my words did not seem to make much of an impression on her. I had not given her enough time to digest her second interview, and I had not strongly counteracted the White talk that characterized my previous interview with both Amy and Michelle. While she did express sincere remorse for quick judgments and low expectations, our conversation never moved on to an admission of racism, or to Amy's sense of responsibility for it.

Conclusion

As the above discussions show, all of the women I spoke with were influenced by racism in ways that became obvious to them during these firm but respectful confrontations. Our trusting relationships, the guidance I offered, and, likely, the comfort of our shared Whiteness had helped them to peel away the stifling veneer of color-blindness and then articulate their honest thoughts about people of color and English-language learners, including the children they tutored. The deficit thinking, stereotypes, and low expectations they shared were revealing in and of themselves. However, the purpose of being more "honest" about one's racism without taking responsibility for it is dubious at best. As the interview with Amy and Michelle illustrates, Whites engaging in such honest discourse for the first time can easily fall into the trap of White talk as they put their efforts into congratulating one another for their honesty and rescuing one another from critical examination of their own racism.

Until I confronted them and asked them to be accountable for what they had said, the women I spoke with felt comfortable sharing their beliefs, but they did not automatically problematize these beliefs. Indeed, they did not seem to really *hear* their own words until I brought them to each speaker's attention. Until these gentle confrontations, each young woman had characterized herself as loving, tolerant, and supportive of "all children." Most had also characterized themselves as "open-minded" and "progressive" regarding racial matters. Despite the negative beliefs they shared about people of color and English-language learners, all of the tutors believed they would be able to successfully teach children who were different from themselves ethnically, culturally, racially, and linguistically. That is, they held these contradictory beliefs until they were confronted about them and asked to explain and take responsibility for them. These confrontations enabled tutors to finally recognize the racism in their own words. In addition to problematizing the beliefs they held about others, this recognition compelled them to problematize the idealistic images they had constructed of themselves, often for the first time.

CHAPTER 5

Changes of Heart:
How Tutors Came to
Recognize Their Racism

As illustrated in the previous chapter, tutors found the firm but respectful confrontations about racism, aided or unaided by transcriptions, disconcerting. Nevertheless, these confrontations seemed to have a very strong, positive impact on seven of the nine tutors. Over the course of our conversations, these seven tutors eventually turned a critical eye to their own positionalities as White women influenced by, and perpetuating, racism. Because these women planned to spend their careers teaching children, the adoption of this critical perspective was especially important (Adams, Bell & Griffin, 1997; Banks & Banks, 2003: Lawrence, 1998; McIntyre, 1997; Sleeter, 1993; Tatum, 1999; Wink, 2000). Although they did not want to work against the successes of their students, they realized they might do just that if they remained oblivious to their own positionality as White women and to their own racism. Becky and Amy were the only tutors who did not seem to be strongly moved by these discussions. In analyzing these dialogues about racism, it became clear to me that the young women for whom these conversations were successful were the ones who turned a critical lens on their own beliefs, deconstructed them, and then began to reconstruct them. This was no small feat considering that the truths we construct for ourselves are, in the words of Pajares (1992, citing Rokeach, 1968), "taken-for-granted beliefs about physical and social reality and self, and that to question them is to question one's own sanity. As such, they are deeply personal, rather than universal, and unaffected by persuasion" (p. 309). As many scholars in the area of teacher beliefs argue, changing deep-seated beliefs in the minds of adults is often next to impossible (Butt, Raymond & Townsend, 1990; Doyle, 1997; Lortie, 1975; Nespor, 1987; Pajares, 1992, 1993; Paine, 1989; Rokeach, 1968).

However, seven of the nine tutors I spoke with appeared to have strong changes of heart as a result of this intervention. As I analyzed the paths these women took to changes in both heart and beliefs, I found that they seemed to move through seven distinct steps that concluded with a sincere admission of racism and recognition of their role in perpetuating it. These seven steps are a combination of my efforts to lead tutors in dialogue that was critical of their racism and their efforts both to resist and recognize their racism. During my meetings with each young woman, I was not aware of these steps as such. Only through careful analysis of our conversations did they come to light.

Step 1: Opening the Floodgates
and Recognizing One's Own Racism in the Torrent

In order to enable tutors to talk honestly about racism, a trusting relationship had to be established and then maintained (Brown, 1994a, 1994b; Krashen & Terrell, 1983; Freire, 1970/2000; Henry, 1998; Magolda, 2000; Titone, 1998; Wink, 2000). By the time I began confronting tutors about their racism, I had gotten to know each of them for more than two months through our interviews and our twice-weekly class. By their own admissions, they felt "safe" discussing these controversial issues with me. At the start of our interviews about racism, I had encouraged each woman to talk honestly and freely about whatever was on her mind that day. Thus, our conversations started with their catharses. This process was an invitation to put one's beliefs on the table, strip them of "political correctness," and take a careful look at them. Because I told tutors we were going to talk about Whiteness, racism, and their beliefs about the children they tutored, they were anxious to talk about these issues. Indeed, most women seemed to "pour their hearts out" as they did so.

As they talked freely about their thoughts and their frustrations, those who were very sensitive began to hear the racism that tinted their words. That is, they began to realize that the truths they had constructed were not "immutable entities that exist[ed] beyond individual control or knowledge" (Pajares, 1992, p. 309) after all. Rather, as we talked, they started to see the socially constructed nature of their beliefs about their students. When they spoke freely, the beliefs that rose to the surface sounded different than they expected. To the surprise of many, their beliefs sounded racist. Because tutors genuinely did not want to be racist, some, like Elizabeth, paused in their commentary to rationalize what they were saying. These tutors emphasized that even though they *sounded* racist, they certainly *were not* racist. However, by denying their own racism even as they heard it or saw it in their words, their "evidence base [was] totally discredited" (Pajares, 1992, p. 317). That is, what they believed to be absolutely "immutable," the fact that they were good people and not racist, began to seem more debatable than absolute. The moment tutors recognized this, they sought to "correct" their images and, thus, reaffirm their goodness in light of this discrediting.

Step 2: Calling Attention to Contradictions

Even though some tutors readily heard or saw the racism in their own words, they did not want to believe it; thus they rationalized or made excuses, such as Elizabeth's comment that "[I] would be willing to put my personal opinions aside [if] I'm going to be teaching children [of color]"; Michelle's comment that "[I] can hold things back when I need to and, luckily, most people don't notice"; and Ashley's comment that "[I] really work hard not to put across anything . . . because it's not them; it's not their fault." Believing that "unless they [were] deliberately challenged" (Pajares, 1992, p. 316), the beliefs of tutors would not change, it was my responsibility to call attention to the excuses tutors were making and to "deliberately" challenge them.

This kind of challenging questioning is the very opposite of White talk (McIntyre, 1997). Rather than comforting tutors by encouraging their "stock" stories (Delgado, 1995b, p. 66) and engaging in unifying in-group discourse (Delgado, 1995b) such as White talk (McIntyre, 1997), I drew attention to the fallacies they were presenting. I had to do this again and again in each of our conversations about racism, always in a gentle, respectful but unwavering manner. Relentlessly drawing attention to racism was difficult for me. It was exhausting, especially since it was very important for me not to alienate tutors. After all, in addition to sharing their thoughts about racial matters with me outside of class, they were also students in my class. It would have been much easier to just let the conversations move on to less controversial subjects. However, this persistent challenging was absolutely crucial in disrupting the original, deficit-filled beliefs the women had held and in helping them move their perspective from an outward gaze on children to an inward gaze on the self.

Step 3: Sighting and Then Denying the Tip of the Iceberg

By drawing attention to their contradictions, I helped tutors catch a glimpse of their own racism and the subsequent shakiness of the "evidence base" (Pajares, 1992, p. 317) upon which they were relying to affirm their own lack of racism. At this point in each conversation, it seemed to me, for a moment, that each tutor had been able to link her own racism to the larger system of advantage and disadvantage in our society. That is, they seemed to recognize the hulking iceberg hidden beneath the visible tip. Elizabeth, for example, admitted that she was unfairly judging the child she tutored and then said, "I sit here and I listen to myself and it's freaking me out." Similarly, Claire admitted, "I think—I think I kind of sound defensive and I don't want to be racist, but, I am. I really think [I am]." In our joint interview, even Amy and Michelle had admitted that "[I] feel like we're being so racist." However, while these admissions were certainly breakthroughs, they were not the ends of our journey together. All women except for Becky, who denied her racism inexorably, and Ashley and Megan, who admitted their racism to themselves before we began our discussions, quickly followed this first admission of racism with strong denial.

This first admission of racism was so frightening and painful that nearly all the women next sought the comfort of White talk to alleviate their negative feelings. Amy and Michelle successfully used this kind of talk to unburden themselves of, and feel empowered by, their deficit thinking. As Michelle said later, "I felt like I was being more honest than racist." Elizabeth also strongly denied her racism after she first glimpsed it. When I asked if she was ready to admit her racism, she passionately responded, "No. Absolutely not." Rachel similarly commented that, "I don't think that I'm a terrible person . . . "I'm sure [racism] affects me. But, I don't think it *negatively* affects me." However, because I did not participate in White talk, no tutors after Amy and Michelle were able to engage in it. Because I did not encourage their avoidance techniques, our conversations remained focused on race and racism. Because the tutors were beginning to see that their nonracist beliefs were, in fact, racist and that their "immutable" good hearts could, in fact, harm children, their "representations of reality" were seriously challenged. They retreated into the safe place offered by denial in order to protect their beliefs. However, it was once again my duty to challenge them.

Step 4: Constructing and Challenging Easy Answers

Because I did not allow the tutors the luxury of White talk, most of them chose another means to deflect responsibility for the racism they glimpsed in themselves. They constructed easy answers that would mitigate any racism that might influence their teaching. Nearly always, the easy answer was a resolve to "be more aware." When they did this, I challenged them by calling attention to the fragility of this answer. Elizabeth was actually able to hear the problems with the easy answer she constructed even as she posited it. She realized her racism could influence her even if she was not "consciously" aware of it. Thus, she began to be critical of her own "immutable" beliefs about the world, and she was also able to catch a glimpse of the influences of society on her beliefs about the child she tutored. For other tutors, I tried to draw attention to the same weaknesses Elizabeth had recognized. This technique did not work for Becky or Amy, who never seemed to realize the drawbacks of the easy answers they posited. It is likely that they were not able to recognize the social influences on their beliefs.

Step 5: Drawing Attention to the Bigger Picture

Once tutors realized the uselessness of easy answers, I drew attention to the bigger picture; that is, I tried to make the connection between the racism that influenced them and the challenges many children of color, including English-language learners, face in American schools. For many of the women, this connection was a devastating blow as it brought more concrete attention to the fallacies of their own "nonracist" or "antiracist" identities. Through this connection, Elizabeth realized that "White teachers are culturally constructed to be racist"; Rachel realized that "My expectations were really low"; and Gen realized that "teachers," more than any other factor, influenced her decision to drop out of high school. These young women realized that, in many ways, their lives had been full of lies. The tangible, negative effects of a teacher's racism, even if it is unintentional and unacknowledged, stunned many tutors. Elizabeth's comments that "It's frightening because you don't want to inflict it on others, especially kids" summed up the feelings of many tutors at this point. Through this intervention, they realized that their own personal prejudices were not benign, but, rather, evidence of a larger social problem.

Step 6: Coming to Terms with Recognition and Responsibility

Finally seeing this connection led most tutors to recognize their own racism, to sincerely admit it, and to take responsibility for their role in perpetuating it. Through this intervention we peeled away layer after layer of "stock" stories (Delgado, 1995b), fictions about people of color (Davis, 1995), fictions about the inherent goodness of White teachers (McIntyre, 1997), and numerous excuses for maintaining the status quo (Tatum, 1999). As we did this, the tutors' beliefs about the children, themselves, and much of the world were revealed. The beliefs that now lay bare in front of us were ugly assortments of deficit thinking and racism. They were so ugly and so obvious that no one who got to this point could continue to deny them. Reaching this point, thus, made for a very powerful moment. Elizabeth was devastated and started sobbing. Gen was disgusted at herself, and emphasized, "I don't want to be racist. And—I don't want to [be a deficit thinker] either." Michelle and Rachel both felt terrible. Megan realized that she was not as far along in her rejection of racism as she had initially thought. Claire was impressed by how undeniable her racism was "in black and white." Ashley realized that with thoughts such as hers, she should not teach American children. The realization that, despite their best intentions, they could still harm children with their racism was a devastating blow for almost every tutor with whom I spoke.

Because Becky and Amy never admitted their own racism, they did not come to these discombobulating conclusions. They maintained outward perspectives on the deficits of children and their families rather than inward perspectives on their own weaknesses. Perhaps Becky would not reflect on her own contributions to racism because she already considered herself to be very strongly antiracist. Her friends and the man she was dating also thought of her as antiracist and agreed that many of her deficit thoughts were "normal" rather than racist. Her beliefs were very hard to challenge because they were strongly respected and encouraged by important people in her life. Becky also had a very strong personality and was very self-confident, even resilient, in light of many of the obstacles she had overcome in her education. A tendency toward self reflection and a desire to deconstruct long-held beliefs may have been qualities she long ago rejected because of the negative effects they could have had on her life. I imagine that with more time, more meetings, and more reflection on her own words, Becky might have eventually admitted her own racism and seen the effects it could have on children. However, it is possible that this kind of critical intervention just did not work for her.

The limitations of my conversation with Amy, on the other hand, seemed to be due, in great part, to my own foibles. Each tutor needed time to contemplate her interview transcriptions at her own pace. Indeed, other tutors took up to three weeks to reflect on them. Because I forgot to send Amy the transcriptions of our second meeting, and then asked her to read them at our third meeting, I disrupted her approach to reflecting on the information. Consequently, when I brought up the notion of her own racism, she simply rejected it, likely because she had not had time to deeply think about the effects of her own words. Meeting with nine different women and moving at their individual paces allowed me, in a sense, to lose track of Amy. I forgot about the White talk that had characterized our last conversation. Moreover, it is possible that I became so comfortable with my intervention technique that I forgot how many individual differences contribute to successful discussions about White racism. Because of her sensitive, reflective nature, I do feel that, had I been more organized, the intervention with Amy likely would have been more successful.

Step 7: Moving Past the Impotence of White Guilt

As tutors realized their own racism, and the possible consequences this racism could have on their teaching careers, many of them became distraught. They felt terrible. Elizabeth, for example, was devastated. After she wiped away her tears and explained her feelings, she fearfully asked me, "What do you—what do you think?" She was worried that I would think less of her. Scholars in the area of teacher beliefs point out that "People are often loath to engage in discussions that touch on what they feel are their most deeply held beliefs" (Pajares, 1992). This is true because no one wants her or his basic beliefs about the world to be challenged. Successfully challenged beliefs necessarily result in the construction of new perspectives on the world (Delgado, 1995b; Tatum, 1999). Constructing this new perspective necessitates the difficult, often distressing mapping of something previously uncharted.

Learning to view the world in a more critical, more race-sensitive manner is particularly challenging and frightening for those just embarking on this journey (Helms, 1990; Howard & Denning del Rosario, 2000). Few if any antiracist scholars would argue that White Americans can sincerely realize their own racism without feeling despair at the same time. Rodriguez (1998), for example, writes that coming to terms with racism necessarily provokes feelings of "trauma," "unsettlement," and "bafflement" (p. 34). Citing Baldwin (1963), Karp (1981), and Katz (1977), Helms (1990, p. 59) adds that coming to terms with the racism entangled with Whiteness provokes "feelings of guilt, depression, helplessness, and anxiety" that exacerbate the negativity associated with White identity. Helms terms this painful first stage of racial realization *disintegration*, signifying the collapse of a previous, uncritical way of looking at the world. As Elizabeth astutely noted, most middle-class White Americans are taught to think of themselves as open-minded, racially tolerant, and good. Racism is considered an abstract, horrible mind-set that ignorant, hate-filled people embrace, not a condition that invisibly affects all White Americans. Thus, seeing racism in the self necessarily draws a connection between the self and something that is very often perceived to be evil. It can be horrifying and immobilizing.

While many would argue that these frightening, unsettling feelings are necessary in coming to terms with racism and Whiteness, few would advocate for becoming permanently immobilized. In Helms's (1990) stages of White racial identity, disintegration is just the second stage—the first stage of racial consciousness. Because disintegration is such a painful stage, many individuals choose to "avoid further contact" with people of color or look for information that indicates "either racism is not the White person's fault or does not really exist" (p. 59). These strategies are clearly counterproductive to developing an antiracist White identity. Kincheloe and Steinberg (1998) add that the goal of critical self-reflection about race and Whiteness should not be "White guilt" (p. 14), "White nihilism" (p. 21), or simply dominant culture "angst" (p. 12) because these constructions are ineffectual and enervating. Rather, they argue that a reconstituted White identity should focus on "unlearning racism" and "encouraging insight into the nature of historical oppression and its contemporary manifestations" (Kincheloe & Steinberg, 1998, p. 19). Helms (1990) would likely agree. She suggests that there are four more stages of White racial-identity development that Whites must go through in order to develop a White identity that is truly antiracist. The disintegration stage is just the beginning.

Stages of White Racial Identity Development

With all this in mind, when Elizabeth crumbled at the end of our second conversation, I sought to help her move forward. When she asked me, "What do you—what do you think?" I answered that I thought she was going through the disintegration stage of White racial identity development as presented by Janet Helms (1990). Writing in the field of psychology, Helms presents a stage model of White racial identity development in her book, *Black and White Racial Identity: Theory, Research, and Practice*. This model is a theoretical tool helpful in understanding Whiteness and its relationship to racism. It is not "the truth," and it is not infallible; rather, it is a theoretical tool that can be helpful for those interested in better understanding Whiteness and racism. Helms's model is the most used and most respected White identity model in the social sciences (Carter & Goodwin, 1994; Howard & Denning del Rosario, 2000; McAllister & Irvine, 2000; Tatum, 1992, 1999). In it, she proposes six stages of White racial identity that can help White people better understand the complexities of their racial positionality.

The first stage, contact, is characterized by "naïve curiosity about or fear of people of color" (Howard & Denning del Rosario, 2000, p. 132). Most Whites begin their examinations of racial identity here. The second stage, disintegration, is characterized by "discomfort or guilt, shame, and sometimes anger when faced with recognition of one's own advantage based on race" (p. 132). As described above, the disintegration stage lives up to its name. Whites in this stage of identity development "begin to see how much their lives and the lives of people of color have been affected by racism in our society" (Tatum, 1999, p. 98). As Tatum (1999) notes, one's belief in the American ideal of meritocracy is greatly challenged and often shattered in this stage. The third stage, reintegration, is a stage of denial where "anger and fear" are redirected "towards people of color, who are seen as a source of discomfort" (p. 132). This stage comes about as a way of dealing with the guilt provoked in the disintegration stage. Firm comments such as "Black people/Hispanics are racist too" characterize this stage. Without perseverance and not a small amount of courage, it is very easy to remain in this stage indefinitely.

If one can break free of the reintegration stage, she or he can move on to the pseudo-independent stage, which Helms describes as "the first stage of redefining a positive White identity" (p. 60). In this stage, feelings of White superiority are abandoned, but the residual White identity is negative. Individuals in this stage may try to "help" people of color "help themselves," as they do not yet see the responsibilities of Whites in the battle against racism. Moreover, those in the pseudo-independent stage may negatively characterize Whiteness and feel uncomfortable in their own skin. Only when the individual begins "the quest for a better definition of Whiteness" does she or he move out of this stage and "into the immersion/emersion stage" (p. 62). This fifth stage is characterized by an acceptance of Whiteness and a search to "replace White and Black myth and stereotypes with accurate information about what it means and has meant to be White in the United States as well as in the world in general" (p. 62).[1] Individuals in this stage are explorers with lots of questions. The sixth and final stage proposed by Helms is autonomy, which is characterized by a positive White identity coupled with active antiracist attitudes and actions. Those who make it to autonomy can spend the rest of their lives working to better understand themselves and to fight against racism. While autonomy is the goal, those who reach this stage do not have all the answers and do not suddenly lead un-racist lives. Because racism permeates our society, to be completely un-racist is impossible (Scheurich, 1993). Rather, those in the autonomous stage realize the pervasiveness of racism, the contribution of Whites to racial inequality, and the power they have to actively work against it.

Becoming an autonomous, actively antiracist individual is not an easy transformation, nor is it clearly defined (Thompson, 2003). One must constantly self-reflect on her or his beliefs, actions, and positioning as a someone who remains advantaged by "the system" of racial inequality despite her or his antiracist actions. Anyone looking for easy ways to "unlearn" racism and become an un-racist person will be disappointed. Autonomy and antiracism must be thought of as lifelong experiences. The challenge to overcome racism never ends, although the strength one finds in understanding her or his White positionality makes the struggle less difficult than it initially appears.

During my interview with Elizabeth, I happened to have Helms's (1990) book at hand, so I passed it to her and briefly discussed the stages with her. I told her that it was often a comfort to me to find my own emotional traumas discussed in the detached, reserved voice of academics. Helms's discussion of White racial identity is systematic and accessible. I thought it would help Elizabeth see that, of course, she was not alone in her feelings. I also thought it might help her to continue examining her racial development because it would help her recognize what stage might come next. Because this seemed to be such a good idea for Elizabeth, I decided to give Helms's (1990) chapter four, titled "A Model of White Racial Identity Development," to all the women I spoke with after our discussions about racism. In this chapter, Helms includes a self-assessment readers can use to gauge their own placement on her scale. It is not a scientific measurement tool but rather another tool for self-exploration. I suggested that all women read the chapter, complete the self-assessment, and then bring it to our subsequent interview for more discussion.

Responses to Helms's Chapter

Just as the transcriptions served as a strong tool to reinforce what Elizabeth, Ashley, and Gen had discovered about themselves in our interviews, the Helms (1990) chapter on White racial identity development made a very strong impression on most of the tutors. Many of them were surprised and relieved to read about what they were going through in print. Michelle, for one, breathlessly exclaimed,

> This is an eye-opening experience! I never—I guess I just don't think about racial issues so much. And when I was reading this part, it talked about "Ask a White person what he or she is racially and you may get the answer Italian, English, Catholic or Jewish" [Helms, 1990, p. 50, citing Katz & Ivey, 1977, p. 486]. And how it says White people don't see themselves as White and I *totally* agree with that! If you asked me what my race—when you asked that in class, I thought of White because I'd already read this article. But, I don't even know if I would have said White without reading this article.

Later in our conversation, when we talked about passive racism Michelle interrupted me, asking, "You mean more like what I have probably?" I was delighted that Michelle named her racism in this manner, similar to a disease she could treat. She told me that she realized, "I try to be as nice and heartwarming as possible to other—other types of people, but I feel like maybe I don't think about it enough and I don't question myself enough." These words clearly indicate Michelle's new critical perspective.

After completing the self-assessment, Michelle assessed herself as falling primarily in the contact stage, with her attitudes progressing toward the more advanced stages, while her behaviors lagged behind. She told me, "I can't help but that I got a bad score," explaining that she lived and grew up in all-White areas and that all of her friends were White. By a "bad score," Michelle meant that she scored primarily in the early stages of White racial identity. I assured her that she could not receive a "bad score," and explained that this was just a tool to help her better understand herself. After our talk, she explained, "Now I can see that I am more in the beginning stage." It seemed that Michelle had developed a language with which to talk about her own racism.

Claire was similarly moved by the Helms (1990) chapter. In showing me her chart, she laughed lightly and said in a resigned manner, "I thought I was so racist after I did this." I asked her to explain what she meant, and she said, "I guess because it was so high on some things and, honestly, I don't relate to anything to try to help change the world with racism. I really don't. I just kind of tend to my own business." In her self-assessment, like Michelle's, her attitudes were charted as more advanced than her behaviors. Although her behaviors scored highly in the contact and reintegration stages, she felt that the reintegration stage described her feelings best. I agreed with this assessment and told her that the defensiveness she had admitted to earlier was an indicator of this stage. As it had done with Michelle, this chapter helped Claire to better articulate her thoughts about racism. At this point in our semester together, it was very easy for her to talk about the subject.

Rachel also seemed to be strongly affected by the Helms (1990) chapter. She thought she could pinpoint herself in the disintegration stage and explicitly pointed out this descriptive sentence:

> It is probably during this stage, for instance, that the person first comes to realize that in spite of mouthings to the contrary, Blacks and Whites are not considered equals and negative social consequences can besiege the White person who does not respect the inequalities. (Helms, 1990, p. 58)

Rachel explained that

> I recognize that not everybody's really equal in our society. . . . I'm quick to say that, "Everybody should be treated equally"; but—I know—I feel like *I* should be treated equally, you know, being Jewish and whatever. But I know that if it was something that somebody could see, that I wouldn't be.

I understood Rachel's comments as indicating an important change of heart. In all our previous meetings, she had talked a great deal about the importance of "treating everybody the same," and the ideal of being "color-blind." It was clear that she had been thinking a lot about our last interview, as well as her transcriptions, and Helms (1990) chapter. She also told me that she was taking an African American literature class that likewise contributed to her change of heart. Like the others, Rachel's attitudes outscored her behaviors in Helms's self-assessment tool. Also like the other tutors, she made a strong showing in the contact stage. This assessment helped her realize that, despite her intentions, her actions lagged behind her more "progressive" attitudes.

Most, but not all, of the tutors found themselves primarily in the contact stage. Megan's score placed her more solidly in the latter three stages of White racial identity: pseudo-independence, immersion/emersion, and autonomy. Elizabeth also showed behaviors and attitudes more consistent with immersion/emersion than contact. This was surprising considering that I had expected her to fall more strongly in the disintegration stage. However, it was certainly true that talking about race and racism had made an exceedingly strong impact on Elizabeth. It is possible that she moved across the stages quickly. It is also possible that the Helms model is not necessarily linear or that the model does not accurately represent Elizabeth's unique experience. Amy's scores were more or less even across the stages. Although her attitudes showed few contact characteristics, her behaviors were strongly situated in that stage. Becky's scores were a similar mismatch of contact behaviors and more advanced attitudes. Gen was the only tutor whose attitudes and behaviors made the strongest showing in the autonomy stage. Indeed, her life was very multicultural, although she did not seem to be consciously aware of it. I must again caution, as Helms did, that this self-assessment is not part of a larger "validated scale," and it is not a scientific tool; rather, it is a "workshop activity" meant to help those interested in their racial development roughly assess themselves.[2] While Becky was very critical of this self-assessment and disliked its 1–4 (strongly disagree–strongly agree) scaled format, all the other tutors enjoyed quizzing themselves with this activity. For them, it seemed to work as a tool that reinforced what we had already discussed. It also gave them more insight into all six stages of Helms's White racial identity model, and helped them envision their own journeys toward active antiracism. As a tool for further enhancing consciousness-raising, this activity seemed very useful for nearly all of the tutors.

Responses to Supplementary Materials

In the time that passed between our previous interviews and these interviews about the Helms chapter, SLA students had also read Peggy McIntosh's (1988/1997) article "White Privilege and Male Privilege: A Personal Account of Coming to See Correspondences through Work in Women's Studies" for our class. This very compelling article includes a list of 46 "special circumstances and conditions" that seem, to the author, to be merited by White skin color more than any other quality (i.e., economic position, gender, etc.). This article made a very strong impression on several SLA students. The most compelling condition that McIntosh listed, for many SLA students, was number 46: "I can choose blemish cover or bandages in 'flesh' color and have them more or less match my skin" (p. 294). A few students, including Ashley, told me that after reading this article, they rushed to a drugstore to see if this was really true. By doing this, Ashley learned that the make-up color she used was called "natural." She was amazed that her own White skin color was truly considered "normal" by the world around her. She told me that the White girlfriend she had dragged along to the drugstore thought she was "completely crazy."

Something else that made a strong impression on Ashley was another article we read in class, Jim Scheurich's (1998) "Highly Successful and Loving Public Elementary Schools Populated Mainly by Low-SES Children of Color: Core Beliefs and Cultural Characteristics." As the title indicates, in this article, Scheurich outlines the beliefs and cultural characteristics that distinguish some highly successful schools with large populations of English-language learners and children of color. A key characteristic of these schools is that they have very "loving" environments, where all teachers, administrators, and staff show love for the students and support for each child's success. In our third meeting, Ashley excitedly told me that "I want to be a teacher like Scheurich talks about—I know I have my biases, I know I'm not like that now— but, I want to be a teacher who believes all students can succeed." All these tools, from the transcriptions to the articles, affected tutors and reinforced the message that they had biases that could influence their teaching, despite their best intentions.

A Note of Caution

Although I present a seven-step intervention methodology here, I must caution that this is certainly not a cookie cutter-type "technique" that should be used for all antiracist endeavors with preservice teachers. Indeed, the women presented here were all volunteers who could have ended our conversations anytime they wished. Imposing this approach on a class where students do not have the choice to opt out might be problematic. In addition, as with any collection of individuals, the women I spoke with were unique and showed different propensities for critical self-reflection, denial, and the desire to change. Each woman also had a different background articulating and dealing with her own racism and the racism of others. Because of this, Ashley was quick to admit her racism with little denial, while Becky, in contrast, never admitted to racism and continuously denied it. Both Ashley and Megan had started their journeys toward antiracism before they met me. Ashley had done so simply by naming her own words as racist. Amy and Gen had never given any thought to Whiteness, and very little thought to racism, before we met. Rachel and Becky both considered themselves strongly antiracist before they were confronted with the racism in their own words. While confrontation deeply affected Rachel, it seemed to leave Becky untouched. Nevertheless, seven distinct steps did emerge as I analyzed our conversations. Most tutors passed through each of them. It is possible that a curriculum could be developed that would seek to move students through all seven of the stages. However, that curriculum would have to be very flexible, as well as individually tuned, in order to merit success. For a different group of people, it is possible that the steps presented here would be inadequate. Only future research can tell.

Themes That Arose in the Confrontation of Racism

Desire To Talk about Racism and Whiteness

In the analysis of this intervention, several clear themes arose. These themes were remarkably consistent across the tutors I interviewed and many SLA students. First, tutors *wanted* to talk about racism and White identity, subjects they had long considered taboo. As I have said many times throughout this book, racism is almost always discussed in either a very heated, passionate, or political manner, or through the masks of political correctness and color-blindness. Once trust was established and tutors felt comfortable opening up about their true feelings, they felt unburdened in many ways. As Elizabeth stated, "I hope I was some help. My ideas aren't very clear because I'm just—trying to—starting to be aware of everything.

But I'll be glad to talk about it anytime. I mean, I *like* talking about it." Similarly, in discussing the analysis of her own racism Megan enthusiastically said, "I want to start up working with it again." As we talked more, it became clear that she believed there were very few venues where she could seriously, and yet safely, explore her own racism. Like Elizabeth, she was very eager to talk about racism once she felt comfortable doing so.

Desire Not To Be Racist

The second theme that arose was that the tutors did not want to be racist. In the beginning of our explorations when they first glimpsed their racism, they were shocked and confused. Because they did not want to be racist, they quickly denied it. However, the more we talked, and the more we teased out the ways in which racism did affect their beliefs and actions, the more they felt even stronger about not wanting to be racist. Other SLA students shared similar insights in their journals, as the following two examples illustrate:

> Wow. Lecture last Thursday left me stunned. It completely changed not only how I looked at the way I'm tutoring or my thoughts on this class, but also how I look at myself, my background and experience in education, and the overall future teacher that I am endeavoring to become. . . . Shamefully I have to admit that there were ideas, concepts, and prejudices (and there probably still are!) in me that I didn't even know existed until lecture. I have always thought of myself as an open-minded, well-traveled, non-prejudiced person, but I realize that I still have many views of myself as a more powerful person than those people of color. McIntosh [1988/1997] writes that this is "obliviousness about White advantage." Not that it ever came out as racial remarks or even would be something that I would verbalize (in fact this is even hard to write!), but it is much more masked. My expectations for minority students and false concepts of Mexican migrants especially were degrading. Why did I assume that [this child's] parents never read to her? Why was I surprised when I found out that they read to her often in Spanish AND English? Because of hidden prejudice. . . . I can't say that this information had dramatic results in my time with [the child I tutored]. We still chatted, we still read, and nothing outwards seemed to be very different. But I know that I have changed. Inside I saw her much differently today. Perhaps the results will come later.

***

> Today I noticed that Ms. Brown and I were the only White people in the [tutoring] classroom. After reading the McIntosh [1988/1997] article, I made much more aware of my Whiteness. I certainly hope that I have not expressed any biases to my students. Though I cannot pinpoint an example of my prejudice or biases, I know that I'm not perfect and that they are there. I did want to add I'm very conscious now and try to be careful. As pointed out by the article, these biases are very subtle and unconscious many times.

Through journal entries such as these, as well as class discussions and tutor interviews, it became clear that our discussions and activities concerning White racism and the biases teachers bring with them into the classroom were greatly appreciated by SLA students. While many students were skeptical at first, once they realized they were influenced by racism, they wanted to do everything in their power to mitigate its results. Serious self-reflection was the first step they took.

Association of Goodness with Antiracism

This self-reflection led to the desire for action at least in part because tutors thought of racism as a quality only "bad," "terrible," "disgraceful," "horrible" people shared. Several expressed their beliefs that good people could not be racist. This is the third theme that arose in the intervention. Elizabeth, for example, stressed that "I *know* I'm not a bad person. I *know* I have a good heart. I think I have a better heart than a lot of people I see." Rachel's comments that she could not be racist because, "I don't think that I'm a terrible person," and Becky's comments that "I'm not as racist as a lot of people. . . . I think I'm a lot more open-minded" reveal similar thoughts. Becky was the only one who never lost faith in this argument. In coming to terms with one's own racism, a person necessarily has to make the connection that she or he can be a good person and still be racist. This new realization blows away the notion that racism is only hate-mongering and requires a necessary restructuring of beliefs (Delgado, 1995b; Helms, 1990; Tatum, 1999). Even the most loving teachers can still be racist. Moreover, despite their altruistic hearts and their efforts to "hide" their racism, it is still possible for their racism to hurt the children they teach.

Realization of the Superficiality of Most Discussions of Racism

Once tutors realized the extent to which racism had influenced their own lives, they were stunned. In particular, they were shocked that they had never before heard racism discussed in this personal manner, with focus on Whiteness and responsibility. This became the fourth theme of the intervention. Most often, racism is discussed as an outside, abstract force that has little to do with Whites personally. In most of the courses they had taken that addressed children of color or English-language learners, preservice teachers had been encouraged to look at the deficits and differences these children brought with them into the classroom. Almost never had they been directed to look at their own deficits, biases, and racism. As Elizabeth said, "It's a big deal, but I don't think it's made a big deal because I have *never* even thought about it like this." The more she thought about it, the more it became clear to her that White people hold racism at an arm's length. As she said, White people talk about racism, "but you don't really think about that you have the views inside you whether you put them there or not." Several times in our conversations, Elizabeth commented that most people "just don't get it." That is, they never take more than a superficial glance at the racism that is "out there," nor the racism that resides inside each individual White person. Michelle's comment that "We are hiding so much from the world today" relays the same message.

Development of a Language of Race and Racism

The fifth theme that emerged was that, through all our conversations and confrontations, tutors began to develop a language with which to talk about racism. Color-evasion had characterized the language of all tutors at our first meeting, but continued attention to racism and Whiteness forced a more specific language of race and racism to emerge. Michelle, for example, began to talk about passive racism as something "like what I have probably," much like a disease she could treat. Similarly, Ashley was able to ask if her own prejudices showed up in her journal, and Claire was able to explicitly admit that, "I am definitely, definitely racist." Being able to name one's own racism was no small feat considering that earlier in the semester, every young woman except for Megan had felt that she "had no prejudices."

The development of this new language of race and racism is a significant accomplishment for several reasons. First, this new language enables racism to be discussed in a more neutral, less emotional, less politically charged, and less threatening manner that ultimately made our conversations very productive. Those tutors who admitted their racism and learned to talk about their Whiteness no longer needed to keep these two entities at arm's length. By examining the racism that existed in their own persons, they were able to examine the effects racism and Whiteness had on their attitudes, beliefs, and perceptions about the children they tutored. Becky, in contrast, persistently described racism as "ridiculous" and "silly," something she could "never" feel. This characterization made it even harder for her to admit her own racism. Because she never made this admission, she had no reason to reflect on her own racism and the consequences it could have on her teaching. Becky also maintained her original belief that children are children, so, in her mind, there would be no reason to alter her teaching beliefs or practices to account for cultural, ethnic, racial, and/or language differences. Tutors who admitted their racism and their Whiteness, on the other hand, became capable of doing something about it.

Desire to Do Something about Racism and the Invisible Privileges of Whiteness

Doing something about racism became the sixth theme that emerged during the intervention. Once tutors admitted their racism, they were anxious to counteract it by any means possible. Elizabeth, for example, called me a few weeks after we had stopped meeting for interviews and told me that she had gone to a bookstore to buy a book for Martin. She was looking for a book he could relate to in some fashion and found that nearly all the books available on his fourth grade reading level were geared toward middle-class White-American children. All the characters were White, and the stories were told through a White middle-class gaze. After looking through several different bookstores, she finally found a book with Latina/o characters and bought it immediately. However, when she got home, she read the book and realized that the family in the story was somewhat negatively stereotyped, with too many family members and not enough beds. Elizabeth called me because she was unsure whether she should actually give this book to Martin or not. She did not want to give him a White-centered book, but she did not want to put down his own culture by giving him a book she thought might be full of stereotypes either. Together we decided that she would give Martin this book, but that they would read it together and deconstruct the stereotypes it portrayed. She was anxious to learn what Martin thought about the story and the characters.

Ashley was taken aback by a similar discovery. Because she tutored in a library, she had a lot of time to read through a variety of children's books. In our last interview, she expressed amazement that many of the Spanish-English bilingual books she had read were geared toward White middle-class American children. They were simply White-American stories with White-American characters that were translated into Spanish. She lamented that most of the children she tutored would not be able to relate to the characters or storylines presented in the books. Together, we came up with the idea of asking the children to retell or rewrite the stories from their own cultural perspective, changing the characters and the storylines as needed or wanted. We took this idea even further by discussing the merits of asking children to write their own little books that centered on their culture and their language. Together, the children and the teacher/tutor could translate the story into English. Considering that Ashley started this study as someone who was "sick of" Latina/o children, this was a remarkable change of heart.

Once again, the tutors I interviewed were not the only SLA students making these kinds of insights. In her journal, another student shared her own epiphanies and how they had affected her tutoring. She wrote:

> In class the other day we discussed the need for teachers to "share power." I couldn't believe what a narrow outlook I have had on this whole tutoring experience. I had no thought before of what I was learning from [the child], but more how I was her role model and that she was under my "authority." Again in this class I was humbled and changed the way I looked at this tutoring experience. On my way to tutor I spent time thinking about class and what I wanted to learn from [the child] today. Instead of explaining and teaching all English words, I spent time [having] her teach me Spanish. It was so refreshing. She enjoyed it and so did I (she laughed quite heartily at my accent). I can't believe how just changing the way I look at myself as a teacher could make such a difference.

Just a few days after these comments, the same student wrote, "I have such a long way to go and I know that I'm only scratching the surface. But at least I'm that far, which is a lot farther than I was in September." Like Claire, she vowed to "work on it."

Over the course of the semester, it became clear that most of the tutors I interviewed and many SLA students wanted to learn more about their Whiteness, their racism, and the ways these two entities are perpetuated in American society. Admitting their racism was an extremely difficult, heartrending process for the young women who shared their thoughts with me. However, once they made this admission, they became deeply self-reflective and self-critical. They were amazed that no one had ever talked to them about their own roles in racism before. Once they saw the connection between their own thoughts and actions, and racism at the societal level, they adamantly wanted to do something about it. Moreover, they were *grateful* that, through our dialogues, their Whiteness and their racism had been revealed.

Although I was surprised by this gratitude, perhaps I should not have been. After all, preservice teachers are generally a kindhearted, passionate group of preprofessionals who are strongly devoted to children. If being a good teacher for children requires serious self-reflection about racism and actions to work against it, it should not be surprising that most of the tutors I got to know were enthusiastically willing to take on these challenges. At the end of the intervention, I became convinced that by keeping the notion of a personal responsibility for racism from preservice teachers, teacher educators are keeping from them valuable information the students, in reality, crave. This omission in teacher preparation is akin to refusing to tell someone they have a contagious disease despite the fact that, once the disease is recognized, it can be treated.[3] Tutors who admitted their racism and the privileges of their Whiteness and then took action against these effects in small but significant ways were just beginning the treatment. Already, it was making a difference.

CHAPTER **6**

Becoming Empowered by Recognizing Racism

While the notion of empowerment through education is usually discussed in relation to those who are traditionally marginalized in society, groups of individuals whom Freire (1970/2000) terms "the oppressed," I believe that many tutors—individuals who, as members of the dominant, White group, are traditionally considered "the oppressors"—became empowered through the admission of their own Whiteness and racism. By empowered, I mean that through our dialogues, many tutors learned "to critically appropriate knowledge existing outside their immediate experience in order to broaden their understanding of themselves, the world, and the possibilities for transforming the taken for granted assumptions about the way we live" (McLaren, 1989, p. 186). As they did this, they developed "belief in [their own] capability and competence" (Ashcroft, 1987, p. 145). As the stories in the previous chapter illustrate, most tutors ultimately found discussion of racism and Whiteness – even their own racism and Whiteness – to be illuminating and rewarding.

In addition to developing this new lens of vision, several tutors also began to change their behaviors to actively work against their own racism and to challenge the racism and White privilege that is perpetuated through maintenance of the status quo. Through these actions, which emerged from our dialogues and their deep self-reflections, these young women began to transform their worlds. In Freire's (1970/2000) words, they developed "conscientizaçâo"; that is, they began a "process of developing consciousness . . . that is understood to have the power to transform reality" (Taylor, 1993, p. 52). Through conscientizaçâo, tutors uncovered the "social reality" (p. 61) that they were privileged by their skin color, language, and culture, while the children they tutored were marginalized by theirs. Moreover, they discovered that the privileges, obliviousness, and myriad other norms of White in-group membership directly affected their own relationships with the children they tutored, to the children's disadvantage. This was a shocking, painful realization for those who came to it. However, once they admitted this social inequality, which affected and benefited each one of them, they sincerely wanted to change it.

By reflecting on their worlds and acting on them, most tutors began the process of praxis (Freire, 1970/2000). As Taylor (1993) explains, "praxis can be defined as the action and reflection of people upon their world in order to transform it. . . . What is actually required, according to Freire, is *active reflection* and *reflective action*" (p. 56). By the end of our time together, most of the tutors I interviewed and some SLA students had begun the process of praxis by, at the very least, changing their behaviors with the children they tutored. Claire, Michelle, Gen, and Rachel became very critical of their own positionality and sought to change their individual behaviors. Megan became more deeply aware of the biases entangled within her Whiteness and began to ponder what kinds of actions to take. Elizabeth and Ashley actively started to work against the status quo by criticizing curriculum materials and learning more about the perspectives their tutees brought to each lesson. While Becky consistently resisted any notion of her own racism and its possible effects, by our final interview, Amy at least had realized that thinking antiracist thoughts was not enough to counteract the system of advantage. With the understanding that praxis is the cycle of reflecting on the world, acting to change the world, and then reflecting on the world once again (Freire, 1970/2000), it was clear that most tutors began this process by the end of our time together.

Something I need to clarify is that I am not presenting the White, female, preservice teachers from varying economic backgrounds presented in this study as "the oppressed." In fact, I am making a statement to the contrary. Though tutors can be thought of as oppressed due to their gender and, for some, their economic status, throughout this book, I have emphasized the perspective that these women are members of the oppressing White dominant group. That is, in this kind of Marxist/Freirian language, they are "the oppressors." Nevertheless, these women, and I daresay all White people in America, are *oppressed by* racism, even as it benefits them/ us. By stating this, I do not mean to suggest that White people are the *victims* of racism. Nor do I mean to dismiss or diminish the real, exhausting, and oftentimes overwhelming, effects of racism on the lives of people of color in this country. What I do wish to argue is that racism has damaging effects on everyone who lives in a racist society such as ours (Feagin & Vera, 1995; Helms, 1990; Tatum, 1999). Through our discussions, tutors indicated that they were *damaged* by racism in ways ranging from their deep-seated fears of people of color, to their deficit thoughts about their own classmates and the children they tutored, to their desires to live and work geographically separated from people of color, to the guilt these desires engendered within their own hearts.

The Lies We Tell Ourselves

One of the most striking findings of this investigation is that racism damaged tutors by fooling them into thinking they were not racist. These White, female, preservice teachers believed they were exceedingly "open-minded" and racially tolerant when, in fact, they were not. In many ways, their constructions of self were perforated with lies. The way racism is commonly understood in this country, as the hate-filled idiocy of extreme groups, contributes to the lies White people, such as the tutors presented here, tell themselves/ourselves. In analyzing the comments of tutors, it became apparent that the racism affecting them was not that different from the racism affecting hate groups and active racists. Fear, deficit thinking, racial separation, and racial superiority characterize the racial philosophies of the Ku Klux Klan just as much as it did the philosophies of the tutors. The only real differences between the racial philosophies of tutors and hate groups were that, in normal life, tutors rarely voiced their thoughts about race, while hate groups angrily shout them. Moreover, tutors always emphasized that their thoughts were not based on hate, while hate groups and active racists usually do not deny the hatred involved in their message. Although the ways in which the tutors and hate groups or active racists articulate their philosophies are different, the philosophies themselves are remarkably similar. I suggest that if passively racist White people realized that the connections between their own racial philosophies and those of actively racist "racists" were so close, passively racist White people would almost certainly want to reassess their racial philosophies. That is, they would want to deconstruct the lies they (and society) have been telling themselves.

Deconstructing the Construct of Racism

This first lie we Whites tell ourselves is that we are not racist. As I have emphasized throughout this book, White people tend to keep racism at arm's length. We easily see it in the words and actions of others; yet we make excuses when we see it in ourselves. Moreover, labeling our own negative thoughts about people of color small "prejudices" rather than racism once again draws attention away from our problem and stymies efforts to treat our condition. Naming the racism that affects all White people in the United States is an essential step in taking responsibility for it. Only when we take responsibility for racism on a personal level will we be able to see a connection between our own actions and the larger effects of racism in society. Indeed, seeing the connections between themselves and the "bigger picture" made a very strong impression on most of the tutors presented here.

Part of taking responsibility for racism is recognizing the racism inherent in the role model and savior personas generated for and by teachers who work with children of color and English-language learners. Colleges of education, tutoring programs, schools, teachers, administrators, and volunteers all contribute to the construction of the teacher as savior. Very often, the only information preservice teachers have about children of color and English-language learners is that they are in dire need of being rescued from their family, their culture, their economic class, and their language. Teacher education courses contribute to these role model and savior constructions first by emphasizing the deficits of children of color and English-language learners and, second, by omitting any discussion—or any challenging discussion—of the biases that teachers bring with them to the classes and the children they teach.

Deconstructing the notions of role model and savior had a strong effect on several tutors. Michelle, who began tutoring with a strong need to feel appreciated and respected as a role model, had a clear change of heart during the semester. In one of her later journal entries she wrote of the children,

> They are not only role models to me because they are so successful at learning a second language, but they're also role models because they work so hard, and do their best 100% of the time. They also have to use such a large bit of patience at all times. I truly do not know if I could learn as they do all day at school. It makes me so proud of them!!!

Michelle's last several journal entries were full of strong connections to our class readings, as well as a great deal of self-reflection. In addition to turning a critical eye to her own biases, she became very critical of the tutoring program where she volunteered. Throughout this change of heart, Michelle's enthusiasm for teaching never waned. In fact, as she got to know the children better, and as she shared more power and authority with them, her enthusiasm seemed to grow. Through her journals and our conversations, it became apparent that she had developed a great deal of respect for the kids. Michelle could not have generated so much sincere respect for Cristobal and Valerie had she not deconstructed the racism, the privilege, and the power inherent in her own positionality and the ways these entities influenced her thoughts about the children.

Deconstructing the Neutrality of Whiteness

A second lie that must be deconstructed is the fabrication that Whiteness has no boundaries, no kind of in-group membership, or any historical significance. That is, Whiteness must be situated within time and space so that White people, such as the tutors presented here, have a better understanding of the ways in which their/our "group" contributes to racism, inequality, society as we know it, and the education of English-language learning children of color. Situating Whiteness helps "displace" Whiteness "from its unspoken (perhaps unspeakable?) status" in American society (Frankenberg, 1997, p. 3). "Displacing" Whiteness from the neutral position it occupies, and then "reemplacing it" (p. 3) as a characteristic of an American ethnic group with historical ties to imperialism and racism, is an important effort to pull Whiteness free of the invisibility that envelopes it.

However, coming to terms with Whiteness must not be synonymous only with coming to terms with White guilt. Just as children of color become empowered through the development of a strong, "confident cultural identity" (Cummins, 1986, p. 32), White people, such as the tutors presented here, can only become racially secure and aware if they/we also develop a strong sense of cultural identity. While some may scoff at this idea because Whites make up the dominant force in American society and American culture is, in many ways, White culture (Hale, 1998), this is still an important issue because *White people do not realize this is the case*. Many, if not most, White Americans believe, as Elizabeth did, that, "White people are just lost. And they don't know where they fit in." The autonomy stage of White racial identity that Helms (1990) delineates is a positive White identity that is coupled with active antiracist attitudes and actions. Historical understanding of the situatedness of one's own cultural and racial identity, as well as confidence in this culture and identity, are virtually prerequisites for successful antiracist endeavors

(Helms, 1990; Kincheloe & Steinberg, 1998). Understanding the histories of marginalized racial and ethnic groups in this country also lends to one's understanding of historical and contemporary Whiteness. Racial and cultural confidence and historical understanding will also likely diminish the fear that comes with "giving up" and "displacing" some of the privileges inherited with Whiteness and the backlash that accompanies this fear. This new understanding worked for Elizabeth. As she developed a stronger, more confident White identity, she began to feel less resentment toward people of color who she had initially felt were unfairly demanding too much attention and too many privileges. As she gained a stronger historical understanding of her own privilege, she also sought to do more to counteract the racism pervading the status quo. A positive White identity gave Elizabeth the strength to relinquish many of her earlier fears about losing power and sharing center stage with people of color. Elizabeth was exceptional because she was an especially thoughtful, self-reflective young woman. However, she was certainly not unique; many other tutors followed the same path she took to racial awareness and confidence.

Donning New Eyeglasses

By realizing their own positionality, the tutors began to recognize how their own perspectives had been shaped by society, their families, their teacher education program, and themselves. Through this realization, they were able to label their understanding of "reality" as a perspective shaped by myriad factors, including their membership in the dominant American group. Using Delgado's (1995b, p. 65) metaphor, they became aware of the "eyeglasses" that had been shaping their vision of themselves and the children they tutored. Once they became aware of these eyeglasses, they became very critical of them. Taylor (1993) suggests that, as the result of this kind of consciousness-raising,

> An individual experiences the redefining of their total boundary systems and a recreating of their own self-image. Inevitably, that must lead on to the validation or rejection of the individual's cultural base, which includes the common codes of accepted behaviour ... (p. 69)

Indeed, most tutors became critical of, and began to reject, some of the "normal" aspects of their education. Ashley and Elizabeth, for example, became critical of the White-dominated curriculum that made up their education. Elizabeth became very suspicious of multicultural-type classes that mentioned racism without challenging White positionality. In one of our later interviews, she explained that, "I just think it's sad that people can go through life and not think about . . . anything. I mean they are just *numb.*"

Nearly all of the tutors I interviewed and several SLA students made an effort to share what they had learned about racism and Whiteness with their friends and family. Rachel, Amy, and Michelle, being good friends, had the benefit of comparing and contrasting what each of them had learned with one another. Elizabeth decided to share her transcriptions with her boyfriend in an effort to open his eyes to the racism that influenced his words, as well as her own. She also wanted him to read the McIntosh (1988/1997) article on White privilege. In our last interview, she told me that she wished she could make him participate in a similar intervention so his ideas would necessarily be challenged. Similarly, Claire decided to share her transcriptions with her sister so her sister would recognize how racist her seemingly benign comments could sound to other people. Nearly all the tutors wanted to keep learning about and talking about racism and Whiteness. They were clearly developing a critical perspective on education and beginning to back their insights with action. Reimer (1971, p. 96) suggests that this kind of development is evidence of "true education."

The Need for Support

As our semester together wound to a close and many tutors expressed their enthusiasm for continuing discussions of racism and Whiteness, a caveat of this investigation emerged. It ended too soon, and tutors were left without scaffolding that would help them continue their explorations. All the tutors for whom the intervention was successful—Elizabeth, Gen, Rachel, Claire, Ashley, Michelle, and Megan—expressed a willingness to continue our conversations. They seemed to have developed some amount of dependence on the cathartic and yet self-critical dialogues we had engaged in for more than four months. These dialogues were challenging, dynamic, and exciting. They also enabled us to get to know each other intimately through the sharing of our beliefs, our thoughts, and our weaknesses. Moreover, through these dialogues, each tutor began to feel empowered to make great changes in her life. Ashley vowed to become a more loving teacher. Elizabeth decided that she needed to travel internationally with her boyfriend. As I mentioned earlier, she also put off her marriage plans until her boyfriend's feelings about other races and cultures changed. Many tutors began to notice the stereotypes and inequality perpetuated in standard curricula. These seven tutors vowed to work toward developing an antiracist White identity (Helms, 1990; Titone, 1998).

However, once our interviews finished at the end of the semester, the tutors were largely on their own in developing this change in identity. Helms (1990) cautions that Whites who seek to reject racism and become actively antiracist often have a lonely journey. She writes that those who eventually abandon the journey "receive much support in an exclusively White environment for the development of individual racism as well as the maintenance of cultural and institutional racism" (p. 59). She also writes that most Whites will abandon this journey if it is inconvenient for them. Thus, while seven of the nine tutors I got to know this semester expressed a very strong desire to become White allies (Titone, 1998) in the fight against racism, it is possible that this enthusiasm will wane without more support from other Whites and people of color. Although I encouraged each tutor to get in touch with me through e-mail and the telephone whenever they needed encouragement, this minimal amount of communication is not enough to ensure the success of their transformations. They need encouragement from all sides.

Freire (1970/2000) addresses this concern by advocating solidarity among those endeavoring to make changes. He uses the argument that "the oppressed" can rely on their numbers for strength, and emphasizes that leadership must come from within oppressed groups. Examining the oppression of "the oppressors" is different in many ways. The powerful in-group solidarity created by Whites is most often used to derail in-depth self-reflection about the role of Whites in racism and consequent antiracist action in order to maintain White power (Delgado, 1995b; Helms, 1990; McIntyre, 1997; Moon, 1999; Rodriguez, 1998). Whites seeking to become White allies in the fight against racism thus have to struggle against the dominance and the privileges of their/our own racial and cultural group. White talk (McIntyre, 1997) and the stories that maintain the superior position of Whites in our society (Delgado, 1995b) are tools Whites will use to continually divert attention away from antiracist efforts. Often, this is done with the intention of making the White person who struggles with her or his own racism feel better. The invisibility of Whiteness and the unnamed state of its privileges exacerbate group attempts to reach toward a more critical, antiracist stance. I believe that the intervention I present here found some measure of success because I met with each tutor individually. By doing this, I avoided in-group collusion in the maintenance of power. I also consistently challenged attempts to subvert the message that Whites have an individual responsibility for racism.

However, once the tutors became critical of their own privileges and their own racism, they did not have a solidarity with others who made similar insights to help them make a large-scale difference. Moreover, they became somewhat dependent on me to help them on their journey. For these tutors, I kept in touch for a while and did my best to offer encouragement for, and insights into, their paths to antiracism. From these tutors, I have learned a great deal about improving antiracist education, especially the importance of solidarity on the path to antiracism. I offer these insights with the hope that they help future teacher educators and teacher education students transform their thoughts into antiracist actions.

It is naïve to believe that the recommendations I offer here will be embraced and adopted by universities and teacher education programs; after all, these institutions are charged with reproducing the status quo. The racism that is a part of the status quo is generally ignored or passively defended by the dominant culture as evidence of rigor, intellectualism, fairness, and "normalcy" rather than racism. Recognizing that "racism is an integral, permanent, and indestructible component" (Bell, 1992, p. ix) of the status quo would certainly be a radical, subversive, change to the system. By maintaining the status quo, we maintain order, tradition, and "the way things are." But, look at the costs: myriad numbers of children of color and English-language learners spend their unhappy school careers in special education or other remedial classes. Oftentimes, their school experiences are short. In the region where I presently teach, Latina/o students have a 50 percent dropout rate (Brown, 2005). At the same time, White teachers and administrators locally and around the country believe they are doing all the right things to help these same children. The system is clearly not working. Changes need to be made on every level, from policy to teaching methodology. The system that currently exists needs to be subverted.

The recommendations that I offer below are small-scale specifics that might together foster more discussion of racism and White positionality among White teacher education students in their teacher preparation experience. However, the infrastructure that must be in place to support these changes in teacher education is necessarily large scale. I offer these suggestions as a challenge to teacher education programs that truly desire to improve the education of children of color and English-language learners by improving the education of teachers.

Recommendations

Model a Supportive Teacher Education Classroom Environment
That Encourages Critical Discussion

One of the most important things a teacher education instructor can do is model the kind of teaching and classroom environment she or he is encouraging her or his own students to adopt. I want my own students to create safe classrooms that encourage critical thinking about the issues present in this book and promote cooperation among students, so I model that kind of classroom. Something I've found very effective is modeling aspects of culturally relevant teaching as presented by Ladson-Billings (1994). In particular, I place a lot of emphasis on the class as family. To paraphrase Ladson-Billings, in such a classroom the teacher-student relationship is "humanely equitable" and extends "beyond the class-room and into the community"; the "teacher demonstrates a connectedness with all students"; the "teacher encourages a 'community of learners'"; and the "teacher encourages students to learn collaboratively. Students are expected to teach each other and be responsible for each other" (p. 55).

In a multicultural and social justice education class that I presently teach, we develop this family quality by meeting in my home to get to know one another, by learning one another's names, by working in groups, and by requiring that students lead part of each class discussion. Through-out our time together, I actively mentor students, requiring that present-ing students share their lessons with me before class so we can together ensure they are successful. Through these and many other activities, stu-dents learn that they can depend on me, that they must depend on one another to succeed, and that becoming a successful teacher is a learning process. As the semester progresses, it becomes clear that students gen-uinely care about one another. They make sure absent students receive assignments; they help one another articulate complex thoughts about our subject matter; they challenge classmates to think more critically; and they offer encouraging words to those willing to take risks.

In the beginning of the semester, before we know each other well and before students understand the critical nature of the course, I clearly and repeatedly articulate our focus on equity in the k-12 classroom. I encour-age students to talk about race and racism as I address color-blindness as a troublesome, passively racist discourse. Addressing these issues clearly and repeatedly lets students know that the "typical" responses to multicultural and social justice education (to be more aware, to "celebrate" diversity, to emphasize we are all the same and that children are children whether they are "Black, Brown, or purple with polka dots," etc.) are unacceptable in this class.

Students' first assignment is to read Beverly Daniel Tatum's (1999) book *Why Are All the Black Kids Sitting Together in the Cafeteria? and Other Conversations about Race*. Because students are initially skeptical of Tatum's definition of racism as a "system of advantage based on race" (p. 7), the definition I use throughout this book, and defensive of their own racial positioning (most students are White), I give them time to vent.

I pass out note cards and allow students to write whatever questions and comments they might have about the book anonymously. I then spend much of our class period answering their questions, giving examples of systematic racial inequality, and asking them to share more examples. We read this book over several class periods and then students are asked to write an autobiographical racial identity paper that highlights when and how they "discovered" their own racial/ethnic identity, whether it was years ago or as a result of our class. Students are nervous about this project at first, but they often find the assignment to be cathartic and enlightening. This self-reflective paper on race serves as an excellent beginning for the deep, critical discussions we will continue to have about racism and equity in schooling throughout the semester.

This entwined focus on critical multicultural/social justice education and class as family enables students to take risks and think "outside the box" regarding issues of diversity, equity, racism, etc. Because I initially articulate and rearticulate the critical focus of our class and introduce Tatum's book as a framework for the ways we will discuss race and racism, White talk is not an issue in this course after the first few class periods. The family-like support students give each other focuses instead on helping one another make connections between the readings and the real world and the individual and society. The camaraderie students develop in this class hopefully gives them a sense of solidarity that will help them maintain their dedication to issues of equity in education long after the semester is over. For more information on setting up antiracist, critical teacher education classrooms focused on multicultural and social justice education, see Derman-Sparks and Phillips' (1997) book *Teaching/Learning Anti-racism* and Adams, Bell, and Griffin's (1997) book *Teaching for Diversity and Social Justice: A Sourcebook*. The following recommendations are built on this initial recommendation of instilling a family-like quality in the teacher education classroom.

Integrate Studies in Whiteness into Teacher Education Curriculum

A second recommendation is that investigations into White identity, White privilege, and White racism become fundamental aspects of *all* teacher education courses. As U.S. children become more diverse and U.S. teachers become more homogenous, a multicultural/social justice lens with some emphasis on Whiteness should filter all our examinations of curriculum, students, and teachers. Critical multiculturalists such as Sleeter (1992b, 1994) also recommend that readings focused on Whiteness and racism become part of the multicultural canon and that a critical multicultural lens influence all aspects of teacher education. A class on multicultural issues is not enough to make a strong, lasting imprint on most teacher education students because it does not go far enough in challenging long-held beliefs (Lortie, 1975; Pajares, 1992, 1993). Indeed, the tutors who were most moved by our examinations of racism were immersed in multicultural-type classes that repeated the message that Whites are privileged and made connections between the individual and society as a whole. During this study, Elizabeth took three classes that focused on race and culture. Indeed, she said that all these classes at once were "a sign" that she needed to look at issues of race and culture more seriously. Rachel, Michelle, and Megan were also taking—or had just taken—classes in the multicultural aspects of education, African American literature, and African American culture.

Through this investigation, I learned that African American and other ethnic group-centered courses made a very strong impression on the tutors. Certainly, the African American literature course I took as part of my own masters program made a similarly strong impact on me. I had no idea so much great literature had been omitted from the traditional Western-European, White, male-dominated literature canon that I had come to know as an undergraduate English major. By adding a critical multicultural/social justice dimension to all teacher education classes, the message that the dominant White perspective is not the neutral, normal state of things would be reinforced daily. Through this kind of incessant attention to the markedness of Whiteness, few students would be able to avoid developing a critical stance regarding the status quo. Re-situating Whiteness in this manner would reconstruct the dominant group as "cultural *mestizaje*"; that is, a culturally and racially mixed group that influences and is influenced by all other groups making up, and continually recreating, the United States (Kincheloe & Steinberg, 1998; McLaren, 1998). Such a reframing of Whiteness would necessarily disrupt its neutrality.

Name White Racism in Teacher Education Classes

Teacher educators hesitant to make "a big deal" out of racism and Whiteness should be comforted by the fact that within a trusting, safe environment, the White preservice teachers I met with very much *wanted* to talk about the role of Whites in racism. Once we together named racism as part of ourselves and our worlds, tutors were very anxious to learn more about it, to reflect on their own contributions to racism in society, and to make changes in themselves to actively counteract racism. Many of them even sought to actively "change" their family and friends. Long after the SLA class finished and I stopped meeting with the tutors, several still e-mailed me for advice; some of them even sent me articles on education and racism. As an instructor of multicultural/social justice education courses in the present time, I continue to have these kinds of experiences with teacher education students. Our discussions of racism, Whiteness, and social inequities make strong impressions on many of them.

In reflecting on this investigation and the accomplishments of the tutors, I remember that the biggest barrier I faced in initially confronting racism was my own insecurity in doing so. I was afraid that I would cause emotional uproar and chaos. Moreover, I was afraid that, due to my own inexperience, I might make things worse; that is, I might contribute to the resentment and backlash of Whites, entities that are extremely counterproductive to multicultural education and efforts towards social justice. Indeed, many antiracist endeavors seem to have had this effect on participating teachers and teacher education students (see, for example, Berlak, 1999; Henze, Lucas & Scott, 1998; McIntyre, 1997; Sleeter, 1994). In finally getting up the nerve to conduct an antiracist investigation that included intervention, I sought to learn from endeavors that seemed unsuccessful. In doing this, I tried to build on strategies that seemed to have worked well and to avoid those that seemed to have contributed to backlash. Discussed below are two qualities that became the foundation of the project I share in this book and make a strong contribution to its success. Antiracist educators wanting to experiment with intervention regarding White racism in teacher education classes may benefit from modeling these aspects of the project.

Trusting Relationships The first quality critical to antiracist intervention is trust—initial trust and trust developed through contact (Freire, 1970/2000). This trust must be unwavering. Moreover, the trust crucial to opening up dialogues about race and racism must be interwoven with support. Whites learning to talk about these issues are learning a new language; as any new speakers of language inevitably do, new speakers of the language of race and racism make serious faux pas that easily offend. Teachers of this new language must remain supportive and guide their students to more stable ground. Teaching the language of race and racism is very similar to teaching English to nonnative speakers. As ESL teacher educator Brown (1994b, p. 23) states, teachers of language must "overtly display a supportive attitude to [their] students." They also must be patient and remember that learners are sophisticated, wholly functioning beings in their first language. Important also is Titone's (1998) advice that antiracist educators must know their own positionality well and must provide consistently strong leadership to those they are teaching. Talking with Amy and Michelle certainly highlighted the importance of this advice for me.

Students Are Learners Above all, it is important to remember that students are *learners*. Working with my own students in this investigation helped clarify our roles of teacher and student. As I discussed earlier, I did try to soften my "robes of authority" by sharing power with tutors through reciprocity and storytelling. I also learned much from them that influenced my own teaching style and the intervention methods I took. So, in that sense, I was a teacher-student and tutors were students-teachers (Freire, 1970/2000). However, despite all the sharing of power, tutors still saw me as a "teacher" whose role was to guide them through our explorations of racism. Indeed, as an instructor, that was my job. There was no way around it. Tutors seemed to truly appreciate this role distinction. Several times, when I pointed out their own racism, they commented that they were "still learning." When I emphasized to Michelle that I was not "attacking" her but drawing attention to something she needed to reflect on, she expressed these feelings, saying,

> It's not offending me! It's not offending me! I mean, because I know—in my mind, I'm thinking, "She is doing this for a study and that's why . . ." I guess, I mean, I don't like being called racist but I've learned to set things aside. Like "know when to hold them." You know, that song?

Our trusting, supportive interview environment, which was reinforced by a trusting, supportive classroom environment, and our defined roles as teacher and student helped Michelle absorb the attention we placed on her racism. As she said, she could handle this kind of intervention. Eventually, Michelle and many of her classmates expressed that they *appreciated* this kind of intervention. They wanted to learn more and they were willing to act on what they learned. It is thus our responsibility as teacher educators to broach the topic of White racism more often with our students in manners that are infused with trust, support, and leadership. Only then can we hope for positive results.

Require All Teacher Education Students To Take Classes in Second Language Acquisition

In addition to implementing a critical sociocultural lens and pointedly addressing racism and Whiteness, teacher education classes should give more attention to English-language learners in the mainstream classroom. At least 17 percent of school-age children in the United States are estimated to be speakers of languages other than English (NCES, 2003b), and 18 percent are estimated to be the children of immigrants (U.S. Census, 2000b). Latinas/os now account for the largest minority ethnic group in the United States, at 12.5 percent of the population (U.S. Department of Commerce, 2001). While all teachers had a 50 percent chance of teaching English-language learners 10 years ago, it can be assumed that teachers getting their credentials now will be more likely than not to teach non-native speakers of English. Rather than focusing only on the challenges English-language learners bring to the mainstream classroom, it is to every teacher's and every child's advantage that these children be thought of as great assets to every classroom (Collier, 1995; Gardner, 1985; Gonzalez et al., 1995). There is even some evidence to suggest that bilingualism boosts measurable intelligence (see Gardner, 1985). Indeed, through English-language learners, mainstream U.S. students and mainstream teachers can learn a great deal about different cultures, different languages, and different ways of looking at the world. These new perspectives must be thought of as *benefits* to U.S. teachers, schools, and children. Most classes that focus on the English-language learner take the opposite, deficit approach with dire results.

Because bilingual education programs have been eliminated or severely cut back throughout the United States, more and more English-language learners are being mainstreamed in regular classrooms (Krashen, 2000/2001). Therefore, most English-language learners spend the majority of their school careers with teachers who are not trained in language acquisition or the related area of second-language literacy development (Hudelson, 1994). Like the tutors I got to know, many mainstream teachers confuse verbal and written fluency with intellectual skill and assess their English-language learners as less intelligent than their native English-speaking students. Many times they wrongly assess these children as learning-disabled (Cummins, 1994). In 1983, it was reported that "Latino students in Texas were overrepresented in the 'learning disability' category by more than 300%" (Cummins, 1994, p. 39, citing Ortiz & Yates, 1983). Data taken from a 1998–1999 California study show that English-language learners were "seriously overrepresented" in special education by 27 percent (Artiles, Rueda, Salazar & Higareda, 2002, p. 119). This should be seen as a crime against humanity.

Better education for teachers is the key to better education for English-language learners. While not every teacher can become a bilingual teacher, every teacher can learn the fundamentals of English-language teaching and English-language learning. All teacher education students should be required to take a class in SLA that focuses on theories and methods. Moreover, methods that work for English-language learners should be a fundamental aspect of every subject matter class. In the extremely important field of education for English-language learners, good intentions are inadequate. Finally, special education teachers must be asked to guard against the over-referral of English-language learners to special education classes simply because of language skill. All teachers should realize that special education is often a "one-way ticket" (Cummins, 1994, p. 59). Ignoring the need to better train teachers who will likely work with English-language learners is tantamount to turning our backs on these children.

Improve Field Experiences

Part of improving teacher education to better meet the needs of English-language learners is improving the field experiences that put preservice teachers in contact with English-language learners, often for the first time. Many times these field experiences are also the first experiences White middle-class preservice teachers have with children of color. While these preservice teachers may claim, as Rachel did, to enter the field experience with no expectations, in reality, they often have constructed images of English-language learning children of color that are full of deficits (Valencia, 1997). Teacher education classes, visiting principals, the media, and daily life have contributed to these constructions. Indeed, as a rather extreme example, I can share that a student I once taught gave a presentation on Latina/o culture by showing a clip of a Cheech and Chong movie and explaining that Latinas/os smoked a lot of marijuana, talked incessantly about drugs, cursed a great deal, and had little ambition in life. The most shocking part of this presentation, to me, was that she seriously believed what she was presenting. I suggest that teacher educators need to assume that stereotypes and misinformation contribute to the background knowledge most White preservice teachers have about English-language learners and children of color. Therefore, it is necessary to address these misperceptions before preservice teachers are asked to tutor or observe children.

Because teaching is taught in an apprenticeship manner, people who want to become teachers spend dozens to hundreds of hours observing and tutoring children in schools even before they begin student teaching. While we teacher educators realize the value of "real" contact with "real" children, we oftentimes forget that our students are not professionals. During the semester I interviewed tutors, most teacher education classes at our university required a field component; however, few classes required a reflective, dialogic activity through which the field experience could be assessed by the instructor—like the journals SLA students kept of their tutoring experience.

In order to meet accreditation standards, many field experiences are required to be in schools with high populations of children of color and children from low socioeconomic backgrounds. Many teacher educators believe that experiences with low-income children of color help prepare teachers to better work with these populations and that these particular field experiences lend assistance to the children who need help the most. There are many truths to these beliefs; but, it is also true that teacher education students bring misperceptions, stereotypes, biases, and racism regarding children of color and English-language learners with them into these field experiences. This "baggage" that comes from living in a racist society is rarely addressed in teacher education programs. Because of these preconceptions, such field experiences often contribute to, rather than deconstruct, stereotypes, racism, and desires to teach in suburban, predominantly White schools. This approach to teacher education also contributes to the constructs of teachers as role models and saviors. Preservice teachers very often consider the time they spend in these field experiences to be charity work that is a necessary rite of passage for a teaching certificate. Once they have their certificate, most hope to start their careers in the suburbs. While I believe that tutoring English-language learners is an exceptional way to relate theory to real life, I also believe that a number of changes should be made to ensure that English-language learners benefit from these encounters at least as much as preservice teachers do. In the present state of things, English-language learners are often disadvantaged and exploited by the field service requirements of preservice teachers. The recommendations I suggest are outlined below.

Offer More Supervision

First, preservice teachers need more supervision in their tutoring experiences. It is unacceptable that simply because they are adults, they are considered experts who know what is best for children. As my conversations with the tutors and my observations of their tutoring sessions show, tutors made a lot of mistakes with, and have many misperceptions about, the children they tutored. Many times they shared these misperceptions with the children's teachers and sought to influence their education plans in erroneous ways. Their interventions usually worked to the *disadvantage* of the children rather than to their advantage. One way to change this situation would be to make classes such as SLA that require a field component, site-based. That is, these classes could meet at schools with large populations of English-language learners. Tutoring in a classroom or tutoring lab could be accomplished in the first part of each class meeting, with the following time devoted to analyzing the lessons and relating theory to practice. The instructor would be present in both the tutoring lab and the following class; thus, she or he would be privy to the various strengths and weaknesses of her or his students. This would also enable instructors to relate class material directly to the tutoring situation. Because so many schools are desperate for tutors, this option seems reasonable. Willing schools must also have classroom space available for the teacher education class to meet afterwards. The schools and the teacher education classes would also have to develop trusting, reciprocal relationships that would benefit both equally. Moreover, the value of this arrangement for the schools and the university classes would have to be acceptable to both parties. This arrangement would ensure that tutoring experiences benefit both the children and the preservice teachers.

Ensure Good Placements

Another critical factor in improving field experiences is the need to place preservice teachers in schools with exemplary learning environments. Teacher education students are influenced by their own school experiences and the teachers with whom they work, perhaps even more strongly than by the teacher educators who teach them (Lortie, 1975; Pajares, 1992, 1993). A teacher's or program's negative assessments of a student's language skill, culture, and home life readily rub off on apprentices. Teacher education students are oftentimes accepting and uncritical of the teachers and programs where they work. Thus, it is important that they be placed in environments that are supportive of all children. It takes time to find these schools, as "nationally recognized" programs often tout measurable test scores rather than atmosphere. For example, Willow Elementary, the school where Elizabeth and I tutored, was nationally recognized for student achievement, but, nevertheless, encouraged its Spanish-speaking children to be ashamed of their home language and culture. Moreover, children in the tutoring lab, nearly all of whom were children of color and English-language learners, were encouraged to fail rather than succeed. Teacher educators need to spend time searching for schools and teachers who model loving, supportive, academically challenging environments for all their students. Collaborations with communities and colleagues will certainly help this endeavor. I realize this suggestion is much easier to offer than to implement, but the importance of working with successful teachers of ELLs and children of color cannot be overstated.

Improve Student–Community Relationships

Another aspect of improving field experience is improving the relationships between teacher education students and the communities they enter to tutor and observe. In effect, tutors and communities had no relationship during the tutoring experiences I investigated. Several tutors were afraid of the neighborhoods where they tutored and thought of them as "risky." After tutoring, they got in their cars, locked their doors, and drove away. Thus, even though they spent 10 hours in various low-income neighborhoods that were not predominantly White, they maintained a great deal of distance between themselves and these communities. Additionally, tutors thought of themselves as "helpers" who entered these neighborhoods in order to perform charitable good deeds that community members could not, or would not, do themselves. There are a number of problems with this situation. This approach supports the beliefs that preservice teachers are performing charitable acts for communities in need; that tutors' own culture, language, and ways of living are superior to those of the children they are "helping"; and that White middle-class teachers are the tacit role models and saviors for children of color and English-language learners. None of these forms of deficit thinking of the other and superior thinking of the self are challenged or deconstructed in any fashion in this situation.

In order to change these beliefs to benefit both children and preservice teachers, I suggest that preservice teachers enter the communities where they do their fieldwork as learners rather than authorities. Gonzalez et al.'s (1995) work in funds of knowledge is a good model for a teacher's transformation into learner. The funds of knowledge philosophy is that immigrant and cultural minority children and their families have an abundance of skills and knowledge that are enormously important but not traditionally recognized or valued by the dominant American society. Acting as learners, teachers spend time with these families, get to know them, and incorporate what they learn into their own teaching. Spending several hours over the course of a semester with one or two families is enough to break down some of the distance between teachers and their students.

Learning about the community and breaking down distance can take other forms as well. Wilhelm, Cowart, Hume, and Rademacher (1996) have found success with something they call "the community plunge." In this activity, preservice teachers work in groups to explore the community where they teach in numerous ways. After their exploration, they meet at a local restaurant with their instructors to "debrief" and "probe their attitudes, feelings, and insights about the area and their future students" (p. 52). Haberman and Post (1998) go a step further by requiring the student teachers in their Metropolitan Milwaukee Teacher Education Program (MMTEP) to actually live in the communities where they teach. Tutors I met with lived only a few miles from the schools where they tutored, yet the cultural, racial, and economic differences separating them from the children they tutored made the geographic distance seem vast. Breaking down the psychological distance requires much more quality time in the community.

A novel way to dismantle this distance would be to require preservice teachers to learn a valuable skill from members of the community where they tutor. In this capacity, they would be put into the role of student, while community members assume the role of teacher. The topic to be taught could be Spanish language, Latina/o literature, Latina/o culture, community history, or something else the local community deems important for future teachers to learn. Of course, a focus on Latina/o culture is most appropriate when the children being taught are Latinas/os. If the children being tutored are Vietnamese, Cambodian, or from any other background, aspects of their culture should be highlighted. These cultural aspects must not be static, superficial items of culture such as traditions and holidays but dynamic, meaningful aspects of culture. The skills taught by local community members also must be appreciated by teacher educators and teacher education programs. Offering university credit for these lessons is essential, as credit is a major indicator of value. Moreover, preservice teachers should be given the time to commit to these lessons. Preservice teachers and student teachers are notoriously pressed for time during their teacher preparation programs. Rather than spreading these future educators even more thinly, I suggest that their commitments be reassessed and then streamlined. Moving a class such as SLA to a site-based format would alleviate some of the time pressures for students and open up time for lessons from the community. In addition to its other many strengths, learning from community members would directly challenge the constructions of teacher-as-role-model and-savior.

Another important aspect of getting to know the community would be to learn more about its history. SLA students had little historical knowledge of the town where they went to school and tutored. They did not know that the town had a history of racial segregation during the Jim Crow era (1890s – 1960s) that prevented people of color from getting gas or water hookups if they lived on the west side of the main highway until 1967. They did not know that some predominantly African American and Mexican American parts of town had been all White before mandatory desegregation efforts in the 1960s and 1970s. Many Whites moved rather than allow their children to attend racially integrated schools. The Whites who stayed typically had children who had already graduated high school; thus the Whites in the area tended to be of retirement age. Learning more about the ways that race has influenced history and that history has influenced race would add an eye-opening dimension to teacher education, underscoring the fact that we are all makers of history. If classes on local community histories are not available, teacher education students could be assigned research projects to get to know the community through interviewing community members and examining historical documents in local libraries and city halls. The ways that the past influences the present is an important dimension of such a project.

Require Reflective Assignments

All these modifications to field service will be for naught unless preservice teachers are continually asked to reflect on the time they spend with the children they tutor and their communities. They must also be encouraged to critically reflect on the presuppositions they bring with them to the tutoring situation. Moreover, instructors must constantly challenge these presuppositions and encourage students to challenge one another. Interactive journals are an excellent tool for encouraging this kind of challenging reflection. SLA students kept a journal that detailed tutoring lessons taught, connections made to class discussions and readings, and beliefs about tutees. Students were required to write one journal entry per tutoring session. I collected these journals several times during the semester, read them thoughtfully, and gave extensive feedback to each student. Reading each journal helped me to better understand each student in the class. In addition, interacting with students through their journals enabled me to help them with their tutoring, even when I could not personally observe all 76 of them. SLA students regularly evaluated these journals as the most meaningful assignment in the class.

While I highly value interactive journals, assignments that encourage serious reflection and the development of a critical stance also certainly contribute to enriched learning. One such assignment could be for the tutor and child tutored to generate their own goals for the time they spend together. At the end of the semester, each could evaluate herself or himself, as well as her or his partner. Another assignment would be to tape-record a number of tutoring sessions. Preservice teachers could choose their best session, make a transcription of the audiotape, and then critically assess their contributions as tutor. The course instructor would evaluate the criticalness of each student's assessment rather than the quality of the tutoring session. The possibilities for insightful, meaningful class assignments are truly limitless. See Schön (1983, 1987, 1991) and Fairbanks (1998) for much more on the topic of nurturing reflective practitioners.

Change Status of Students

The final recommendation I have for improving field experiences is admittedly idealistic. Like most towns in the United States, the town where this study took place is strongly segregated by class and race. It is a town of White schools and schools of color, with very little mixing of the two. In order to find English-language learners or children of color, students in search of field experiences have only to cross the highway. Because color and economic class are so tightly connected in this town, tutoring children of color almost always means going into a low-income community. Thus, over the years, the students in the SLA class have learned to associate Latinas/os with poverty. Working with people "in need" without reflecting on the positionality of the teacher seems to have contributed to the teacher as savior and role model constructions. Indeed, numerous SLA students over the years have gotten a kind of "high" from showering children with small tokens such as candy, lunches, soft drinks, books, etc. Most tutoring programs discourage gift-giving, as do I. However, many students still continued to give small gifts because they saw it as an opportunity to fulfill small needs or wants and to elevate their own status.

In assessing this situation over the years, I have often wondered what kinds of beliefs preservice teachers would construct for English-language learners and people of color who maintained a socioeconomic status higher than their own. I wonder this because, before getting certified to teach public school, I taught English as a second language to students from backgrounds much wealthier and much more powerful than my own. When I taught children at a Japanese *juku*, that is, an intensive study center, my classes were monitored by a camera in the back of the classroom. Parents were able to observe classes through a screen in the principal's office or in person at any time, which they often did. Later, I taught at an expensive private language school in the United States. Some of our students were the children or grandchildren of presidents and prime ministers. When I misjudged students or made mistakes with the English language, students would complain to our school director. Seven students actually transferred out of my class the day I answered, "I don't know" to a question. Students and their families held a great deal of power in these schools. Because of the status of the students, deficit comments about them, their culture, their language, or their families were cause for dismissal. In contrast to these students, the children who preservice teachers around the country are encouraged to tutor most often comprise the least wealthy and least powerful residents in their communities. These children are commonly taken advantage of, misunderstood, ill-treated, and shipped off to special education classes. The parents of these children, many of whom have not had successful experiences with education, or are new to this country, often maintain a faith in the system (Rose, 1989; Trueba, 1998). Thus, many children are at the mercy of their teachers and the novice preservice teachers who work with them.

My idealistic recommendation then, is that this situation changes. Perhaps the quickly shifting population dynamics will lead to effective changes, eventually. As these groups gain more economic and educational power, they will, hopefully, rail against the system. The Latina/o population in the university town described in this book alone nearly doubled between 1990 and 2000. The numbers of "other" races and ethnicities more than tripled in the same time period. These changing population trends are common across the United States. As Freire (1970/2000) emphasizes, true change for oppressed groups must come from within those groups; leadership from the oppressors on behalf of the oppressed is always suspect. However, people in the dominant group can make changes among themselves/ourselves to facilitate these larger societal transformations as well. Naming their/our racism is the first step.

Future Research

The possibilities for further research on the topic of White racism in teacher education abound. What is most compelling is the possibility of moving from individually focused attempts at antiracist intervention to intervention in classroom settings. This change of venue would lead to new challenges for success. Trust, vulnerability, and reciprocity would take on new meanings in a classroom environment. Moreover, students would have to learn to challenge the beliefs and statements of other students in a firm but supportive manner. Specifically introducing the notions of White talk (McIntyre, 1997) and deficit thinking (Valencia, 1997) would likely make these quagmires easier to name and then avoid. As discussed earlier, I have had some success in creating this kind of environment in the multicultural education/social justice-focused classes that I presently teach. More research could also be conducted regarding the seven steps toward the recognition of White racism that I present here. It is possible that these seven steps can be adapted for classroom use. However, it is also possible that they are best suited for the tutors presented here. Only future research can explore their usefulness in antiracist efforts.

While studies in Whiteness and White racism must continue, I also suggest more collaboration between White researchers and researchers of color. Critical White studies is an exciting area for many racially progressive, self-critical Whites who want to make a difference in the world. Indeed, I am certainly one of these. However, there is an undeniable safety to studying

Whiteness. Although Scheurich (1993) cautions against it, it is easy for critical White scholars to think of themselves as "the good Whites" who are, heroically, examining the deficits of their own racial group. Indeed, criticism from scholars of color about the growing field of Whiteness are oftentimes brushed off as irrelevant, nonacademic, or mean-spirited. Critical White scholars defend their actions with the (true) statement that White racism must be dealt with in every manner possible. However, while critical examination of Whiteness is necessary, perhaps especially in education, it can be separating. That is, while it creates a much-needed critical solidarity among Whites, it oftentimes, once again, relegates people of color to "the other," to "them." It also can usurp center stage in discussions of multiculturalism (Sheets, 2000). I think it is important for those engaged in critical explorations of Whiteness to realize this. As we work to "enlighten" our own racial group to our acts of oppression and our invisible privileges, we must also open ourselves to partnerships with people of color, and to their criticisms. As many critical race theorists of color argue, the invisible privileges and aspects of race that are hard for the dominant group to recognize often appear to people of color in bold Technicolor (Bell, 1992; Chennault, 1998; Delgado, 1995b). Thus, when Whites scoff at this criticism, they/we are once again asserting their/our privilege to do so.

By working together, White researchers and researchers of color can open a myriad of doors to critical inquiry. As cultural and racial insiders, we can together critically explore not only White teachers, but their/our relationships with teachers of color, children of color, and the communities where they/we teach. Through this kind of inquiry, White teachers may be moved from center stage. Rather than exploring just one aspect of education, intergroup collaboration will enable more holistic pictures to emerge. This seems, to me, to be a very exciting opportunity for future research (see Obidah & Teel, 2001 for an example).

One final point I must emphasize is that I believe it is essential to share data and final reports with volunteers who participate in Whiteness and White racism research projects. This sharing increases the accountability of researchers and solidifies the trust created in the data collection process. It also helps expose and name Whiteness and racism, adding to the development of a new language of race and racism. In this way, the investigation itself becomes a form of praxis (Freire, 1970/2000). If we as teacher educators are truly devoted to the growth of our students and ourselves, we must be brave enough to share our findings with those we have examined and listen attentively to their points of view. Those of us committed to antiracist research must also be willing to remember that our branch of research is a new one to which no one has all the answers. We must remember that we are learners even as we hope to teach others. Only through collaboration can we develop a new language with which to talk about these things and with which we can construct a new way of looking at the world.

Measures of success for antiracist teaching comprise another area for future research. Questionnaires and commentary are simply not enough to indicate that beliefs about children of color and English-language learners have actually changed. Such measures are not an indication of changes in behavior at all. Rather, preservice teachers and teachers should be studied more often in the actual classroom setting where behaviors can be compared and contrasted with stated beliefs. Teachers should also be studied in a longitudinal fashion. Preservice teachers are just developing their teaching philosophies and ideologies. Almost assuredly, they are more open to change than teachers who have actually been practicing their beliefs for a number of years. Moreover, the collegial pressure to conform to school practices, even if they oppose teacher education theory, can be overwhelming. Lessons learned in the "Ivory Tower" can, and often do, seem irrelevant once a teacher is in her or his own classroom. Thus, long-term studies where preservice teachers are studied again as novice teachers, and perhaps even again as seasoned professionals, will offer some assessment of the effectiveness of antiracist teacher education practices. Until long-term studies are conducted, we can never truly know the value of these seemingly transformational interventions.

Additionally, more research needs to be conducted on the effects of Whiteness and racism on practicing teachers and the children they teach. Preservice teachers are, in many ways, all too convenient. As teacher educators, we have quite a bit of control over our students. Our students look up to us as authority figures as well as experienced teachers. That is the beauty, as well as the detriment, of working with preservice teachers. Practicing teachers who have their own experience to guide them, as well as a healthy skepticism for teacher education and educational researchers, are a critical source for further inquiry. These teachers influence preservice teachers and novice teachers at least as strongly as teacher education programs do. It is likely that they have a stronger influence on new teachers because they spend more time with them as mentors, friends, and colleagues.

A Final Comment

As most White Americans realize, racism is an excruciatingly difficult subject to discuss (Howard & Denning del Rosario, 2000). The color-blind, color-evasive era we live in adds to this difficulty by masking our thoughts and stifling our language (Frankenberg, 1993; Omi & Winant, 1986, 1994; Sleeter, 1993). However, in order to move beyond this era of false egalitarianism, we must talk about race and racism (Howard & Denning del Rosario, 2000; Tatum, 1999). Through language, we must unearth our own true feelings and bring them into the light of day for critique. Because this is difficult for us, and because we have few models, this process is often awkward and sometimes even frightening. However, as we learn to name, discuss, and take responsibility for our racism, we will begin to develop a stronger, more helpful language with which to talk about racism in society, including the privileges of Whiteness. By doing this, we can begin to look past the era of color-evasiveness and toward a new era of, perhaps, color-embrace.

Until we gather the courage to name racism in the world around us and within ourselves, teaching philosophies such as "All children can succeed at high levels" are empty slogans at best. At worst, they are cruel lies we tell our students, their families, and even ourselves. If we, as educators, sincerely adopt the belief that all children can succeed, we must then turn a critical lens inward and examine our own roles in ensuring this success. Specifically, we must be willing to examine the barriers we put in the way of our students' successes. For White people, racism that benefits Whites is one of these barriers. The kind of self-exploration that I am suggesting here takes courage and confidence. It also takes resilience. Whites who bravely decide to embark on this journey may find that it is even harder than they first imagined (Helms, 1990; Obidah & Teel, 2001; Tatum, 1999). They may realize that they expect to be appreciated as "good Whites" (Scheurich, 1993) just because they have entered this journey. Whites, however, do not deserve medals for their/our efforts to be less racist. Rather, they/we must consider this effort to reflect on and constantly challenge the racism in their/our lives as their/our duty. Those of us who work with children of color on a daily basis are especially obligated to critically examine our beliefs and our intentions. The successes of our students are truly at stake.

Although this journey takes courage, and although our feelings may sometimes get hurt, the results can be amazing. Ashley, for example, began our semester together by talking about how much she hated working with Spanish-speaking children, even calling some of them "our little coconuts." However, by examining her own racism and the contribution it made to the education of children of color, she made an incredible turn around. By the end of our time together, she desperately wanted to become a "loving" teacher for children of color. As she said, "I know I'm not like that now—but, I want to be a teacher who believes all students can succeed." She also started to speak Spanish again, something she had not done since she moved to our college town. Elizabeth made a similar transformation. When we met, she was greatly frustrated by what she perceived to be the ethnocentrism of people of color. By the end of our time together, however, she realized the peripheral nature of people of color in school curricula and school materials. Amazed at this realization, she desperately wanted to change things by, at least, bringing more diverse materials into her own classroom. Several tutors gained a new perspective on the world by examining and confronting their own racism.

With this new perspective came a new love for teaching. Rather than continuing to view their tutees as troubled children with "hard" home lives, limited intellectual skills, and little chance for success, through this new perspective, most tutors began to see the children in a new, positive light. Michelle, for example, began to think of the children she tutored as her role models because of the amount of dedication they put into their studies, most of it being in their second language. An impressive feat indeed. Through many of their stories, it became clear that tutors began to look at teaching in a whole new way; that is, they began to think of it as an exciting, dynamic profession in which they would always be growing as people. They also began to look at their English-language learning students of color in a new light as valuable assets with much to offer teachers and other students. Without critically examining their own positionality, the tutors would have had no reason to reconstruct their beliefs about the roles of teachers and the roles of students.

The findings shared in this book offer an optimistic picture that things can change for the better. Preservice teachers who think of themselves as entirely without prejudices can learn to turn a critical lens on their own beliefs and, indeed, their own racism. This new critical perspective can help them change their teaching methods, their beliefs about their students, and even their beliefs about themselves. I have to caution, though, that these are the short-term conclusions that I have found. The passive racism that characterizes our society and our schools is a pervasive, oftentimes overwhelming, force. It is quite possible that the young women I got to know who gained a new perspective on the world will slowly, or even quickly, revert to their old ways of thinking (Helms, 1990; Pajares, 1992). In our e-mail contact just one month after our interviews had finished, for example, Rachel again expressed her desire to be "a role model, especially in an environment where [kids] may not have anyone to look up to." Old habits die hard. Tutors may also learn to embrace a deficit-based school culture once they start teaching, despite their intentions to the contrary. The passive racism that permeates our society ensures that the struggle to become an antiracist individual remains a struggle.

However, during our time together, the White preservice teachers I got to know *wanted* to talk about race, White identity, and White privilege, despite their initial hesitations. Moreover, once they saw their own racism, they wanted desperately to change. Their beliefs that racist teachers should not be in the classroom never wavered. The students I got to know through this investigation might just become the kinds of teachers I would like my own children to have in the future: teachers who know how to talk about race and racism; teachers who are confident enough in their own racial, cultural, and language backgrounds to value the racial, cultural, and language backgrounds of all their students; and teachers who truly love children and are able to help them all succeed. As teacher educators, it is our responsibility to raise the topics of race and racism more frequently and more firmly with our students so they can develop these skills. Together, we and our students can iron out this awkward language of race, learn to talk about our honest feelings, and work to change them. As we change ourselves and help others to change, we thus change the world. It is imperative that we not let our fear of entering the discussion prevent us from doing so.

Notes

Introduction

1. All names of people, schools, and places are pseudonyms.
2. King's (1991) "dysconscious racism" can be defined similarly to Tatum's (1999) notion of passive racism. Specifically, King writes, "Dysconscious racism is a form of racism that tacitly accepts dominant White norms and privileges. It is not the absence of consciousness, but an impaired consciousness" (p. 128).

Chapter 1

1. In order to ensure that my meetings with tutors would not influence their grades in the SLA class, all tests were objectively graded by a Scantron machine, and my teaching assistant graded the papers of the young women who talked with me. I read the tutoring journals of all students and assigned them either credit or no credit but not an actual grade.
2. All italics used in quotations throughout this book highlight the emphasis speakers gave particular words. No italics in quotations are added by the author.
3. During the semester we spent together, the fall of 1999, White students made up 64.6 percent of our university's undergraduate population. American Indians accounted for only .4 percent of the same population, African Americans only 3.9 percent, Asian Americans, 14.5 percent, Latina/os 13.7 percent, and foreign students, including exchange students, 3.1 percent. Whites accounted for 63.6 percent of the of the entire student body population.

Chapter 5

1. In her chapter on White identity development, Helms specifically focuses on White and Black Americans. Because SLA students were tutoring children of Mexican origin and sharing their beliefs about people from a wide variety of ethnic backgrounds, my conversations with them focused on "people of color" rather than only Blacks or African Americans. I believe Helms's work is still an appropriate reference here because the White students in this study tended to view Blacks and all other people of color as "Others." Thus, their own White identities were partially constructed in contrast to these perceptions. Tatum (1999) and Howard and Denning del Rosario (2000) discuss Helms's 1990 model with similar modifications.

2.   I should mention that there are several errors in Helms's (1990) self-assessment tool. The reintegration and disintegration stages are out of order and Helms includes questions that measure disintegration attitudes but not behaviors. Therefore, those taking this inventory have no means by which to measure disintegration behaviors. Because this was an impromptu kind of "workshop activity" and not a scientific measurement tool, I decided to go ahead and use this imperfect exercise.

3.   I must emphasize that while racism can be treated throughout an individual's life, I do not suggest it can be "cured." The best disease metaphor for racism is a lifelong condition that can be managed through daily treatment.

References

Adams, M., Bell, L., & Griffin, P. (Eds.) (1997). *Teaching for diversity and social justice: A sourcebook.* New York and London: Routledge.

Alba, R. (1990). *Ethnic identity: The transformation of White America.* New Haven, CT and London: Yale University Press.

American Psychological Association. (2001). *Publication manual of the American Psychological Association* (5th ed.). Washington, DC: American Psychological Association.

Anstrom, K. (1996). Defining the limited English proficient student population. *Directions in Language and Education, 1*(9), 1–6. National Clearinghouse of Bilingual Education.

Apple, M. (1998). Foreword. In J. Kincheloe, S. Steinberg, N. Rodriguez, & R. Chennault (Eds.), *White reign* (pp. ix–xiii). New York: St. Martin's Press.

Artiles, A., Harry, B., Reschly, D., & Chinn, P. (2002). Overidentification of students of color in special education: A critical overview. *Multicultural Perspectives, 4*(1), 3–10.

Artiles, A., Rueda, R., Salazar, J., & Higareda, I. (2002). English-language learner representation in special education in California urban school districts. In D. Losen, & G. Orfield (Eds.), *Racial inequality in special education* (pp. 117–136). Cambridge, MA: Harvard University Press.

Ashcroft, L. (1987). Defusing "empowerment:" The what and the why. *Language Arts, 64,* 142–156.

Baldwin, J. (1963). *The fire next time.* New York: Dell.

Ball, S., & Goodson, I. (1985). Understanding teachers: Concepts and contexts. In S. Ball, & I. Goodson (Eds.), *Issues in education and training series: Vol. 3. Teachers' lives and careers* (pp. 1–25). London and Philadelphia: Falmer.

Banks, J. (1991). A curriculum for empowerment, action, and change. In C. Sleeter (Ed.), *Empowerment through multicultural education* (pp. 125–141). Albany: State University of New York Press.

Banks, J. (2003). Multicultural education: Characteristics and goals. In J. Banks, & C. M. Banks (Eds.), *Multicultural education: Issues & perspectives*, (4th ed.) (pp. 3–30). New York: John Wiley & Sons, Inc.

Banks, J., & Banks, C. M. (Eds.) (2003). *Multicultural education: Issues & perspectives* (4th ed.). New York: John Wiley & Sons, Inc.

Behar, R. (1993). *Translated woman*. Boston: Beacon.

Behar, R. (1996). *The vulnerable observer*. Boston: Beacon.

Bell, D. (1992). *Faces at the bottom of the well*. New York: Basic Books.

Bell, D. (1995). Property rights in Whiteness – their legal legacy, their economic costs. In R. Delgado (Ed.), *Critical race theory: The cutting edge* (pp. 75–83). Philadelphia: Temple University Press.

Bell, L. A. (2002). Sincere fictions: The pedagogical challenges of preparing white teachers for multicultural classrooms. *Equity & Excellence in Education*, 35(3), 236–244.

Berlak, A. (1999). Teaching and testimony: Witnessing and bearing witness to racisms in culturally diverse classrooms. *Curriculum Inquiry*, 29(1) 99–127.

Berlak, A., & Moyenda, S. (2001). *Taking it personally: Racism in the classroom from kindergarten to college*. Philadelphia: Temple University Press.

Berryman, J. H. (1998). Canada's courts say teachers must be role models. *Professionally Speaking*. Ontario College of Teachers. Retrieved April 9, 2006, from http://www.oct.ca/publications/professionally_speaking/june_1998/-role.htm.

Blum, J. (1978). *Pseudoscience and mental ability: The origins and fallacies of the IQ controversy*. New York: Monthly Review Press.

Boog, B., Coenen, H., Keune, L., & Lammerts, R. (1996). *Theory and practice of action research. With special reference to The Netherlands*. Tilburg, The Netherlands: Tilburg University Press.

Bonilla-Silva, E. (2003). *Racism without racists: Colorblind racism and the persistence of racial inequality in the United States*. Lanham NY, Boulder CO, New York, and Oxford: Rowman & Littlefield.

Boyle, S. P. (1962). *The desegregated heart*. New York: William Morrow.

Brodkin, K. (2000). *How Jews became White folks and what that says about race in America*. New Brunswick, NJ and London: Rutgers University Press.

Brooks, M. (1989). *Instant rapport*. New York: Warner Books.

Brown, C. (2005, March 6). Looking at 50/50: Cache, Logan districts tackle low Hispanic graduation rate. *Herald Journal*, p. A3.

Brown, H. D. (1994a). *Principles of language learning and teaching* (3rd ed.). Englewood Cliffs, NJ: Prentice Hall.

Brown, H. D. (1994b). *Teaching by principles: An interactive approach to language pedagogy*. Englewood Cliffs, NJ: Prentice Hall.

Butt, R., Raymond, D., & Townsend, D. (1990, April). *Speculations on the nature and facilitation of teacher development as derived from teachers' stories*. Paper presented at the annual meeting of the American Educational Research Association, Boston.

Calabrese, R. (1989). Public school policy and minority students. *The Journal of Educational Thought, 23*(3), 187–196.

Carter, C., & Rice, C. L. (1997). Acquisition and manifestation of prejudice in children. *Journal of Multicultural Counseling and Development, 25*, 185–194.

Carter, R. T., & Goodwin, A. L. (1994). Racial identity and education. In L. Darling-Hammond (Ed.), *Review of research in education, 20*, 291–336.

Cazden, C., & Leggett, E. (1981). Culturally responsive education: Recommendations for achieving Lau remedies II. In H. Trueba, G. Guthrie, & K. Au (Eds.), *Culture and bilingual classrooms: Studies in classroom ethnography* (pp. 69–86). Rowley, MA: Newbury House.

Chabram-Dernersesian, A. (1997). On the social construction of Whiteness within selected Chicana/o discourses. In R. Frankenberg (Ed.), *Displacing Whiteness: Essays in social and cultural criticism* (pp. 107–164). Durham, NC and London: Duke University Press.

Chennault, R. (1998). Giving Whiteness a black eye: An interview with Michael Eric Dyson. In J. Kincheloe, S. Steinberg, N. Rodriguez, & R. Chennault (Eds.), *White reign* (pp. 299–328). New York: St. Martin's Press.

Chubbuck, S. M. (2004). Whiteness enacted, Whiteness disrupted: The complexity of personal congruence. *American Educational Research Journal, 41*(2), 301–333.

Collier, V. (1995). Acquiring a second language for school. *Directions in Language and Education, 1*(4), 1–12. National Clearinghouse of Bilingual Education.

Connelly, M., & Clandinin, J. (1994). Telling teaching stories. *Teacher Education Quarterly, 21*(1), 145–158.

Conrad, J. (1902). *Heart of darkness.* New York: Doubleday, Page & Company.

Cummins, J. (1986). Empowering minority students: A framework for intervention. *Harvard Educational Review, 56*, 18–36.

Cummins, J. (1994). The acquisition of English as a second language. In K. Spangenberg-Urbschat, & R. Pritchard (Eds.), *Kids come in all languages: Reading instruction for ESL students* (pp. 36–62). Newark, DE: International Reading Association.

Darling-Hammond, L., & Sclan, E. M. (1996). Who teaches and why: Dilemmas of building a profession for twenty-first century schools. In J. Sikula (Ed.), *Handbook of research on teacher education* (2nd ed.). New York: Macmillan.

Davis, F. J. (1991). *Who is Black? One nation's definition.* University Park: The Pennsylvania State University.

Davis, P. (1995). Law as microaggression. In R. Delgado (Ed.), *Critical race theory: The cutting edge* (pp. 169–179). Philadelphia: Temple University Press.

Debates and Proceedings in the Congress of the United States, 1789–1791, 2 vols. (1834) Washington, DC.

Delgado, R. (Ed.) (1995a). *Critical race theory: The cutting edge.* Philadelphia: Temple University Press.

Delgado, R. (1995b). Legal storytelling: Storytelling for oppositionists and others: A plea for narrative. In R. Delgado (Ed.), *Critical race theory: The cutting edge* (pp. 64–74). Philadelphia: Temple University Press.

Delpit, L. (1995). *Other people's children.* New York: New Press.

Derman-Sparks, L., & Phillips, C. B. (1997). *Teaching/learning anti-racism*. New York: Teachers College Press. 117.

Diller, J. V., & Moule, J. (2005). *Cultural competence: A primer for educators*. Belmont, CA: Thomson Wadsworth.

Donato, R., Menchaca, M., & Valencia, R. (1991). Segregation, desegregation, and integration of Chicano students: Problems and prospects. In R. Valencia (Ed.), *Chicano school failure and success: Research and policy issues for the 1990s* (pp. 27–63). London: Falmer.

Doyle, M. (1997). Beyond life history as a student: Preservice teachers' beliefs about teaching and learning. *College Student Journal, 31*, 519–531.

Dulay, H. C., & Burt, M. K. (1977). Remarks on creativity in language acquisition. In M. Burt, H. Dulay, & M. Finocchiaro (Eds.), *Viewpoints on English as a second language* (pp. 95–126). New York: Regents.

Edelman, M. W. (2000). On mentors and the making of a life. *The College Board Review, 189–190*, 3–5.

Ellison, R. (1947/1980). *Invisible man*. New York: Vintage Books.

Enrolled Acts and Resolutions of Congress. (1789–1996). An act to execute certain treaty stipulations relating to the Chinese, May 6, 1882. General Records of the United States Government, Record Group 11, National Archives.

Erickson, F. (2003). Culture in society and in educational practices. In J. Banks, & C. M. Banks (Eds.), *Multicultural education: Issues & perspectives* (4th ed.) (pp. 31–58). New York: John Wiley & Sons.

Fairbanks, C. M. (1998). Preservice teachers' reflections and the role of context in learning to teach. *Teacher Education Quarterly, 25*(3), 47–68.

Fanon, F. (1967). *Black skin, White masks* (C. L. Markmann, Trans.). New York: Grove Press.

Feagin, J. R., & Feagin, C. B. (1978). *Discrimination American style: Institutional racism and sexism*. Englewood Cliffs, NJ: Prentice-Hall.

Feagin, J., & Vera, H. (1995). *White racism: The basics*. New York: Routledge.

Field, S. L. (1996). Historical perspective on character education. *The Education Forum, 60*, 118–123.

Fillmore, L. W. (1989). Language learning in social context. The view from research in second language learning. In R. Dietrich, & C. F. Graumann (Eds.), *Language processing in social context* (pp. 277–302). Amsterdam, New York: North-Holland/Elsevier Science Pub. Co.

Flagg, A., & Flagg, P. (1988). More Black teachers are needed as role models for Black students in our schools. *College Student Journal, 22*, 315–316.

Foley, D. (1997). Deficit thinking models based on culture: The anthropological protest. In R. Valencia (Ed.), *The evolution of deficit thinking: Educational thought and practice* (pp. 113–131). London: Falmer.

Foley, D. (1998). On writing reflexive realist narratives. In J. Shacklock, & J. Smythe (Eds.), *Being reflexive in critical educational and social research* (pp. 110–129). London: Falmer.

Foshay, A. W. (1996). Character education: Some observations. Historical perspective on character education. *The Education Forum, 60*, 130–134.

Frankenberg, R. (1993). *White women, race matters: The social construction of Whiteness.* Minneapolis: University of Minnesota Press.

Frankenberg, R. (1994). Whiteness and Americanness: Examining constructions of race, culture, and nation in White women's life narratives. In S. Gregory, & R. Sanjek (Eds.), *Race* (pp. 62–77). New Brunswick, NJ: Rutgers University Press.

Frankenberg, R. (1997). Local Whitenesses, localizing Whiteness. In R. Frankenberg (Ed.), *Displacing Whiteness* (pp. 1–33). Durham and London: Duke University Press.

Franklin, B. (1751). Observations concerning the increase of mankind. In L. Labaree (Ed.) (1961), *The papers of Benjamin Franklin* (Vol. 225–234). New Haven, CT: Yale University Press.

Freire, P. (1970/2000). *Pedagogy of the oppressed* (30th anniversary ed.) (M. B. Ramos, Trans). New York: Seabury.

Fuller, M. L. (1994). The monocultural graduate in the multicultural environment: A challenge for teacher educators. *Journal of Teacher Education, 45*(4), 269–277.

Gabaccia, D. R. (2002). *Immigration and American diversity: A social and cultural history.* Malden, MA and Oxford, UK: Blackwell Publishers.

Gardner, R. C. (1985). *Social psychology and second language learning.* London: Edward Arnold.

Gibbs, L. J., & Earley, E. J. (1996). Character education: A challenge for staff developers. *Journal of Staff Development, 17,* 36–40.

Giroux, H. (1997). *Channel surfing.* New York: St. Martin's Press.

Giroux, H. (1998). Youth, memory work, and the racial politics of Whiteness. In J. Kincheloe, S. Steinberg, N. Rodriguez, & R. Chennault (Eds.), *White reign* (pp.123–136). New York: St. Martin's Press.

Giroux, H., & McLaren, P. (Eds.) (1994). *Between borders.* New York: Routledge.

Glesne, C., & Peshkin, A. (1992). *Becoming qualitative researchers: An introduction.* White Plains, NY: Longman.

Goldwin, R., & Kaufman, A. (Eds.) (1988). *Slavery and its consequences: The constitution, equality, and race.* American Enterprise Institute.

Gonzalez, N., Moll, L., Tenery, M., Rivera, A., Rendon, P., Gonzales, R., & Amanti, C. (1995). Funds of knowledge for teaching in Latino households. *Urban Education, 29*(4), 443–470.

Goodson, I. F. (1981). Life histories and the study of schooling, *Interchange, 11*(4), 62–76.

Goodson, I. F. (Ed.) (1983). *School subjects and curriculum change.* London: Routledge and Kegan Paul.

Grant, C., & Sleeter, C. (2003). Race, class, gender, and disability in the classroom. In J. Banks & C. M. Banks (Eds.), *Multicultural education: Issues & perspectives,* (4th ed.) (pp. 59–81). New York: John Wiley & Sons, Inc.

Haberman, M., & Post, L. (1992). Does direct experience change students' perceptions of low income minority children? *Midwestern Educational Research, 5*(2), 29–31.

Haberman, M., & Post, L. (1998). Teachers for multicultural schools: The power of selection. *Theory into Practice, 37*(2), 96–104.

Hale, G. E. (1998). *Making Whiteness: The culture of segregation in the South, 1890–1940.* New York: Random House, Inc.

Hale, R. (1996). Reflections on the importance of role models. *Black Issues in Higher Education, 13,* 22–23.

Hartigan, J., Jr. (1999). *Racial situations: Class predicaments of Whiteness in Detroit.* Princeton, NJ: Princeton University Press.

Helms, J. (1990). *Black and White racial identity: Theory, research, and practice.* New York; Westport, CT; London: Greenwood Press.

Henry, A. (1998). *Taking back control: African Canadian women teachers' lives and practices.* Albany: State University of New York Press.

Henze, R. C., Lucas, T., & Scott, B. (1998). Dancing with the monster: Teachers discuss racism, power, and White privilege in education. *The Urban Review, 30*(3), 187–210.

Herrnstein, R., & Murray, C. (1994). *The bell curve.* New York: Free Press.

hooks, b. (1989). *Talking back: Thinking feminist, thinking Black.* Boston: South End Press.

Hopwood v. State of Texas, 78 F.3rd 932 (5th Cir. 1996).

Horwitz, E., Horwitz, M., & Cope, J. (1986). Foreign language classroom anxiety. *The Modern Language Journal, 70,* 125–132.

Howard, T. C., & Denning del Rosario, C. (2000). Talking race in teacher education: The need for racial dialogue in teacher education programs. *Action in Teacher Education, 21*(4), 127–137.

Hudelson, S. (1994). Literacy development of second language children. In F. Genesee (Ed.), *Educating second language children: The whole child, the whole curriculum, the whole community* (pp. 129–158). Cambridge, UK and New York: University of Cambridge.

Ignatiev, N. (1995). *How the Irish became White.* New York: Routledge.

Ignatiev, N. (1997). The new abolitionists. *Transition, 73,* 199–204.

Ignatiev, N., & Garvey, J. (1996). *Race traitor.* New York: Routledge.

Ivek, I. (1994). Lev S. Vygotsky (1896–1934). *Prospects, 24*(3–4), 761–85.

Jones, D. M. (1997). The curse of Ham. In R. Delgado, & J. Stefancic (Eds.), *Critical White studies: Looking behind the mirror* (pp. 255–257). Philadelphia: Temple University Press.

Jorgensen, D. L. (1989). *Participant observation: A methodology for human studies* (Vol. 15). Newberry Park, CA: Sage.

Karp, J. B. (1981). The emotional impact and a model racist attitude. In B. P. Bowdser, & R. G. Hunt (Eds.), *Impacts of racism on White Americans* (pp. 87–96). Beverly Hills, CA: Sage.

Katz, J. H. (1977). The effects of a systematic training program on the attitudes and behavior of White people. *International Journal of Intercultural Relations, 1*(1), 77–89.

Katz, J. H., & Ivey, A. E. (1977). White awareness: The frontier of racism awareness training. *Personnel and Guidance Journal, 55*(8), 485–488.

Kimmel, E. B., & Rudolph, T. (1998). Growing up female. *Yearbook (National Society for the Study of Education), 97*, 42–64.

Kincheloe, J., Steinberg, S., Rodriguez, N., & Chennault, R. (Eds.) (1998). *White reign*. New York: St. Martin's Press.

Kincheloe, J., & Steinberg, S. (1998). Addressing the crisis of Whiteness: Reconfiguring White identity in a pedagogy of Whiteness. In J. Kincheloe, S. Steinberg, N. Rodriguez, & R. Chennault (Eds.), *White reign* (pp. 4–29). New York: St. Martin's Press.

King, J. (1991). Dysconscious racism: Ideology, identity and the miseducation of teachers. *Journal of Negro Education, 60*, 133–146.

Klarman, M. (2004). *Jim Crow to civil rights: The Supreme Court and the struggle for racial equality*. New York: Oxford University Press.

Kolchin, P. (2002). Whiteness studies: The new history of race in America. *The Journal of American History, 89*(1), 154–173.

Kolchin, P. (2003). *American slavery: 1619–1877*. New York: Hill and Wang.

Krajewski, R. J. (1999). Caring with passion: The 'core value.' Interview with E. L. Bailey. *NASSP Bulletin, 83*, 33–39.

Krashen, S. (2000/2001). Bilingual education works. *Rethinking Schools, 15*(2), 1–7.

Krashen, S., & Terrell, T. (1983). *The natural approach: Language acquisition in the classroom*. Oxford, UK and New York: Pergamon Press; San Francisco: Alemany Press.

Ladson-Billings, G. (1994). *The dreamkeepers: Successful teachers of African American children*. San Francisco: Jossey-Bass.

Ladson-Billings, G. (1999). Preparing teachers for diverse student populations: A critical race theory perspective. *Review of Research in Education, 24*, 211–247.

Ladson-Billings, G., & Tate, W. F. IV (1995). Toward a critical race theory of education. *Teachers College Record, 97*(1), 47–68.

Lambert, W. E. (1974). Culture and language as factors in learning and education. In F. E. Aboud, & R. D. Meade (Eds.), *The fifth western symposium on learning*. Bellingham, WA: Western Washington State College.

Lara-Alecio, R., Irby, B. J., & Ebener, R. (1997). Developing academically supportive behaviors among Hispanic parents: What elementary teachers and administrators can do. *Preventing School Failure, 42*, 27–32.

Lawrence, S. (1998). Research, writing, and racial identity: Cross-disciplinary connections for multicultural education. *The Teacher Educator, 34*(1), 41–53.

Leonardo, Z. (2002). The souls of White folk: critical pedagogy, Whiteness studies, and globalization discourse. *Race Ethnicity and Education, 5*(1), 29–50.

Lewis, O. (1965). The culture of poverty. *Scientific American, 215*, 19–25.

Lincoln, Y. S., & Guba, E. G. (1989). Ethics: The failure of positivist science. *The Review of Higher Education, 12*, 221–240.

López, G. R. (2001). Revisiting White racism and educational research: Critical race theory and the problem of method. *Educational Researcher, 30*(1), 29–33.

Lopéz, H. I. (1995). The social construction of race. In R. Delgado (Ed.), *Critical race theory: The cutting edge* (pp. 191–203). Philadelphia: Temple University Press.

Lortie, D. (1975). *Schoolteacher: A sociological study.* Chicago: University of Chicago Press.

Lynch, E., & Hanson, M. J. (1998). *Developing cross-cultural competence: A guide to working with children and their families.* Baltimore: Paul H. Brooks Publishing Co.

Magolda, P. (2000). Being at the wrong place, wrong time: Rethinking trust in qualitative inquiry. *Theory into Practice, 39*(3), 138–145.

Martinez, R. L. (1991). A crisis in the profession: Minority role models in critically short supply. *Vocational Education, 66,* 24–25.

Marx, S. (2000). An exploration of preservice teacher perceptions of second language learners in the mainstream classroom. *Texas Papers in Foreign Language Education, 5*(1), 207–221.

Mayeroff, M. (1971). *On caring.* New York: Harper & Row.

McAllister, G., & Irvine, J. J. (2000). Cross-cultural competency and multicultural teacher education. *Review of Educational Research, 70*(1), 3–24.

McIntosh, P. (1988/1997). White privilege and male privilege: A personal account of coming to see correspondences through work in women's studies. In M. Andersen, & P. H. Collins (Eds.), *Race, class, and gender: An anthology* (pp. 291–299). Belmont, CA: Wadsworth Publishing Company.

McIntyre, A. (1997). *Making meaning of Whiteness: Exploring racial identity with White teachers.* Albany: State University of New York Press.

McLaren, P. (1989). *Life in schools.* New York: Longman.

McLaren, P. (1998). Whiteness is . . . The struggle for postcolonial hybridity. In J. Kincheloe, S. Steinberg, N. Rodriguez, & R. Chennault (Eds.), *White reign* (pp. 63–75). New York: St. Martin's Press.

McWhirter, E. H., Hackett, G., & Bandalos, D. (1998). A causal model of the educational plans and career expectations of Mexican American high school girls. *Journal of Counseling Psychology, 45*(2), 166–81.

Melnick, S., & Zeichner, K. (1998). Teacher education's responsibility to address diversity issues: Enhancing institutional capacity. *Theory into Practice, 37*(2), 88–95.

Michaels, S. (1980, March). *Sharing time: An oral preparation for literacy.* Paper presented at the Ethnography in Education Research Forum, University of Pennsylvania, Philadelphia.

Miller, S. M. (1952). The participant observer and over-rapport. *American Sociological Review, 17,* 97–99. Also in: G. J. McCall, & J. I. Simmons (Eds.) (1969), *Issues in participant observation* (pp. 87–89). Reading, MA: Addison-Wesley.

Moon, D. (1999). White enculturation and bourgeois ideology: The discursive production of "good (White) girls." In T. Nakayama, & J. Martin (Eds.), *Whiteness: The Communication of Social Identity* (pp. 177–197). Thousand Oaks, CA; London; and New Delhi, India: Sage Publications.

Moorehead, M. A. (1998). Professional behaviors for the beginning teacher. *American Secondary Education, 26*(4), 22–26.

Nakayama, T., & Krizek, R. (1999). Whiteness as a strategic rhetoric. In T. Nakayama, & J. Martin (Eds.), *Whiteness: The Communication of Social Identity* (pp. 87–106). Thousand Oaks, CA; London; and New Delhi, India: Sage Publications.

Nash, G. B. (1999). *Forbidden love: The secret history of mixed-race America.* New York: Henry Holt.

National Center for Education Statistics. (2001). Dropout rates in the United States: 1999. Retrieved April 4, 2006, from http://nces.ed.gov/pubs2001/dropout.

National Center for Education Statistics. (2003a). Overview of public elementary and secondary schools and districts: School year 2001–02: Statistical analysis report. Washington, D.C.: Lee McGraw Hoffman.

National Center for Education Statistics. (2003b). The condition of education 2003 in brief. US Department of Education: Institute of Education Sciences. Retrieved June 26, 2006, from http://nces.ed.gov/pubs2003/2003068.pdf.

National Center for Education Statistics. (2005a). The condition of education 2005. Indicator 4. Racial/ethnic distribution of public school students. Retrieved April 4, 2006, from http://nces.ed.gov/programs/coe/2005/section1/indicator04.asp.

National Center for Education Statistics. (2005b). Violence in U.S. public schools: 2000 school survey on crime and safety. Statistical analysis. Retrieved April 4, 2006, from http://nces.ed.gov/pubs2004/2004314.pdf.

National Education Association. (2003, August). Status of the American public school teacher 2000–2001. Washington, D.C.: NEA RESEARCH. Retrieved April 4, 2006, from http://www.nea.org/edstats/images/status.pdf.

Navarro, M. (2003, November 9). Going beyond Black and White, Hispanics in Census pick "other." *New York Times,* Late Edition - Final, Section 1, Page 1, Column 2.

Nespor, J. (1987). The role of beliefs in the practice of teaching. *Journal of Curriculum Studies, 19,* 317–328.

Nisbett, R., & Ross, L. (1980). *Human inference: Strategies and shortcomings of social judgment.* Englewood Cliffs, NJ: Prentice Hall.

Noddings, N. (1984). *Caring, a feminine approach to ethics and moral education.* Berkeley: University of California Press.

Noddings, N. (1994). *The challenge to care in schools: An alternative approach to education.* New York: Teachers College Press.

Noddings, N. (1999a). Caring and competence. *Yearbook. National Society for the Study of Education, 98,* 205–220.

Noddings, N. (1999b). *Justice and caring: The search for common ground in education.* New York: Teachers College Press.

Obidah, J., & Teel, K. (2001). *Because of the kids: Facing racial and cultural differences in schools.* New York: Teachers College Press.

O'Brien, E. (2004). "I could hear you if you would just calm down": Challenging Eurocentric classroom norms through passionate discussions of racial oppression. In V. Lea & J. Helfand (Eds.), *Identifying race and transforming Whiteness in the classroom* (pp. 68–86). New York: Peter Lang Publishing.

Ogbu, J. (1992). Understanding cultural diversity and learning. *Educational Researcher, 21*(8), 5–14.

Omi, M., & Winant, H. (1986). *Racial formation in the United States: From the 1960s to the 1980s.* New York: Routledge and Kegan Paul.

Omi, M., & Winant, H. (1994). *Racial formation in the United States: From the 1960s to the 1990s.* New York and London: Routledge and Kegan Paul.

Onyekwuluge, A. B. (2000). Adult role models: Needed voices for adolescents, multi-culturalism, diversity, and race relations. *The Urban Review, 32*(1), 67–85.

Ortiz, A. A., & Yates, J. R. (1983). Incidence of exceptionality among Hispanics: Implications for manpower planning. *NABE Journal, 7,* 41–54.

Paine, L. (1989). *Orientation towards diversity: What do prospective teachers bring?* (Research Report 89–9). East Lansing: Michigan State University, National Center for Research on Teacher Learning.

Pajares, F. M. (1992). Teachers' beliefs about educational research: Cleaning up a messy construct. *Review of Educational Research, 62*(3), p. 307–332.

Pajares, F. M. (1993). Preservice teachers' beliefs: A focus for teacher education. *Action in Teacher Education, 15,* 45–54.

Parker, L., Deyhle, D., & Villenas, S. (1999). *Race is . . . race isn't: Critical race theory and qualitative studies in education.* Boulder, CO: Westview Press.

Pearl, A. (1997). Democratic education as an alternative to deficit thinking. In R. Valencia (Ed.), *The evolution of deficit thinking: Educational thought and practice* (pp. 525–556). Washington, DC: Falmer.

Pettigrew, T. (1975). Preface. In T. Pettigrew (Ed.), *Racial discrimination in the United States.* New York: Harper & Row.

Philips, S. U. (1983). *The invisible culture: Communication in classroom and community on the Warm Springs Indian Reservation.* New York: Longman.

Proweller, A. (1998). *Constructing female identities: Meaning making in an upper middle class youth culture.* Albany: State University of New York Press.

Pyle, W. H. (1915). The mind of the Negro child. *School and Society, 1,* 357–60.

Rains, F. (1998). Is the benign really harmless? Deconstructing "benign" manifestations of operationalized White privilege. In J. Kincheloe, S. Steinberg, N. Rodriguez, & R. Chennault (Eds.), *White reign* (pp. 77–101). New York: St. Martin's Press.

Reimer, E. (1971). *School is dead.* Harmondsworth, UK: Penguin Education Special.

Rodriguez, N. (1998). Emptying the content of Whiteness: Toward an understanding of the relation between Whiteness and pedagogy. In J. Kincheloe, S. Steinberg, N. Rodriguez, & R. Chennault (Eds.), *White reign* (pp. 31–62). New York: St. Martin's Press.

Roediger, D. (1991/1999). *The wages of Whiteness: Race and the making of the American working class.* London and New York: Verso.

Roediger, D. (1999). Is there a healthy White personality? *The counseling psychologist, 27*(2), 239–244.

Rogoff, B. (2003). *The cultural nature of human development.* New York: Oxford University Press.

Rokeach, M. (1968). *Beliefs, attitudes, and values: A theory of organization and change.* San Francisco: Jossey-Bass.

Rose, M. (1989). *Lives on the boundary: The struggles and achievements of America's underprepared.* New York: Free Press.

Ross, T. (1997). White innocence, Black abstraction. In R. Delgado, & J. Stefancic (Eds.), *Critical White studies: Looking behind the mirror* (pp. 263–266). Philadelphia: Temple University Press.

Said, E. (1979). *Orientalism.* New York: Random House.

Said, E. (1987). Representing the colonized: Anthropology's interlocutors. *Critical Inquiry, 13*(2), 205–225.

Scales-Trent, J. (1997). Notes of a White Black woman. In R. Delgado, & J. Stefancic (Eds.), *Critical White studies: Looking behind the mirror* (pp. 475–481). Philadelphia: Temple University Press.

Scheurich, J. (1993). Toward a White discourse on White racism. *Educational Researcher, 22*(8), 5–10.

Scheurich, J. (1998). Highly successful and loving public elementary schools populated mainly by low-SES children of color: Core beliefs and cultural characteristics. *Urban Education, 33*(4), 451–491.

Scheurich, J. (April, 2000). *White antiracist scholarship within/against the academy.* Paper presented at the annual meeting of the American Education Research Association, New Orleans, LA.

Schön, D. A. (1983). *The reflective practitioner: How professionals think in action.* New York: Basic Books.

Schön, D. A. (1987). *Educating the reflective practitioner.* San Francisco: Jossey-Bass.

Schön, D. A. (1991). *The Reflective turn: Case studies in and on educational practice.* New York: Teachers College Press.

Schultz, R. (1997). *Interpreting teacher practice . . . two continuing stories.* New York and London: Teachers College Press.

Schwiebert, V. L., Deck, M., & Bradshaw, M. (1999). Women as mentors. *Journal of Humanistic Counseling, Education and Development, 37*(4), 241–53.

Semali, L. (1998). Perspectives of the curriculum of Whiteness. In J. Kincheloe, S. Steinberg, N. Rodriguez, & R. Chennault (Eds.), *White reign* (pp. 177–190). New York: St. Martin's Press.

Shakespeare, W. (1611/1994). *The tempest.* New York: Washington Square Press.

Sheets, R. H. (2000). Advancing the field or taking center stage: The White movement in multicultural education. *Educational Researcher, 29*(9), 15– 21.

Sheets, R. H. (2001). Trends in the scholarship on teachers of color for diverse populations: Implications for multicultural education. *Equity & Excellence in Education, 34*(1), 26–31.

Shome, R. (1999). Whiteness and the politics of location: Postcolonial reflections. In T. Nakayama, & J. Martin (Eds.), *Whiteness: The communication of social identity* (pp. 107–128). Thousand Oaks, CA; London; and New Delhi, India: Sage Publications.

Shreffler, M. (1998). Raising a village: White male teachers as role models for African American male students. *Journal of Negro Education, 67*(2), 91–95.

Simmons, B. J. (1996). Teachers should dress for success. *The Clearing House, 69*, 297–298.

Sleeter, C. (1992a). *Keepers of the American dream: A study of staff development and multicultural education.* London and Washington, D.C.: Falmer Press.

Sleeter, C. (1992b). Multicultural education: Five views. *Kappa Delta Pi Record, 29*, 4–8.

Sleeter, C. (1993). How White teachers construct race. In C. McCarthy, & W. Crichlow (Eds.), *Race identity and representation in education* (pp. 157–171). New York and London: Routledge.

Sleeter, C. (1994). A multicultural educator views White racism. *Multicultural Education, 1*(39), 5–8.

Sleeter, C. (1995). *Multicultural education, critical pedagogy, and the politics of difference.* Albany: State University of New York Press.

Smith, L. (1961). *Killers of the dream.* New York: Norton.

Solomon, J., & Rhodes, N. (1995). *Conceptualizing academic language.* National Center for Research on Cultural Diversity and Second Language Acquisition. Washington, DC: Center for Applied Linguistics.

Solórzano, D. (1997). Images and words that wound: Critical race theory, racial stereotyping, and teacher education. *Teacher Education Quarterly, 24*(3), 5–19.

Solórzano, D. (2001). Examining transformation resistance through a critical race and Latcrit theory framework: Chicana and Chicano students in an urban context. *Urban Education, 36*(3), 308–42.

Solórzano, D. (2002). The critical race analysis of advanced placement classes: A case of educational inequality. *Journal of Latinos & Education, 1*(4), 215–230.

Spindler, G. (1997). Cultural sensitization. In G. Spindler (Ed.), *Education and cultural processes: Anthropological approaches* (3rd ed.) (pp. 498–512). Prospect Heights, IL: Waveland Press.

Spindler, G. (1999). Three categories of cultural knowledge useful in doing cultural therapy. *Anthropology & Education Quarterly, 30*(4), 466–472.

Spindler, G., & Spindler, L. (1982). From familiar to strange and back again: Roger Harker and Schoenhausen. In G. Spindler (Ed.), *Doing the ethnography of schooling: Educational anthropology in action* (pp. 20–46). New York: Holt, Rinehart and Winston.

Spindler, G., & Spindler, L. (1989). Instrumental competence, self-efficacy, linguistic minorities, and cultural therapy: A preliminary attempt at integration. *Anthropology and Education Quarterly, 20*, 36–50.

Spindler, G., & Spindler, L. (1990). Schooling in the American cultural dialogue. In G. Spindler, & L. Spindler (with E. T. Trueba, & M. Williams) (Eds.), *The American cultural dialogue and its transmission* (pp. 56–69). London: Falmer.

Spindler, G., & Spindler, L. (1993). Cross-cultural, comparative, reflective interviewing in Schoenhausen and RoMayan. In M. Schratz (Ed.), *Qualitative voices and educational research* (pp. 53–92). Hillsdale, NJ: Academic Press.

Spindler, G., & Spindler, L. (Eds.) (1994). *Pathways to cultural awareness: Cultural therapy with teachers and students.* Thousand Oaks, CA: Corwin Press.

Spradley, J. (1979). *The ethnographic interview.* New York: Holt, Rinehart, & Winston.

Stein, N. (1999). *Classrooms and courtrooms: Facing sexual harassment in K-12 schools.* New York: Teachers College Press.

Stewart, J., Meier, K. J., & England, R. (1989). In quest of role models: Change in Black teacher representation in urban school districts, 1968–1986. *The Journal of Negro Education, 58,* 140–152.

Suárez-Orozco, M., & Páez, M., (Eds.) (2002). *Latinos: Remaking America.* Berkeley, Los Angeles, and London: University of California Press and Harvard University: David Rockefeller Center for Latin American Studies.

Takaki, R. (1990). *Iron cages: Race and culture in nineteenth century America.* New York and Oxford: Oxford University Press.

Tatum, B. D. (1992). Talking about race, learning about racism: An application of racial identity development theory in the classroom. *Harvard Educational Review, 60*(1), 1–24.

Tatum, B. D. (1994). Teaching White students about racism: The search for White allies in the restoration of hope. *Teachers College Record, 95*(4), 462–76.

Tatum, B. D. (1999). *"Why are all the Black kids sitting together in the cafeteria?" And other conversations about race.* New York: Basic Books.

Taylor, P. (1993). *The texts of Paulo Freire.* Buckingham, UK and Philadelphia: Open University Press.

Terry, R. W. (1981). The negative impact on White values. In B. P. Bowser, & R. G. Hunt (Eds.), *Impacts of racism on White Americans* (pp. 119–151). Beverly Hills, CA: Sage Publications.

Texas House of Representatives (April 22, 1997). Texas after Hopwood: Revisiting Affirmative Action. House Research Organization: Session Focus. Retrieved May 16, 2006, from http://www.capitol.state.tx.us/hrofr/focus/hopwood.pdf.

Thompson, A. (2003). Tiffany, friend of people of color: White investments in antiracism. *Qualitative Studies in Education, 16*(1), 7–29.

Titone, C. (1998). Educating the White teacher as ally. In J. Kincheloe, S. Steinberg, N. Rodriguez, & R. Chennault (Eds.), *White reign* (pp. 159–175). New York: St. Martin's Press.

Trueba, H. T. (1988). Culturally based explanations of minority students' academic achievement. *Anthropology and Education Quarterly, 19,* 270–287.

Trueba, H. T. (1998). The education of Mexican immigrant children. In M. M. Suárez-Orazco (Ed.), *Crossings: Mexican immigration in interdisciplinary perspectives* (pp. 251–275). Cambridge, MA: Harvard University Press.

Twine, F. W. (1997). The construction of White identity. In R. Frankenberg (Ed.), *Displacing Whiteness: Essays in social and cultural criticism* (pp. 214–243). Durham, NC and London, UK: Duke University Press.

U.S. Census. (2000a). Hispanic origin and race of wife and husband in married-couple households for the United States: 2000. Retrieved April 4, 2006, from http://www.census.gov/population/cen2000/phc-t19/tab01.pdf.

U.S. Census. (2000b). Household and family characteristics of children under 18 years by age, race, and Hispanic or Latino origin, for the United States: 2000. Retrieved April 6, 2006, from http://www.census.gov/population/cen2000/phc-t30/tab02.pdf.

U.S. Census. (2003). School enrollment: 2000: Census 2000 brief. Retrieved April 4, 2006, from http://www.census.gov/prod/2003pubs/c2kbr-26.pdf.

U.S. Department of Commerce. (2001). Overview of race and Hispanic origin: Census 2000 Brief. Retrieved April 4, 2006, from http://www.census.gov/prod/2001pubs/cenbr01-1.pdf.

U.S. Commission on Civil Rights. (2003, March). The Commission, Affirmative Action, and current challenges facing equal opportunity in education. Retrieved May 16, 2006, from http://www.usccr.gov/aaction/ccraa.htm#_ftnref26.

Valdés, G. (1997) *Con respecto: Bridging the distance between culturally diverse families and schools.* New York: Teachers College Press.

Valencia, R. R. (Ed.) (1997). *The evolution of deficit thinking: Educational thought and practice.* London: Falmer Press.

Valencia, R. R., & Solórzano, D. (1997). Contemporary deficit thinking. In R. Valencia (Ed.), *The evolution of deficit thinking: Educational thought and practice* (pp. 160–210). London: Falmer Press.

Valencia, R. R., & Guadarrama, I. N. (1985). The school closure issue in the Chicano community: A follow-up study of the *Angeles* case. *The Urban Review, 16,* 145–63.

Vygotsky, L. S. (1978). *Mind in society: The development of higher psychological processes.* Cambridge, MA: Harvard University Press.

Wellman, D. (1977). *Portraits of White racism.* Cambridge: Cambridge University Press.

Wetherell, M., & Potter, J. (1992). *Mapping the language of racism: Discourse and the legitimation of exploitation.* New York: Columbia University Press.

Wilhelm, R., Cowart, M., Hume, L., & Rademacher, J. (1996). The effects of a professional development institute on preservice teachers' perceptions of their intercultural knowledge and sensitivity. *The Teacher Educator, 32*(1), 48–59.

Wildman, S., & Davis, A. (1997). Making systems of privilege visible. In R. Delgado, & S. Stefancic (Eds.), *Critical White studies: Looking behind the mirror* (pp. 314–319). Philadelphia: Temple University Press.

Winant, H. (1997). Behind blue eyes: Whiteness and contemporary U.S. racial politics. In M. Fine, L. Wiess, L. C. Powell, & L. M. Wong (Eds.), *Off White: Readings on race, power, and society* (pp. 50–53). New York: Routledge.

Wink, J. (2000). *Critical pedagogy: Notes from the real world* (2nd ed.). New York: Longman.

Index